The Life of a General in
Napoleon's Light Cavalry

The Life of a General in Napoleon's Light Cavalry

The Memoirs of Jean-Nicolas Curély

Andrew W Field

Pen & Sword
MILITARY
AN IMPRINT OF PEN & SWORD BOOKS LTD.
YORKSHIRE – PHILADELPHIA

First published in Great Britain in 2023
by Pen & Sword Military
An imprint of
Pen & Sword Books Limited
Yorkshire - Philadelphia

Copyright © Andrew W Field, 2023

ISBN 978 1 39906 586 3

The right of Andrew W Field to be identified as Author of this work
has been asserted by him in accordance with the Copyright, Designs and
Patents Act 1988.

A CIP catalogue record for this book is available from the British Library

All rights reserved. No part of this book may be reproduced or transmitted in
any form or by any means, electronic or mechanical including photocopying,
recording or by any information storage and retrieval system,
without permission from the Publisher in writing.

Typeset in INDIA by IMPEC eSolutions
Printed and bound in the UK by CPI Group (UK) Ltd, Croydon, CR0 4YY

Pen & Sword Books Limited incorporates the imprints of Atlas, Archaeology,
Aviation, Discovery, Family History, Fiction, History, Maritime, Military,
Military Classics, Politics, Select, Transport, True Crime, Air World, Frontline
Publishing, Leo Cooper, Remember When, Seaforth Publishing, The Praetorian
Press, Wharncliffe Local History, Wharncliffe Transport, Wharncliffe True
Crime and White Owl.

For a complete list of Pen & Sword titles please contact
PEN & SWORD BOOKS LIMITED
47 Church Street, Barnsley, South Yorkshire S70 2AS, United Kingdom
E-mail: enquiries@pen-and-sword.co.uk
Website: www.pen-and-sword.co.uk

Or

PEN AND SWORD BOOKS
1950 Lawrence Rd, Havertown, PA 19083, USA
E-mail: Uspen-and-sword@casematepublishers.com
Website: www.penandswordbooks.com

Contents

Introduction		vi
Chapter 1	Enlistment and the Rhine and Moselle	1
Chapter 2	Switzerland	16
Chapter 3	The Army of the Rhine and the Camp of Boulogne	29
Chapter 4	The Austerlitz Campaign of 1805	43
Chapter 5	The Campaign of 1806 Against Prussia	54
Chapter 6	The Campaign of 1807 in Poland	68
Chapter 7	The Campaign of 1809 in Austria	85
Chapter 8	His Campaign in Spain	102
Chapter 9	1812, the Campaign of Russia	118
Chapter 10	The Campaign of 1813 in Germany	151
Chapter 11	1814, the Campaign of France	171
Chapter 12	1815, Waterloo and the Loire	211
Appendix		222
Index		227

Introduction

Jean-Nicholas Curély is probably a name little known to most students of the Napoleonic Wars. As a French cavalry officer, his name is overshadowed by many of Napoleon's best known and most flamboyant senior commanders such as Murat, Montbrun and Kellerman, or the more junior, but equally famous Lasalle, Colbert or even de Brack. Yet to these latter men, who all served with him, there is little doubt that he was well known and much admired, even envied. Indeed, de Brack, best known for his guide to young officers, first published in 1831, *Avant-postes de cavalerie légère* ('Light Cavalry Outposts'), held Curély up as the almost perfect light cavalry commander. In the introduction to his book he wrote,

> A man must be born a Light Cavalry soldier. No situation requires so many natural skills, an innate genius for war, as that of an officer of light troops. The qualities which render a man superior, intelligence, will, strength, ought to be found united in him. Left constantly to himself, exposed to constant fighting, responsible not only for the troops under his command, but also for those who he is protecting and scouting for, every minute finds employment for his mental and bodily faculties. His profession is a tough one, but every day offers opportunities for distinguishing himself; a glorious compensation which repays his toils so much the more, as it shows the sooner what he is worth.
>
> I have often mentioned to you General Curély; sub-lieutenant with me in 1807, he was general [of brigade] in 1813.

But in 1806, being twenty leagues in advance of our army at the head of twenty hussars of the 7th, he carried terror into Leipsic [*sic*], where there were 3,000 Prussians.

In 1809, when fifteen leagues in front of the division to which he belonged, and at the head of a hundred chasseurs and hussars of the 7th and 9th, he passed unperceived through the Austrian-Italian army, which was engaged in reconnoitring, and penetrated to the centre of the staff of the Archduke, the commander-in-chief.

In 1812, at Polosk, at the head of a hundred chasseurs of the 20th, he carried off twenty-four guns from the enemy and took prisoner the commander-in-chief of the Russian army.

Well! This man, so brave, intrepid, strong-willed, skilful, prompt, of such sound judgment in his daring enterprises, was, when in command of a detachment, at once its doctor, veterinary surgeon, saddler, shoemaker, cook, baker, *farrier*, up to the moment when, meeting the enemy, he showed himself to be the most brilliant soldier in the Grand Army.

When he took part in an engagement, the men under his command were always fresher and more ready to fight than others, and their conduct proved this.

Was a man of this sort to be measured by the common standard, and to be kept at the level that ordinary men of the same or of superior rank keep fixed so firmly for great ability? Curély served for fifteen years and always during times of war, before he got his epaulette [became an officer]. Why had he to wait for it for so long? Because those who could have asked for it for him, had not themselves ability enough to recognise his value. He vegetated until a colonel, a man of like character to his own [Colbert], understood him and threw down the obstacle which kept him back. His rapid promotion was then only an act of strict justice, for, if at first it was so slow, the fault rested with others.

If I dwell on this fact, it is only as an example and a warning. Nowhere more than in the army, ought a man study more conscientiously the man under his orders and to turn to account his special qualifications. Nowhere ought the justice which he administers to be more complete, more devoid of the pettiness of *amour propre* [vanity] which are unworthy of a noble heart, and which become a grave and often irreparable wrong, when they basely fetter talent, and deprive the country of the services it might have rendered it. Seniority doubtless has its claim, and a very respectable one also, but it is not the first. Armies in which too much importance is attached to it are always defeated, whilst those in which merit has not always had to submit to its withering demands, have always been victorious. In the case of equal merit, it ought to carry the day.

In 1815, Curély retired; his soul was not one of those which knew how to bend; it was wounded, ill, it preyed on his vital powers and fled a few years ago to re-join those of his noble brothers-in-arms, dead on the battlefields of the Empire, or the scaffold of the Restoration. A wooden cross marks the place which his body occupies in the churchyard of the little village which he had quit thirty years before as a simple volunteer. Why did not death delay? He would have shaken the dust off the flag concealed under his humble straw bed.

A battlefield on the day of victory, a standard taken from the enemy, were the only tomb, the only shroud, worthy of him.

Curély was, to my mind, the archetypal light cavalry soldier. For three years I served under him, and his example and advice will remain forever engraved on my memory and heart. It was by studying him that I learnt the many qualifications required to make a good light cavalry officer and, if later on, left to myself, I have had my little successes, I have often owed them to the study of the vivid recollections which I had retained of him.

Curély's own *Le Général Curély, Itinéraire d'un Cavalier Léger de la Grande-Armée (1793-1815)*, was edited and published by Général Thoumas in 1887. It was based on Curély's original manuscript. Enrolling as a simple trooper, it is clear that Curély initially kept a record of where his service took him, rather than recording in detail his experiences and the actions in which he was involved. However, as his memoirs progress, reflecting his promotions, his more responsible roles and his understanding of the military situation beyond his own individual exploits that he recounts in his early career, the information he recorded and recollected became more detailed. The value of his *Itinéraire* therefore increases exponentially as each campaign passes until in his later campaigns, we are given a detailed insight into the French light cavalry of the time. This in itself is sufficient reason to make his work available to a wider audience, but it also gives us an equally fascinating insight into what makes an exceptional leader and battlefield commander, lessons which would be familiar to military leaders of today.

Whilst Curély's career in the Revolutionary and Napoleonic Wars reflects that of many of his contemporaries in the French army, it stands in stark contrast to those who became officers in many other

European armies, and particularly the British army of the time. In a way, this is one of the most compelling themes that run through his book. For most British officers, their initial commissioning and many of their promotions were purchased, and for those who were promoted from the ranks, their chances of promotion much beyond subaltern rank were almost non-existent. In the French army, 'every soldier had a marshal's baton in his knapsack'; even many of the French marshals had joined the army as a recruit and a lack of education or being of humble background was no bar to commissioning and attainment of senior rank. In the French army, experience and performance on campaign and on the battlefield were the keys to promotion and success, and it will be seen the extent to which Curély was worthy of his own advancement.

Curély's career also gives a fascinating picture of the full spectrum of the roles of light cavalry and how these developed in the later years of the empire after the near destruction of the cavalry arm during the campaign in Russia. In the early chapters, covering the Revolutionary and earlier years of the Napoleonic wars, Curély describes his involvement in deep raids, long range reconnaissances, advance-guard skirmishes and actions against insurgents, the classic roles of light cavalry. It is noticeable that, although he took part in all the major campaigns, he rarely took part in the major battles. Of course, light cavalry were not 'battlefield' cavalry, whose role was to charge formed infantry or cavalry during an engagement, as this was the role of medium and heavy cavalry. As major battles were fought, the light cavalry was responsible for flank and rear protection and feeling for enemy units not on the battlefield. Although light cavalry continued to have such responsibilities after the campaign in Russia in 1812, when much of the French cavalry was destroyed, the reconstitution of the heavy cavalry took so long due to the lack of suitable horse flesh and the need to train recruits, that light cavalry took an increasing role on the battlefield. In 1814, we see Curély leading his regiment in charges on the battlefields on which light cavalry might not previously have been present.

At the end of the 'itinerary', General Thoumas adds an appendix in which Curély reflects on some key events and battles that Napoleon mentioned in his dictation to Las Cases during his exile, which was published as *Mémorial de Sainte-Hélène*. Curély clearly read this and based on his own experiences in various campaigns, felt compelled to comment. His choice of topics is limited, and this short addition sits rather awkwardly at the end of his memoirs. However, in the interests of completeness it was felt that this should be included.

In his own edition, General Thoumas wrote a long introduction in which he traced Curély's career and highlighted the exploits in which he was involved, including some context for each campaign which is missing in Curély's manuscript. I have left Curély's narrative to trace his own career and describe his own achievements but felt that some detail of each campaign (with the extra maps that I have provided) was important context as he understandably focuses on the role that he and his unit played without much detail on the wider campaign. I have chosen to give this at the beginning of each chapter for extra clarity.

Maps. The production of the right number and usefulness of the maps has been a challenge! As will be seen, Curély assiduously kept a record of his movements around Europe, even listing almost all of his overnight stops when travelling. It is hoped that the many maps that have been included will aid the reader in keeping track of Curély's movements. However, the sheer number of places he mentions made it impossible to show them all given the scale the size of the book demands. I have therefore attempted to show all places during operations but have chosen to avoid maps of long journeys of little interest and incident. Furthermore, as the political map of Europe changed over the years, so many of the names of places have also changed and it has become almost impossible to locate many of the small hamlets or villages which are either lost in the vastness of Russia or the complexity of the Austrian empire. Where places do not appear on a map, others that are marked should allow the reader to follow operations without loss of detail. Finally, the number of places mentioned has prevented me from adding any helpful detail of the locations and manoeuvres of other forces involved: for this level of detail I recommend the military atlases or campaign histories that are commercially available.

Chapter 1

Enlistment and the Rhine and Moselle

Jean-Nicolas Curély was born on the 26th May 1774 at Avilliers in Lorraine. He was the son of a labourer and was brought up like many in his day with no education; his mother died in his childhood. He did not await the conscription, but, with the homeland in danger, volunteered on the 5th April 1793 into the 8th Hussars, which was then in garrison at Pont-à-Mousson (south of Metz). The 8th Hussars was raised originally at Compiègne in 1792 to gather up all the deserters who were flocking to Paris. It was given the name of the Hussars of Lamothe.

Curély had joined the army during the war of the First Coalition, the coalition comprising of Britain, Holland, Prussia, Sardinia (in northwest Italy), Spain and Austria. The war lasted from 1792 until 1797 and included fighting in Germany (where Curély was to serve), the Austrian Netherlands (Belgium), the Netherlands and Italy, as well as on the seas. As the French succeeded in each theatre so the defeated countries left the coalition until in 1797 only Britain remained at war with Revolutionary France.

In the short time he was in this regiment it was part of the armée du Rhin *[Army of the Rhine] and with it, Curély took part in his first battle, the battle of Geisberg (better known as the second battle of Wissembourg), where General Hoche defeated the Austrians and Prussians under General Wurmser) on the 26th December 1793. After this battle the allies were forced back onto the east bank of the Rhine.*

At Geisberg the commander of the cavalry was General Donnadieu, who, in his own report, claims to have been immediately nominated as 'general' and declared the 'bravest of the brave' by a decree of the Convention. However, at the battle, having received the order from Hoche to charge, he had hesitated and allowed the favourable moment to pass. Called before a council of war the next day, he was condemned to death for cowardice, despite the Convention's decree, and shot according to Saint-Cyr's memoirs.

The 8th Hussars were then sent to the blockade of Landau under command of the Army of the Moselle and took winter quarters on the Sarre. It was there that Curély was nominated as fourrier[1].

In 1794 the Committee of Public Safety reorganised the army after the huge influx of conscripts. The 8th Hussars were amalgamated with the Legion of the Moselle, also known as Kellerman's Legion, as well as a hundred soldiers from the foreign regiment Royal-Allemand, and a squadron from the Régiment de Saxe. The reformed regiment were renamed the 7th Hussars, but another 7th Hussars was raised in the Vendée. As the two regiments were then amalgamated into a new, single regiment, Curély, apparently because of his small size, and despite having just been promoted to fourrier, was sent to the infantry, though Curély claims it was actually because his captain wanted his horse. However, having left the regiment, instead of moving to the infantry, he made his way to the regimental depot of the 7th Hussars and re-joined his own regiment.

The regimental colonel of the 7th Hussars was Colonel van Morisy, who, after an illustrious time as the regiment's commanding officer, went on to be a brigade commander. He was wounded at the battle of Austerlitz and served in the campaigns of 1806 and 1807. Made Baron of the Empire he was sent to Spain where he was wounded in 1809 and then killed by guerrillas in 1811.

---

[1] A fourrier was ranked as corporal and had the responsibilities of a quartermaster and clerk, distributing rations, allocating accommodation and keeping the squadron's books; they still fought in the line of battle.

The regiment took no part in Napoleon's campaigns in Italy or Egypt, continuing its service in Germany.

In 1795 the regiment was present at the blockade of Mayence [Mainz] where there was a considerable loss of French manpower and materiel. Conditions were terrible and the later Marshal Saint-Cyr described conditions as worse than in the retreat from Moscow. Curély is very critical of how this operation was conducted; the regiment lost 200 men during the blockade. The 7th Hussars were then put under command of Pichegru for the seizing of Mannheim; they served in General Ambert's division. Pichegru was accused of treason after the seizing of this town for splitting his small force on both banks of the Neckar River for the advance on Heidelberg, which resulted in defeat as the two parts of his small army were unable to support each other. The 7th Hussars had been in the advance-guard under the command of Davout, the future marshal, and were able to retire in good order to Mannheim. They then became responsible for screening the lines of Mayence from any surprise by the Austrians. Curély then fought at the second battle of Mayence against Wurmser who commanded 17,000 Austrians against 12,000 French commanded by Pichegru. Defeated, the French were forced to withdraw. Mayence had no option but to surrender, and an armistice was signed to bring the campaign to an unsuccessful conclusion for the French.

In March 1796, the 7th Hussars were reduced in strength from six squadrons to four.

In May, the Austrian Archduke Charles denounced the armistice and hostilities recommenced on the 31st May. In the campaign that followed, the 7th Hussars were a part of the division of Beaupuis, the advance-guard division of Desaix's army corps in the Army of the Rhine and Moselle commanded by Moreau who had replaced Pichegru. Struck down sick, Curély was sent on sick leave and missed the early engagements of the campaign, re-joining in time for the actions at Rastadt, Ettingen, Neresheim and Moreau's retreat. On the 12th August at the action of Bobfingen, the 7th Hussars, forming part of the advance guard with a regiment of infantry, was attacked by a superior force of Austrian cavalry. Two hundred of the French infantry were taken prisoner, but a counter charge by the 7th Hussars released them. Colonel Marisy particularly distinguished himself; having been struck down by several blows, seeing his own regiment nearby, he shouted to them, and the regiment made a charge and rescued him. The regiment drew much praise in Moreau's report on the battle. After an apparently victorious advance to the Danube, Moreau was forced to retreat, during which there were a number of actions which Curély describes, most notably that at Neubourg (14th September) in which the 7th took a leading role in the repulse of the Austrians. At Ettenheim, Curély took an enemy cuirassier prisoner and sold the Austrian's horse to General Desaix. Curély's regiment now found itself back on the line of the Rhine at which it became part of the garrison during the siege of Kehl which surrendered on the 9th January 1797.

There was now a suspension of hostilities for a few months before the short campaign of 1797. Moreau's army only had time to cross the Rhine at Diersheim (20th April) and to push the enemy back in a three-day fight, in which the 7th Hussars fought the Austrians under the command of General Lecourbe. With Marisy continuing as colonel, the 7th Hussars inflicted considerable losses on the Austrian Kaiser Hussars, but hostilities came to an end as Napoleon wanted peace with the Austrians so he could safely launch his expedition to Egypt. This peace was much to the chagrin of the men of Army of the Rhine and Moselle who felt they had the upper hand and were deprived of victory. Despite his relatively short experience, Curély was employed at the general headquarters to carry orders.

I was born on the 26th May 1774 at Avillers in Lorraine; my father was named Jean-Nicolas Curély. My mother, Marie Gasson, had previously been married to a German cousin of my father's and had had six children in this first marriage, and then had four in her second, of which I was the eldest. I was the only one of six boys that took up arms. I was only eight years old when my mother died, whose memory is always in my thoughts. My father was a labourer, and

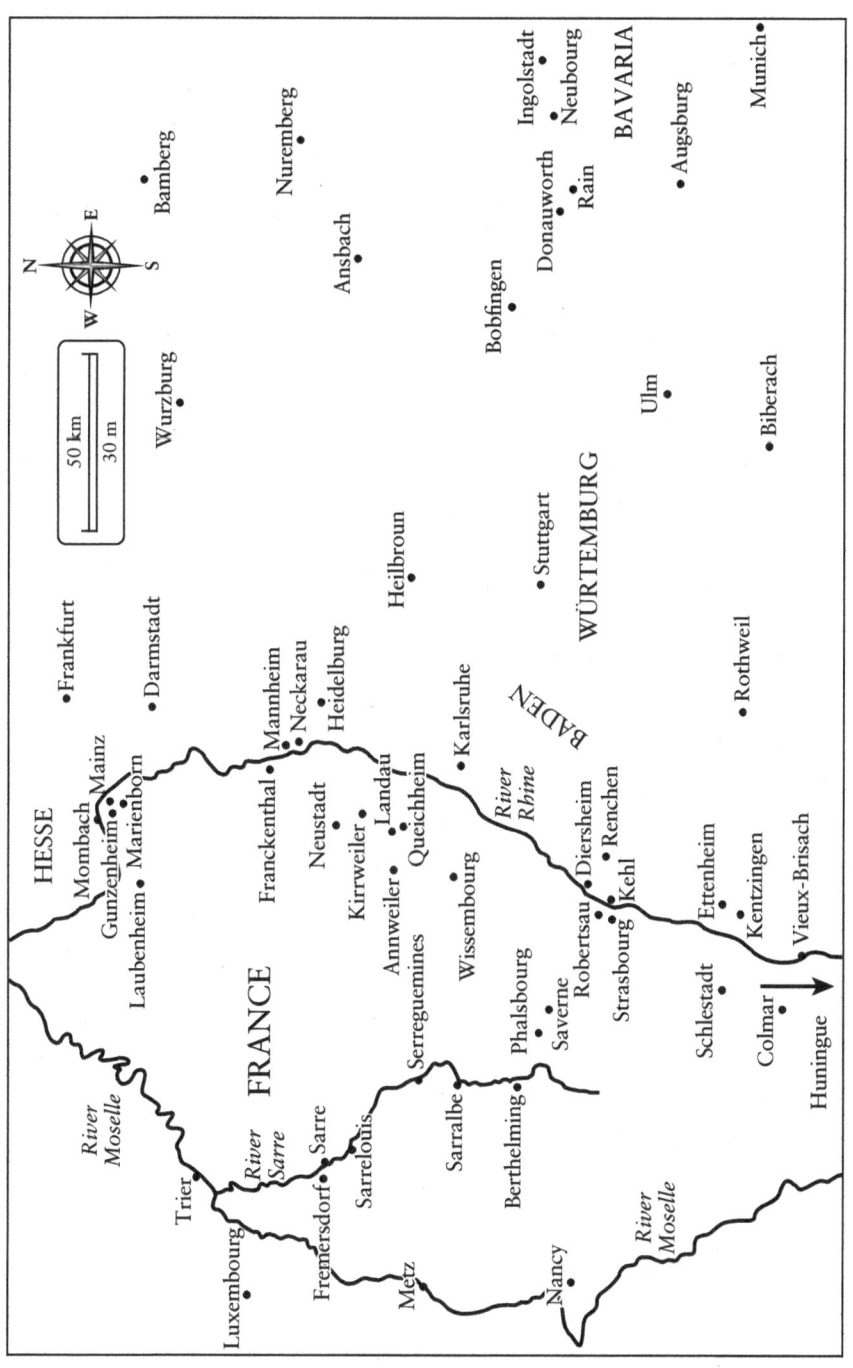

I received no other education than anyone gets in a village, which is the same as saying I received none at all.

I was eighteen and ten months when M. Canton, of Saint-Mihiel, enrolled me, on the 5th April 1793 into the 8th Regiment of Hussars, in which he was an officer. My first garrison was Pont-à-Mousson; I then went to Metz, then to Châlons-sur-Marne and, after six months in garrison there, my military training being complete, I was included in a detachment of a hundred men who left the depot on the 18th October, to join the Army of the Rhine, of which the regiment was a part, and was put into the war companies on arrival at Saverne.

The first combat in which I took part was on the 30th October, in which I made my first prisoner; an Austrian infantryman whose musket, also taken by me, won me fifty Francs in *assignats*[2]. This was an encouragement by the government to procure arms which were lacking. On the following 26th December, I saw my first battle, that of the lines of Wissembourg, won by Hoche who commanded the French army; the Austrians and émigrés lost many men. As for me, the cannonade, which was very lively for a time, caused me no astonishment and when the cavalry, almost all concentrated at a single point, moved off to charge, I suffered an infinite pleasure to see such a mass of cavalry in movement. But we were made to halt, and we remained simple spectators of the struggle.

The next day we marched on Landau, which was blockaded. That day I was one of the scouts of the advance guard; we made many prisoners, but we were only given fifty Francs of *assignats*. We continued our movement of Neustadt, and we had several small encounters with the Prussians, then, winter having become severe, the French army, as well as the enemy armies, went into cantonments. The regiment received the order to move to the Army of the Moselle and arrived in Sarrelouis [Saarlouis] on the 15th January 1794 and

---

[2] Banknotes issued during the French Revolution.

was cantoned at Sarre, between this town and Fremersdorff. There I was nominated *fourrier* on the following 4th April, in M. Canton's company. On the 1st May, the small Army of the Moselle made a movement; it had there, between the Moselle and the Sarre, a serious engagement, but that was without result and the next day the two armies retired, each to its own side and back into cantonments.

Our regiment, composed in part of all the French deserters that had been gathered in Paris and the surrounding area, had been created first in Paris, and then at Compiègne. We know that on the 20th May 1794, this regiment went to be combined with the *légion de la Moselle*, previously of *Kellerman*, and that the two units together took the name of the 7th Regiment of Hussars, but that it started off by discharging a certain number of men, so as not to exceed the established strength. This reform was announced by M. Courcelles, who was provided with the powers of the government. As the lieutenant who provisionally commanded the company in which I was a *fourrier* needed to mount himself; he put me on the list of the hussars discharged because of their height and thus took my horse. I therefore left with the hundred and fifty discharged hussars to enter the 17th Regiment of infantry, that of Auvergne, which was in camp three leagues from Longwy.

Arriving in this town and after having convinced myself during the march that I would be a poor infantryman, I used an old fall from my horse as an excuse to get myself a convalescence pass for a fortnight to go home to my parent's house. Indeed, I passed a fortnight with my father, after which I went to Saint-Mihiel and requested a passport to join the depot of the 7th Hussars which was then at Lunéville. Arriving there, I was received and re-employed in my rank as *fourrier* by the same M. Courcelles who had proceeded to the depot to repeat the operation that he had carried out at my previous regiment; there was no horse for me! I remained at the depot, employed as the *fourrier* with the 11th Company, for each company had its own particular depot, carrying the same number as it and composed of the same men and the same horses, coming and going, as required, from the depot to the regiment and from the regiment to the depot.

Finally, on the 1st September, I left with a detachment to go to find the regiment which was then at Trèves [Triers]. I was placed in my company, the 11th, commanded by Captain Briquet, and in which we found three *fourriers* where there should have been one. In proportion of ranks, there were as many officers and under-officers[3] in all the companies of the regiment due to the last re-organisation.

Before this operation, the 8th Hussars had its depot at Neufchâteau, its war squadrons with the Army of the Moselle and a detachment with the Army of the Vendée, where it later became the 7th *bis* Hussars. In each of these groups, the representatives of the people had nominated officers when and if they wanted; the officers had copied them in nominating the under-officers and it went on like this throughout the Legion of Moselle. This legion consisted of hussars, chasseurs-à-cheval and infantry, almost all of whom were Alsatians or Lorraine-Germans. In sum, the 7th Hussars, composed of twelve companies, each with a strength of seventy-five to eighty men, presented a total strength of around nine hundred men, well-mounted, poorly dressed and of mediocre discipline; a mix of French and Germans who did not get along well and did not understand each other. M. Van Marizy, *chef d'escadron*[4] in the *légion de la Moselle*, a brave soldier, firm and enterprising, had been nominated as colonel of the regiment; he knew with time to reconcile the different spirits in the regiment and to establish the best discipline.

In the month of October, the regiment left the area of Trèves to march to Mayence [Mainz] and had, during the journey, several

---

[3] Non-commissioned officer.
[4] Squadron commander.

engagements with the Prussians who retired in perfect order so that we would have thought we were attending an exercise. Arriving before Mayence, the French army blockaded this place on the left bank of the Rhine; we established a double line of circumnavigation from the village of Laubenheim, above Mayence, to Mombach, situated below the town, passing through Marienborn. At Laubenheim was the attack of the right, at Marienborn the attack of the centre and at Mombach the attack of the left.

Throughout the winter of 1794 to 1795, the army was bivouacked in holes of five to six feet in depth; the lack of rations and the extreme cold resulted in half our men being lost. If, on arriving before Mayence, we had bombarded the place and assaulted it to take it by main force, we would not have lost a quarter of the men which perished during the blockade; the town, once taken, could have been occupied by a strong garrison and the rest of the army could have gone into good cantonments on the left bank of the Rhine. By this ridiculous system of blockade, the regiments lost nearly all their horses for lack of forage. The 7th Hussars who were cantoned at Gunzenheim at first, had several engagements with the Mayence garrison. We were very active, mounting every day at 4am and dismounting at eight [presumably in the evening] on returning to our cantonments. After Gunzenheim, several other villages to the rear of the lines were occupied successively by the regiment, which drew its forage from localities ever further away whilst continuing to carry out its service in the advance posts in front of Mayence. Finally, towards the middle of winter it was decided to send half the regiment five or six leagues in the rear to rest and recuperate. The other half remained in the lines where it was relieved after a month by the first half and so on, the part of the regiment which was going to do service in the blockade carried with it each time enough forage for a month. The countryside was wretched and ruined, and this lasted eleven months.

After so much useless pain, some of the troops were taken from the blockade, amongst which was the 7th Hussars, and 15,000 to 18,000 were sent to Mannheim. Pichegru took command of them, and they crossed the Rhine in the night of the 20th to 21st September 1795 and then moved to Heidelberg. These troops were formed in two divisions, of which one, under the orders of General Dufour, crossed the Neckar a little above Mannheim to follow the right bank. It was beaten and routed, losing all of its cannon as well as its general, who was taken prisoner, and had many men drowned trying to re-cross the Neckar. The other division [commanded by General Ambert], which had not left the left bank of the Neckar, fought with courage; the 7th Hussars, rushed forward by Colonel Marizy, made a brilliant charge and we had already enjoyed some success when we learnt of the defeat of Dufour's division. It was necessary to retire under the walls of Mannheim; the retreat was made at night and in good order.

Sometime after, it is said on the 18th October, the Austrians came to attack us in our bivouacs at one o'clock in the morning. The 8th Hussars, which occupied the road from Neckarau, were surprised and almost entirely destroyed. The 7th, which was on the left, about a quarter of an hour away, mounted up at the first pistol shot and prepared to make a defence. The *grand'gardes*[5] were not surprised even though the Austrians had sent a considerable force against them. Such is the advantage of a well-disciplined force compared to those which are not. In this affair, the regiment resisted the full

---

[5] A *grand'garde*, literally 'large guard', is a guard post thrown forward to provide security to a unit most commonly during the night. It provides the sentries which keep look out and warn the guard of the approach of an enemy. The grand guard maintains a reserve of men who ensure the safe withdrawal of the sentries and are capable of holding up an attacking enemy whilst its parent unit prepares to meet the enemy.

weight of the enemy attacks, were not broken and retreated in the best order under the cannon of Mannheim. The army remained in this position for some time, although the enemy often fired balls into the cavalry's bivouacs. The lines of Mayence having been taken by the Austrians, the French troops who had defended these lines were in full retreat and they arrived at Franckenthal a few days later when the enemy attacked them vigorously. It was necessary to take some troops from the army corps which was covering Mannheim to go to the support of Franckenthal; the 7th Hussars were included in this number, except for a detachment of sixty men who were left in Mannheim, where the garrison amounted in all to about 9,000 men.

The combat of Franckenthal was very murderous, the French were forced to give ground and the 7th Hussars had to sustain a painful retreat; it made it in the greatest order. The army retired between Germersheim and Landau; the 7th Hussars were cantoned in Queichheim. The fortress of Mannheim, blockaded on both banks of the Rhine, surrendered to the enemy on the 22nd November 1795; the garrison was made prisoners of war.

The regiment remained at Queichheim for nearly two months without having a serious engagement with the enemy, who was occupied with the siege of Mannheim. After the capitulation of this place, the two armies went into cantonments and the 7th Hussars was sent to Phalsbourg, where it remained in barracks for the months of January and February 1796. In this garrison, each day, every soldier received half a pound of meat, a pound and a half of bread, salt, vegetables and two *sols*; the officers received double rations and four *sols*. We were far from happy.

From Phalsbourg, the regiment was sent into cantonments in Berthelming in German Lorraine. There it was reduced from twelve companies to eight. About a third of the officers and under-officers were without employment, but they all remained with the regiment; I was classed in the 5th Company where I followed Captain Briquet.

In Spring, the regiment left for the area of Strasbourg; there I fell sick because of a haemorrhage and the colonel granted me a month's sick leave that I went to spend with my father. During this leave, the Army of the Rhine became the Army of the Rhine and Moselle, commanded by General Moreau, and crossed the Rhine at Kehl on the 24th June, and on the 29th won the battle of Renchen over the Austrians. My leave over, I re-joined the regiment the day after this battle, and I re-entered the 5th Company which was still commanded by Captain Briquet.

The regiment advanced with the army and took part in several engagements, notably that of Bobfingen [Bopfingen] on the 5th August 1796. On this day, it found itself under the orders of a general sent on reconnaissance and who, having with him only a regiment of infantry and the 7th Hussars, penetrated almost into the Austrian camp. He was then repulsed and pursued by forces four times his own and almost all the infantry were taken prisoner. In the fighting, Colonel Marizy having been wounded and thrown from his horse, we only realised he was absent when the regiment was rallied. Immediately, by a spontaneous movement, the whole regiment re-took the charge and released the colonel who was already in the enemy's hands. He was a chief loved by all and merited this fine devotion of his regiment. I dismounted to give him my horse, but at the same time a hussar that was closer to him got down from his own on which the colonel was placed. We led him out of danger despite the repeated attacks of the enemy. As to the hussar, he was not qualified for promotion, but he was given the cross of the *Légion d'Honneur*, although he soon retired from the service.

The army continued its march via Donauwerth, Rain, Neubourg [Neuburg] and Ingolstadt. In the engagement that we had in front of this last town, on the 3rd September 1796 (16 Fructidor Year IV), Hussar Nivois, my compatriot and friend, had his thigh taken off by a ball; he died a few hours later. The next day, the army retreated; it was vigorously attacked on the 15th September (28 Fructidor) in front of Neubourg, where the enemy was repulsed with loss beyond a large wood, though a thick fog favoured the march of his columns. On this day, the 7th Hussars made some fine charges and collected up many prisoners. In this affair, Generals Delmas and Oudinot were both seriously wounded and left for dead. The army then retired quietly on Ulm and continued its retrograde march as far as Biberach, where General Moreau gave battle on the 2nd October (11 Vendémiaire Year V) and took from the enemy 5,000 men, eighteen cannon and two colours.

Several days after the battle of Biberach, General Desaix's corps was detached in the direction of Rothweil; Oudinot's division, of which our regiment was a part, encountered an Austrian corps at Ettenheim. General Oudinot charging at the head of the 7th Hussars and the 10th and 17th Dragoons with his arm in a sling, made a battalion prisoner and several cavalrymen. For my part, I took an Austrian cuirassier and his horse prisoner in the middle of the enemy ranks; I was very proud of this capture, for it was the first mounted cavalryman that I had taken. I looked like a child next to this colossus perched on an enormous horse, and this was a subject of amusement for all the troops that saw me bring him back; I sold his horse to General Desaix. We had to fight again at Rothweil to open a path, after which we re-joined the army to cross the Enfer valley, and we had a very serious engagement at Kentzingen in which General Beaupuis was killed. Desaix's corps re-crossed the Rhine under Vieux-Brisach on the 21st November 1796, whilst the main body of the army, under the orders of Moreau, climbed the Enfer valley and crossed the river at Huningue. After the crossing of the Rhine, during which it was not threatened, Desaix's corps went by forced marches to Strasbourg in order to go to occupy Kehl. The 7th Hussars was cantoned in the villages around Strasbourg and principally at Robertsau, from where it provided posts to Kehl.

On the 2nd Frimaire Year V (22nd November 1796), the army attacked the Austrian entrenched camp of which part was taken during the night; but at dawn the enemy re-took the positions he had lost. For my part, crossing the Austrian entrenchments with several hussars and having taken three or four hundred prisoners, we brought them back to the entry point of the French camp, when the enemy charged us and released their men. During this siege, we did not pass a day without fighting until the fort of Kehl surrendered to the enemy on the 20th Nivôse Year V (10th January 1797).

After the surrender of Kehl, the 7th Hussars descended the left bank of the Rhine and took cantonments at Spire and the surrounding area; it remained there quietly for close to three months, occupied with re-mounting and re-equipping itself for a new campaign. At the end of this time, it received the order to go back up the Rhine to be opposite Diersheim on the 30th Germinal Year V (20th April 1797), where it was to execute the crossing of the river. This passage only took place for us the next day and our regiment took a brilliant part in all the fighting which took place there for three consecutive days. A courier from Italy informed General Moreau that the preliminaries of peace had been signed and all hostilities were suspended.

The regiment remained for some time on the right bank of the Rhine, then it re-crossed the river to go into cantonments at Sarralbe, in German Lorraine and to be later sent into garrison at Sarreguemines. We lived there for three months, lacking everything, and receiving no pay; it was impossible for the hussars to live in these conditions, and it was necessary to send the regiment into cantonments in the Palatinate. From the 23rd September to the 2nd October, being in Kerrweiler, it was passed in review by General Schérer, who put me on orders as being the only *fourrier* of the regiment whose accounting was in order. We remained in this country until the 8th February 1798; during this time, the 5th Company in which I was the *fourrier*, occupied the village of Guenzheim and then the town of Wissembourg where, for a month, I was responsible for receiving and sending the despatches of the army general headquarters, then Annweiler, near Landau, the town of Spire and successively two or three villages.

Finally, on the 8th February 1798, the regiment left for Switzerland, passing through Strasbourg, Schlestadt, Colmar and Huningue, where it arrived on the 17th February.

Chapter 2

Switzerland

Curély next saw action during the War of the Second Coalition which ran from 1799 to 1801. The initial members of the coalition were Britain, Russia, Turkey and Austria. The war ended with the Treaty of Lunéville, although the Russians left the coalition in 1799 when they were evicted from Switzerland by Marshal Masséna, the campaign in which Curély was involved. The fighting in Holland between the French and Batavian Republic, and the British and Russians, was ended by the Convention of Alkmaar in the same year after the Russo-British force failed to take Holland, leaving only Austria fighting on. Austria was defeated by Napoleon at Marengo in June 1800, while Moreau also beat them at Hohenlinden before moving on to Vienna. Curély initially served under General Brune in Switzerland.

In February 1798 the 7th Hussars marched into Switzerland in support of their people against the old canton system of government. The Directory sent General Schauenbourg at the head of a corps of 10 to 12,000 men in support of a division under Ménard, drawn from the Army of the Rhine and Moselle which included Curély's 7th Hussars. Hostilities began on the 1st March and the following day the 7th Hussars pushed the Bernese troops in the direction of Soleure. The regiment once more distinguished itself, taking the enemy's artillery in a charge under the walls of that town on the 3rd of March. On the 5th, along with the 8th Hussars, they made a decisive charge at the battle of Fraubrunnen, where 35,000 French took on 20,000 Bernese commanded by General d'Erlach. The French enjoyed a decisive victory which led to the capitulation of the Bernese government after which there was a short break in hostilities.

The break lasted two months, after which the campaign against other cantons continued, drawing the French deeper into the mountains and lakes of Switzerland. The march against Stanz, the capital of Unterwald, was made in two columns, with one squadron of the 7th Hussars with each column. The march took place over some narrow tracks through the mountains, along which the cavalry was forced to dismount and lead their horses. Stanz fell on the 10th December, but the town was sacked by the French soldiers after hearing tales of the mutilation of French prisoners by the Swiss, and the cavalry, including the 7th Hussars, had to be used to re-establish order.

The army was then directed on Lucerne and the first part of the journey was to take place across the lake on which Stanz stood. Curély describes how this journey nearly turned into a disaster for his small fishing boat. The two squadrons with which Curély travelled then moved to Wintterthur where they joined the other half of the regiment.

This invasion of Switzerland led to the intervention of the Russians and Austrians and the 7th Hussars made up part of the French army put under the command of General Messéna who was tasked with stopping the Austro-Russian invasion. With Messéna's army the 7th Hussars took part in the actions at Coire and Feldkirch on the 8th and 23rd March 1799, and at the two battles of Zurich in June and September, as well as the action at Diesenhofen on the 8th October from which the Russians were forced to retreat, ending the campaign. In this final action, Curély was once more to distinguish himself. The army then took its winter quarters, remaining in northern Switzerland and expecting a resumption of the fight against Austria in the Spring of 1800.

On the 21st February 1798, the regiment was near Bienne (in the area of Porrentruy); on the 1st March, the small army commanded by General Schauenbourg attacked the Swiss in front of Soleure; the next day the town opened its gates.[6] On the 3rd March, the army

---

[6] At the moment that the town of Soleure opened its gates, the 7th and 8th Hussars were on the point of capturing all the artillery of the Swiss army.

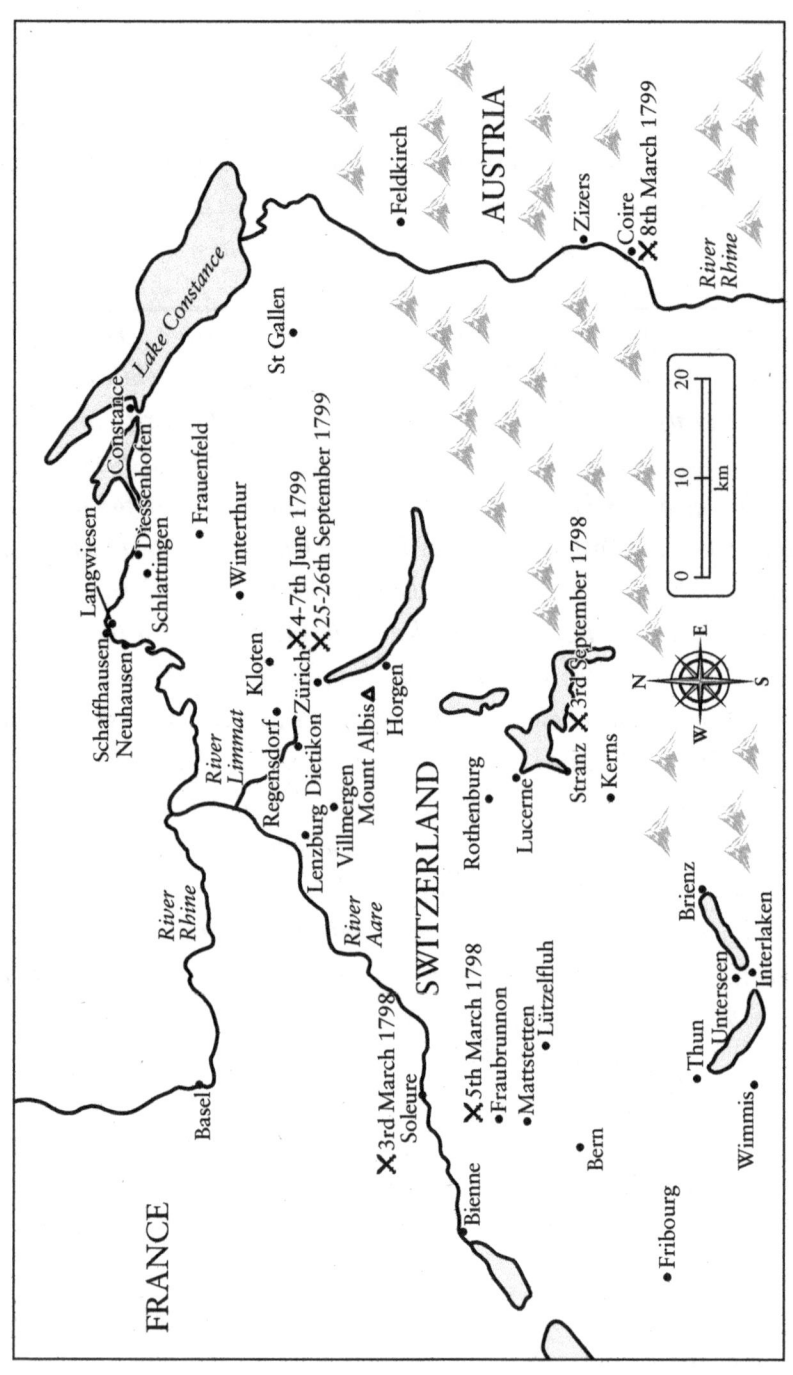

marched on Fraubrunnon and stopped a league from this village, from where I was sent with two hussars to look for forage. We had hardly gone a league to the army's right, when I saw a village which appeared to me to be able to provide the necessary rations, and it was necessary to cross a bridge over a kind of canal to get there. The forage collected, I returned with my two hussars, but I found the bridge occupied by a hundred Swiss infantry. I could not negotiate, and I had no alternative than to either allow myself to be taken prisoner, or to deceive these brave men. I took the second option. The commanding officer was about to give the order to fire on us; I shouted to him that I wanted to talk, and he did so with good grace. I told him that hostilities had ceased three hours ago and that I had been ordered to give this news to all the troops, Swiss or French, that I encountered on my way. He objected that he had drawn musket fire from the area of Fraubrunnen; I heard them as well as him, but I told him that without doubt this was soldiers discharging their arms for sure because hostilities had ceased. The brave man believed me, and my hussars and I passed on.

On the 5th, we fought the good Swiss at the battle of Fraubrunnen; their position was very strong and as well defended,[7] their soldiers, or rather the armed country people, were very brave, but they were turned on their left and then they fled. However, they attempted to reform in front of Berne when the 7th and 8th Hussars, commanded by Colonel Marizy, broke the whole Swiss army by a most brilliant charge.[8] The hussars entered the town of Berne all mixed up with the Swiss; cannons, caissons, baggage, all fell into the hands of the

---

[7] The position of Fraubrunnen is celebrated in history because it was there that the Bernese repulsed the army of Sir de Coucy in 1375; Jomini describes the battle exactly the same as Curély does here.

[8] Jomini, in his *Histoire de la Révolution*, makes a particular mention of this charge.

French. Few prisoners were taken, and we contented ourselves with disarming the combatants and sending them back to their homes. Seeing the rout of their army, the magistrates of Berne carried the keys of the town to the commanding general, who made a treaty with them, after which all the French troops took possession of the town, the gates and the arsenal and made prisoner the regular cavalry which occupied the main square.

In the charge of which I have spoken, a white-haired old man of sixty stood before me; I shouted to him to throw down his musket; as a response, he shot at me at point blank range; happily, I knocked the barrel with my sabre, and I was not hit. He made several bayonet thrusts at me, which penetrated my clothes without wounding me; I was forced to kill him. After having thus tried the courage of an old man armed to defend his country, I wanted to see the Swiss cavalry; I threw one to the ground and took his horse; the old man had showed bravery, the cavalryman did not even try to defend himself.

For two days the regiment was lodged in the town of Berne and then cantoned for some time at Matztelen, between this town and Soleure, then sent to Lutzelfluh to subdue the inhabitants and disarm them. From there it left for Fribourg and stayed there for a month, after which it had to march on the canton of Zug, which was subdued and whose inhabitants laid down their arms at the first sight of French troops. At midnight on the 28th April, the regiment entered Lucerne, remained there for eight hours and then set off for Saint-Gall and was cantoned in the vicinity of this town for a few days. After taking possession of this country, the regiment headed back and took its cantonments on the banks of the lake of Zurich; my company occupied Horgan. We remained in this neighbourhood for a month and the regiment was sent part to Berne and part to Fribourg, where the 5th Company was.

Since our entry into Switzerland, the small cantons of Schwitz, Unterwald, Glaris, Uri and the surrounding area had still not seen a Frenchman. This country is surrounded by mountains that are difficult to climb and unapproachable to vehicles, and it is only for those that move by boat on the lake of the Quatre-Cantons. The inhabitants of these cantons refused to recognise the laws imposed by the French and they had taken up arms, resolved to defend themselves to the death. After negotiations, they were promised that if they laid down their arms, the country would not be occupied by our troops, but they would not listen, thinking themselves impregnable in the shelter of their mountains and their lakes, and reassured in their ideas of resistance by the slowness of the negotiations. The French government therefore ordered a small army corps to march on the canton of Unterwald, composed of the *Légion Noire* [the Black Legion], which since has become the 14th *de ligne*, two other regiments of infantry and two squadrons of the 7th Hussars, of which I was a part. We had no artillery, the tracks not allowing them to move.

We had passed about two months at Fribourg when we received the order to leave on this expedition, and on the 27th August 1798 we slept at Almesing, near Berne, the 28th at Wimmis, two leagues from Thun, where we came to mountains of prodigious height; the 29th at Unterseen, between the lake of Unterseen[9] and that of Thun, the 30th at Brienz on the shores of the lake of this name, the 31st at Kerns in the Oberwald. It was necessary for us to follow the practicable tracks during nearly all this march which were for people on foot only; to the right was a precipice so deep that I did not dare to look down. To the left a mountainside so steep that the tops could hardly be seen; the hussars marched in single file on foot, leading their horses by the bridle. If the Swiss of the small cantons had moved in these defiles, the French would never have been able to penetrate their country by this side.

---

[9] This is how Curély names the smaller part of the lake of Brienz.

Finally arriving on the plain, we employed the 1st and 2nd September to scout the enemy position; there were a number of skirmishes on both sides and the Swiss took three soldiers from us which they returned horribly mutilated. Two of them had their tongues and ears cut off; the third had his eyes pushed in and a hand cut off. These barbarous atrocities made the infantry so angry, and in particular the *Légion Noire*, to which these badly treated soldiers belonged, that our foot soldiers surpassed the Swiss in ferocity during the fighting.

In the morning of the 3rd September, the French troops, formed in column *par peloton*, set off to attack Stanz, the capital of the canton of Unterwald. The town was surrounded by a type of earthen rampart, containing artillery, behind which were deployed all the Swiss troops with the women and children which, each in accordance with their strength, all ran to the defence of their town. Despite the artillery fire and musketry, our soldiers forced the gates and penetrated along the roads of Stanz without hesitating or stopping for an instant. The most terrible carnage then took place. All those taken on the rampart or in the streets were killed with the bayonet. The women, the old people and the children took refuge in the churches; the soldiers of the *Légion Noire* went in, and no one escaped the fury of these men, who wreaked their revenge for their mutilated comrades. Never have I seen such atrocities; the ramparts, the roads, the tracks, the churches, all were full of dead of all ages and sexes. A quarter of the houses of the town were for the most part a prey to the flames; if their occupants and those who had tried to seek refuge trying to save themselves in these burning houses, death awaited them if they left. As to the houses that were not burnt, for the most part, the people who had hidden there had had their throats cut. The officers who managed to save some of them almost fell victim for their devotion, for the furious soldiers seeing them snatching away their vengeance, shot them with their muskets. The commanding general finally re-established order in hunting these madmen. The two squadrons of hussars only drew their sabres to assist the general in this task in preventing, as far as it was in their power, the massacre spreading.

A brigadier[10], whose name I cannot remember but remains conserved in the history of Switzerland, seeing a French infantryman about to plunge his bayonet into the body of a child of three or four years old, stopped the blow and took the child, saying to him, "Poor child! I will be your father." And, indeed, the brigadier took extreme care of the child, who later was able to take it to its parents. A Swiss painter has represented this brigadier in the uniform of the 7th Hussars, saving the child from the blow which would have killed him; at the bottom of the picture is the name of the brigadier with this inscription; *Ich will dein Vater sein* (I will be your father).

For the rest of the day and throughout the night, the two squadrons of hussars were far from being tranquil in the presence of the fire, which continued at several points and the infantry, who were always trying to get back into the town; we finished by putting the fires out. However, order and tranquillity were maintained until the morning of the 4th September. The troops then left this stay of horror, leaving behind them the town with its houses still smoking and its roads still covered in bodies and blood.

The hussars headed towards the lake of the Quatre-Cantons to be embarked on poor fishing boats to go to Lucerne. Going from Stanz to the sides of the lake, we noticed in the fields a Swiss still armed with a club with iron spikes on the end. We ran to him, he wanted to defend himself, but two men disarmed him without harming him; we forced him to follow the column and he found himself embarked with me. In a poor fishing boat, we placed six men and six horses; the horses, striking with their hooves on the planks of the deck, made them bend to the point that we feared at any moment that they would

---

[10] The equivalent of corporal in the French army.

break. Out of these six men we were four friends and immediately we were on board, the task was shared out according to their knowledge of sailing. M. Dey *maréchal de logis* [sergeant] was the grand admiral and at the same time the pilot steering the boat with a long pole. M. Colommier, also *maréchal de logis*, and brigadier Gusler[11] helped to keep the boat moving, a hussar and I held the horses, whilst the Swiss refused to do any work. The boat went to the right and then to the left and after having sailed a distance of about half a league, we decided to return to the point where we boarded; but we could not manage it and it was necessary to surrender ourselves to great efforts to continue on our way. The horses would not be quiet, they fought or tried to drink; the boat was always close to capsizing. Finally, after much hard work, we reached port and the Swiss man disembarked first without anyone noticing until he had escaped. We reckoned ourselves lucky to have arrived. In truth, several of our comrades took more time than us to make the journey, which was not more than three quarters of a league, but, happily, there were no accidents. The journey could not have been conducted in better conditions, for the troop, in arriving on the shore of the lake, found only a few boats good or less good, bigger or not and not a sailor, not a local man. Finally, each did the best they could, and we slept that night at Rothenbourg, close to Lucerne. We went to Saint-Gall via Zurich and Winterhur, where we remained until the 20th October 1798. From there, the regiment was sent into cantonments at Schaffhausen and the surrounding area, and the company was placed at Neuhausen,

---

[11] Brigadier Gusler had been, as a trumpeter, put on orders for his fine conduct at the battle of Rastadt in 1796. He became a lieutenant-general in the wake of and under the reign of Louis-Philippe. He always kept the greatest love for Curély and, after the death of this last, always spoke of his old comrade of the 7th Hussars with expressions of the liveliest admiration.

two hundred paces from the source of the Rhine, where this river fell from a height of eighty feet.

However, a new war was declared with Austria; the 7th Hussars, like all the troops in the small Army of Helvetia, were naturally part of the army commanded by Masséna, who started hostilities by crossing the Rhine close to Coire [Chur] on the 6th March 1799. The enemy was repulsed on the 7th March in front of this town; he was beaten and left many dead on the battlefield, where we made four to five hundred prisoners. On the 13th, the army marched on Zizers and on the 21st on Feldkich, where on the 23rd it attempted an attack that had no result. However, the Army of the Danube, commanded by Jourdan, had been beaten at Stockach and had re-crossed the Rhine. Masséna had to retire and abandon the country of the Grisons; he was invested with the command of the two armies which joined and took position on the left bank of the Rhine. The hussars extended along this river and my company was placed at Langwissen, close to Schaffhausen. This town, which the Austrians seized on the 14th April, is situated on the right bank of the Rhine. The enemy burnt the fine wooden bridge and we remained in position opposite them until the 18th May, the date on which we started to leave the banks of the Rhine to affect our retreat on Zurich. On the 22nd, the regiment encountered the enemy on the road from Winterthur to Schaffhausen [action of Frauenfeld]; the two armies being in contact at various points, I noticed an Austrian hussar who was a little too far ahead. I went forward on his right as if I was heading towards the enemy and I passed him by some distance, finding myself between him and the enemy squadrons; then I quickly returned heading for this hussar, who took me for one of his own. I sabred him, threw him down and took his horse. The army remained the following two days in much the same positions; on the third day, Masséna wanted to push forward a strong reconnaissance and when we had arrived close to the small river Thur, infantry and cavalry were engaged. A large corporal of the Barco Hussars advanced to charge me, I did not think I was strong enough to fight with such a large man; I only took the time to drop my sabre by the sword knot, in the same movement drew my pistols and at the moment that he struck his blow, I lowered my head and placed the end of the barrel of my pistol under his chin. I left him stone dead and took his horse[12].

During the retreat on Zurich, the regiment was constantly ordered to scout the army's left flank. Placed at Regensdorf, two hours from Zurich, on the right bank of the Limmat, it took part in all the engagements of the advance posts which took place on the 31st May, 1st, 2nd and 3rd June, as well as the battle of Kloten on the 5th, 6th and 7th of June [first battle of Zurich]. This battle, which lasted three days, was very bloody; Masséna, without being beaten, decided to abandon his position before Zurich, passed through this town and over the Limmat and deployed on mount Albis, supporting his right on Lake Zug and his left on the Rhine [Reuss]. The regiment had slept at Preisbeck on the 7th, on the left bank of the Limmat; the retreat was made during the night and throughout the next day, without a single musket shot being fired. On the evening of the 8th, the regiment took position at Dietikon, two leagues from Zurich; it remained there for forty-four days, the enemy being repulsed several times. On the 23rd July, the regiment moved forwards to an hour from Zurich and remained there until the 1st August. As it was very tiring at the advance posts, it was relieved there by the 8th Hussars and left for Vilmergen and surroundings, a league and a half from Lenzbourg, on the road to Lucerne. It was then part of the reserve and stayed in these cantonments until the 25th September; that is to say for forty six days. During this time, it received men, horses and

---

[12] General Edward Colbert, to whom Curély was aide de camp during the 1809 campaign, said that this rough *sabreur* had killed the equivalent of a regiment of lancers in his military career.

some equipment from the depot; it was put back into a good state to re-enter the campaign.

On the 24th September 1799, the regiment received the order to start their march during the night of the 24th to 25th; it arrived at Dietikon on the 25th before dawn and crossed the river Limmat towards 5am, on the bridge of boats that the French had thrown opposite the village under fire from the Russian skirmishers. The battle [second battle of Zurich] started over the next two days, the 25th and 26th, and was very bloody. In losing it, the Russians lost all their hopes and all those of the coalition. The enemy's loss was estimated as 21,000 men; this number is grossly exaggerated. However, the carnage was terrible in the town of Zurich. The regiment, which flanked the left of the army, took in two charges, two enemy camps and made numerous prisoners; it lost during the 26th, the bravest of its soldiers, *brigadier* Müller. This battle has been called the battle of Dietikon[13]. On the 27th, the regiment slept at Angerdorf, a league and a half from Zurich, and by successive marches, interspersed with rests, it arrived at Schlattingen on the 7th October, close to Diessenhofen on the Rhine. This was a remarkable journey. A small force of the French army, of which the regiment was a part, was ordered to follow the Russians who were retiring towards the Rhine, while Masséna marched ahead of Sowarow who was descending the Saint-Gothard pass. The column which had the mission of observing Diessenhofen was composed of a squadron of the 7th Hussars, two guns and a regiment of infantry, all under the command of a general[14]. This general deployed our squadron and his artillery on a height which dominated Diessenhofen, while the infantry regiment was well behind, covered by a ditch, which was very useful, as we will see. From time to time we saw some Cossacks

---

[13] History calls it the battle of Zurich.
[14] General Jordy.

and infantry crossing the Rhine on the Diessenhofen bridge, to get onto the right bank. It was a ruse on their part; they had left in the town a body of infantry and cavalry and, as the French were quietly in their bivouacs, I went forward on foot out of curiosity, when I noticed some infantry and cavalry which were moving along the gardens and orchards. I ran as quickly as possible towards the captain, shouting "To horse!" The squadron was hardly in the saddle than it was broken by a body of eight hundred cavalry. The guns were taken and nearly all the gunners cut down. At the same time, Russian infantry arrived at the *pas de course*[15], moving against our infantry regiment which held well and, by a well-maintained musket fire, forced the enemy to retire in disorder, leaving the battlefield covered in their dead. Despite its small number, our squadron retook the charge and forced the Russians to give up the two guns that they had captured. This counterattack had been made on the express orders of Sowarow, demanding from his generals, under pain of death, not to take one more step to the rear. In the evening, our small column beat a retreat towards Vilhausen, where it arrived at 8am. On the 9th, we retook our march to observe the Russians again from close quarters, and we slept at Islikon, then on the 10th at Metzingen, and we arrived near Diessenhofen on the 11th where we found all the Russians had crossed back onto the right bank and burnt the bridge. During this time, another column, in which was the other part of our regiment, was directed on Constance, where it encountered the Russians and French émigrés. After a stubborn fight, these were forced to abandon Constance. Masséna had beaten Sowarow and forced the coalition army to retire onto the right bank of the Rhine. After all these victories, the French army went into cantonments.

---

[15] Running.

Chapter 3

The Army of the Rhine and the Camp of Boulogne

After their defeat in Switzerland, the Russians had withdrawn from the 2nd Coalition, effectively leaving Austria to fight on alone. Napoleon Bonaparte had seized power in France with himself as the First Consul. Threatened by two Austrian armies, one in Germany and one in northern Italy, Napoleon reorganised the French armies. The First Consul moved to take command of the Army of Italy, whilst the 7th Hussars found themselves back in the Army of the Rhine. It was composed of four corps commanded by Generals Sainte-Suzanne, Gouvion Saint-Cyr, Lecourbe and the reserve under General Moreau who was given the overall command. The 7th Hussars, 600 strong, served in the division of General Lorges, part of Lecourbe's corps.

Napoleon's campaign against the Austrian commander in Italy, General Melas, was to culminate at the French victory of Marengo on the 14th June 1800. Operations in southern Germany began on the 1st May and Curély's regiment assisted in the crossing of the Rhine at Stein the same day and at the battles of Engen, Moeskirch and Memmingen on the 3rd, 6th and 10th May. The corps was then detached under the command of General Molitor against the rebels in the Tyrol, seizing Bregenz on the 24th May and took a brilliant part in the actions which resulted in the taking of Feldkirch on the 14th July. On the 13th September, during the armistice that followed this success, Curély was promoted to maréchel des logis chef *(senior sergeant). He had been fourrier for six years, a considerable time, but being responsible for running his company's books, his captain admitted that he had been too valuable to promote.*

When the war restarted in mid-November, the 7*th* Hussars continued as part of Lecourbe's corps, but the corps was not present at the battle of Hohenlinden that was won by Moreau against the Archduke John on the 3*rd* December. On the 9*th*, Lecourbe threw his corps forwards, crossing the Inn at Neubeurn and imprudently crossed the Saale unsupported, upon which he found himself facing the whole Austrian army, now commanded by the much more effective Archduke Charles. However, Lecourbe was saved by the appearance of Decaen's troops at which the Austrians withdrew. It was in this action, on the 14*th* December, that Curély received his first wound when a ball cut his scabbard in two and gave him a heavy bruise on the hip. The pursuit of the Austrians was continued to the east as far as Kremsmünster, shortly after which there was a suspension of arms prior to peace.

After the peace of Lunéville (9*th* February 1801) ended the war, the 7*th* Hussars were garrisoned at Besancon in eastern France, and then in Deux-Ponts [Zweibrücken] in the northeast. On the 17*th* June 1802 Curély was promoted to adjutant sous-officier *(the equivalent of a modern sergeant-major); a rather quicker advancement than his previous one. It was also at this time that Colonel Marisy was promoted to* général de brigade *and left the regiment after nine years in command; he was replaced by Colonel Marx.*

The regiment was then ordered to form three war squadrons and to move to the camp at Bruges, which formed the right of the armée des côtes de l'Océan *(Army of the Sea Coast) which was preparing for the invasion of England. The camp consisted of three infantry divisions and a brigade consisting of three cavalry regiments, of which the 7*th* Hussars was one. The whole was commanded by General Davout (who was to become a marshal of France in May 1804). This army was to become* la Grande-Armée *and Davout's troops were to become its 3*rd* Corps. This army would earn renown at the great battles of Austerlitz, Auerstadt, Eylau, Eckmühl and Wagram. However, the 7*th* Hussars was only to be a part of this corps during the campaign of Austerlitz.*

The Army of the Rhine and the Camp of Boulogne 31

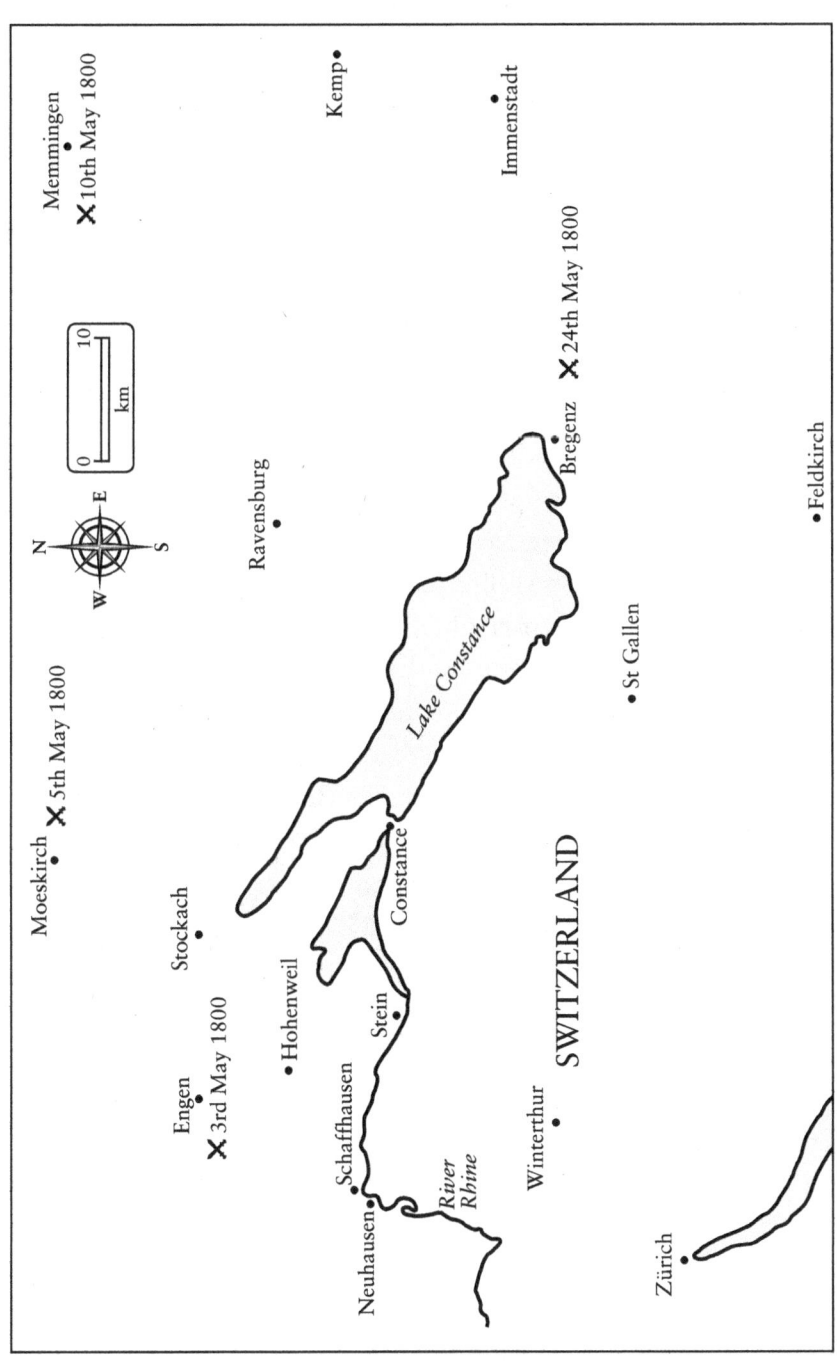

On the 1st May 1800, Lecourbe's corps, of which the 7th Hussars was a part, and which formed the right of the army commanded by Moreau, crossed the Rhine a little below Stein and above Schaffhausen; the Austrians were beaten and the regiment took an artillery piece. The corps slept at Neuhausen, close to the fall of the Rhine. On the 2nd, Lecourbe's army corps marched off to make its junction with the army and slept close to Hohenweil, a fortress which is situated on a high mountain and which surrendered to the French without firing a cannon shot.

On the 3rd, the battle of Engen took place, which the Austrians lost. Whilst Moreau was the victor at Engen, General Lecourbe fought an Austrian corps at Stockach, from which doubtlessly the name the battle of Engen-Stockach came, given by several people who were present. For myself, I took an enemy horse in a charge in which the regiment took part. On the 4th, the main body of the army marched on Stockach; in the morning of the 5th, the whole army moved on Moeskirch and fought another battle with the Austrians which, after in determined defence, were forced to retreat. On the 6th, the army pursued the enemy, and, on the 10th, there was a third battle with the Austrians at Memmingen.

However, on the 22nd May, my regiment received the order to come under the orders of General ***[16] at Brégenz and arrived, at midnight on the 24th, in front of this town which was occupied by the Austrians. The infantry broke down the gates with blows of an axe and we entered Brégenz at the gallop, where we made some prisoners. This detached force, composed of an infantry regiment, two cannon and a company of hussars, formed the extreme right of the army. It took position at Brégenz and remained there until the 11th July, every day pushing reconnaissances towards Feldkirch,

---

[16] The general he does not name is General Molitor, who managed, with a very weak force, to hold in check the whole Austrian army of the Tyrol.

without having any serious engagement either at Brégenz or in the surrounding area. During this time, the main army manoeuvred on the Danube and won the battle of Hochstardt. On the 12th, the troops from Kempten were concentrated with those at Brégenz and they marched together on Feldkirch, which they took from the Austrians after several combats in which they lost many men.[17] On the 18th, we learnt that hostilities had ceased, and the armies went into cantonments.

The regiment left Feldkirch after a series of marches with alternate rests, forced by the necessity of procuring forage. After being moved forward to approach the theatre of war, then to drop back because of the prolongation of the armistice, on the 27th October, it found itself at Vertach, where I was made *maréchal de logis chef* of the company in which I had been *fourrier* and which was still commanded by Captain Briquet.

Thus, from the 4th April 1794 to the 27th October 1800, I had remained for six years, six months and twenty three days as a *fourrier* in the same company. It is true that, two years before my nomination to the rank of *maréchal des logis chef*, I had refused that of *maréchal des logis en second*, not seeing in this rank, nearly always insignificant, any chance of being noticed.

Hostilities about to resume, on the 19th November the regiment left its cantonments in Salmansweiler to observe the Tyrol along the frontier and towards the river Inn, on which was found the main body of the French army. It was part of Lecourbe's corps and did not take part in the famous battle of Hohenlinden, won by Moreau on the 3rd December. After the defeat of the Austrians, Moreau ordered the crossing of the Inn to pursue them and at daybreak on the 9th,

---

[17] This series of combats, after which Molitor seized Feldkirch, defended by superior forces, was particularly glorious for the 7th Hussars, which formed the entire cavalry force of General Molitor.

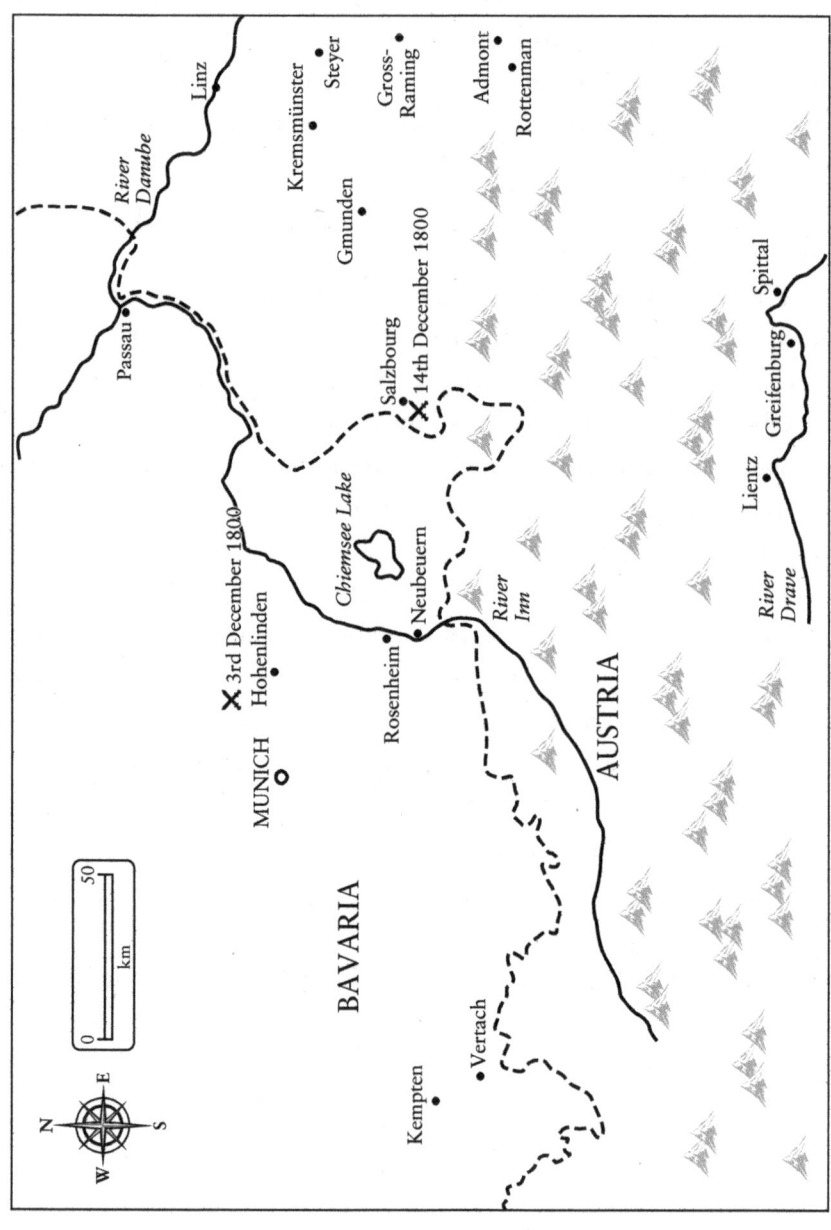

General Lecourbe established a bridge over the Inn at Neubeuern, between Kufstein and Rosenheim, under the protection of thirty guns. The bridge was completed in less than two hours and, towards 9am, the troops crossed it. The enemy had taken position to its rear and was repulsed after a dogged fight. In the evening, the regiment bivouacked close to the Chiemsee lake. The next day, we pursued the enemy and the day after that, the 11th, we arrived at Trauenstein, on the 12th, two and a half leagues from Salzbourg and on the 13th, at Hoffen-Salzbourg; on the 14th, General Lecourbe, having crossed the Saal with his army corps, attacked the Austrians under the walls of Salzbourg, was repulsed and lost many men. In this battle, a cannon ball cut the scabbard of my sabre and made a light bruise on my left leg. On this day, General Lecourbe was accused of wanting to enter Salzbourg first, without waiting for the other corps.[18] The enemy retreated during the night and on the 15th we entered the town; we continued to pursue the Austrians on the road to Kremsmünster and, on the 18th, the army corps passed the night in bivouac, beyond Gmünden, in more than two feet of snow and without fires, in order to hide our movement from the enemy.

On the 19th, we set off in the early hours to arrive at Kremsmünster before the Austrian army, which was retiring on this town by the road from ***.[19] The regiment was deployed as the advance guard, as always, and marched in a countryside that was thickly wooded, without being preceded by infantry. Arriving a league from Kremsmünster, myself, *maréchal des logis chef*, marching at the rear of the 5th Company, I suddenly noticed to my left a post of fifty

---

[18] General Decaen had been sent to cross the Saal upstream; having only a few troops in front of him, he crossed easily. His appearance on the right bank determined the enemy to retreat. Thus, if Lecourbe had waited a day longer, he would have avoided a bloody and pointless engagement.

[19] This name is left blank in the manuscript. It should be Steyer.

Austrian cuirassiers, bivouacking in an orchard covered with trees and surrounded by hedges. Followed without delay by the left of my company, we took the post without firing a shot and for myself, I took three horses. It is good to observe that this post had not noticed either the advance-guard composed of fifty men or our first squadron which had passed by it to the side and, what is more surprising is that our advance-guard, which was supposed to scout the front and flanks of the column, had not noticed this post either, that the 1st Company and all the head of the 5th, had also passed it without seeing it and that it was me who had noticed it first. Immediately that I had taken my three horses, I dismounted my own, which was badly shod and slipping on the snow and ice, and chose to ride, until my own was shod, the best and best shod of the three. A quarter of a league further on, I requested the permission of my captain to leave the company for a moment and to move to the advance-guard to have a ride on my new prize. At the same moment, the advance-guard fell in with an enemy infantry post, which was immediately charged. With my new horse, I crossed alone to the head of the charge and at more than two hundred paces ahead, sabring to right and left, more than 2,000 Austrian infantry were retiring in column. The regiment took them all prisoners, but I did not stop there, and went on to take a good horse in the ranks of the enemy cavalry which was also retiring. We continued to march on the town fighting until night and capturing many men. For us this was the last combat of the campaign. During the night the enemy retreated on Steyer, where the regiment followed on the 21st and where it stayed until the 26th. We found there some guns, caissons and equipages abandoned by the Austrians which were hastening to cross the river.

A suspension of arms had been concluded on the 25th, to negotiate a peace. In consequence of this suspension, the regiment crossed the river and slept successively at Gross-Raming, Admont and Rottenmann. We were in this last town with the émigré dragoons of Condé's corps. All passed quietly and each took a different route the next morning. We pushed as far as Oberwals, Greifenburg and even to Lientz, where we remained from the 9th to the 16th January 1801, to then move on to Greifenburg and Spital. It was then that the Austrian army, with a strength of 25,000 men that had occupied the Tyrol, passed through our cantonments because of the treaty, to go towards Vienna. This force, infantry, cavalry and artillery, were fine looking. If the Austrian general, instead of remaining in the mountains doing nothing, had been called in time to take part in the battle of Hohenlinden, the result could have been different, for on this famous day, the Austrian army was well concentrated and well deployed. A corps of 25,000 men falling on General Richepanse would certainly have beaten him, and he would not have been able to take the Austrian army in the rear as he actually did.

The regiment set off on the 15th March to return to France by Spital, Gmünden, Salzbourg-Hoffen, Hezling, Landsberg, Memmingen, Bettingen close to Ulm, Bertheim close to Ludswigbourg, Besigheim, Heilbronn, Heidelberg and finally crossed the Rhine at Mannheim, having made thirty six stages, intermingled with twenty six days of rest, of which sixteen were at Mindelheim in Swabia. When it crossed the Rhine, the regiment had six hundred mounted men, all old hussars on superb horses; the equipment, the harness and equipment were all in the best state. It was the same across the whole army, infantry and cavalry. We could then start a new war against the whole of Europe and Europe would have been defeated.

After having been cantoned for a fortnight at Franckenthal, the regiment was sent into garrison at Besancon. It remained in barracks there for eight months and twenty-six days, which were eight months and twenty-six days of prison. During this time, the men were disgusted with the service and the horses died of hunger. Such garrisons are most punishing for the cavalry... Happily, I was able to obtain a leave pass to go to Avillers, where I sorted out some family affairs. After my return to Besancon, which was on the 6th January, I again had some distraction; the first two squadrons left this sad garrison to be detached to Gray, but they returned to Besancon on the 20th February. Then the regiment received the order to form a *compagnie d'élite*, composed of a hundred and twenty men chosen from amongst all the other companies, the first squadron was disbanded, and the élite company replaced it. For myself, I left the 5th Company and became the *maréchal des logis chef* of the élite company.

On the 8th June 1802, the regiment left Besancon with the greatest pleasure, to go to Deux-Ponts, where it arrived on the 21st having passed through Rioz, Vesoul, Luxeuil, Plombières, Épinal, Charmes (a stopover), Lunéville, Vic, Morhange, Saint-Avold (a stopover) and Sarrebrück. On the 17th, I was nominated *adjutant sous-officier*.

The rank of *maréchal des logis chef*, which I had held for a year and eight months, is one of the most important; he can send home those who have been reported for exemplary conduct. To ensure obedience, it is necessary to have the best reputation; an established honesty is indispensable and the least blot in this respect puts you out of the reckoning for the lowest rank. It is necessary to be severe but just and know how to command men. It is necessary, as far as possible, to treat them well and however, this good should never be to the detriment of the service. A good *maréchal des logis chef* should be the soldier's father, without ever letting discipline slip. He must also be a model of propriety and good turnout. As far as possible, he must be a good instructor or at least be capable of being one, because to be obeyed it is necessary to know himself how to do what he is asking to be done. It is not by frequent punishments that one makes oneself heard; it is by firmness of character. It is only commanding one's subordinates to do the right things, never swearing at them, being polite to them, but without weakness or favour. The *maréchal des logis chef* is the right-hand man of the captain; all that he does, he does in the name of the captain.

We remained in Deux-Ponts until the 5th May 1803. This town, the ancient residence of the dukes of Deux-Ponts, is good for horses; there is a passable ménage, good barracks, and fine stables so the regiment made progress in its training. The two first squadrons, of which I was a part, left this town on the 3rd May, remaining in barracks for a few days in an old convent in Worms, then in Mayence where they were re-joined by the 3rd and 4th Squadrons and where we remained for four months. Mayence is a strong town, situated on the Rhine; the air there is unhealthy, life very expensive, the hay poor and, by all the reports again, a poor garrison for cavalry. The regiment left it on the 10th September 1803 and went through Bingen, Coblentz, Bonn, Cologne, Juliers and Aix-la-Chapelle, to Maëstricht, where it arrived on the 2nd October and remained on the 2nd and 3rd. During these two days, Colonel Marx, who had replaced Colonel Marisy[20] in command of the regiment, arrived to form three war squadrons that were destined to move to the coast for the expedition to England; the 4th Squadron, composed of all the worst men and horses, was left at Maëstricht. The three war squadrons left immediately and arrived at Bruges on the 15th October, after having passed through Tongres, Saint-Trond, Louvain, Brussels (with a stop), Alost, Gand, Deynse and Thielt.

The headquarters of the regiment and the élite company remained in Bruges; the three squadrons were cantoned in the villages at various distances from the sea and did service on the coast. This situation lasted from the 15th October 1803 until the 17th September 1804. During this time the colonel received from the Minister of

---

[20] Marisy had been promoted to *général de brigade*. He was to distinguish himself in the most brilliant fashion at the battle of Austerlitz, at which he commanded one of the brigades of Kellerman's division, then in the campaigns of 1806 and 1807 at the head of a brigade of dragoons. Sent with this brigade to Spain, he died there in March 1811, assassinated by guerrillas.

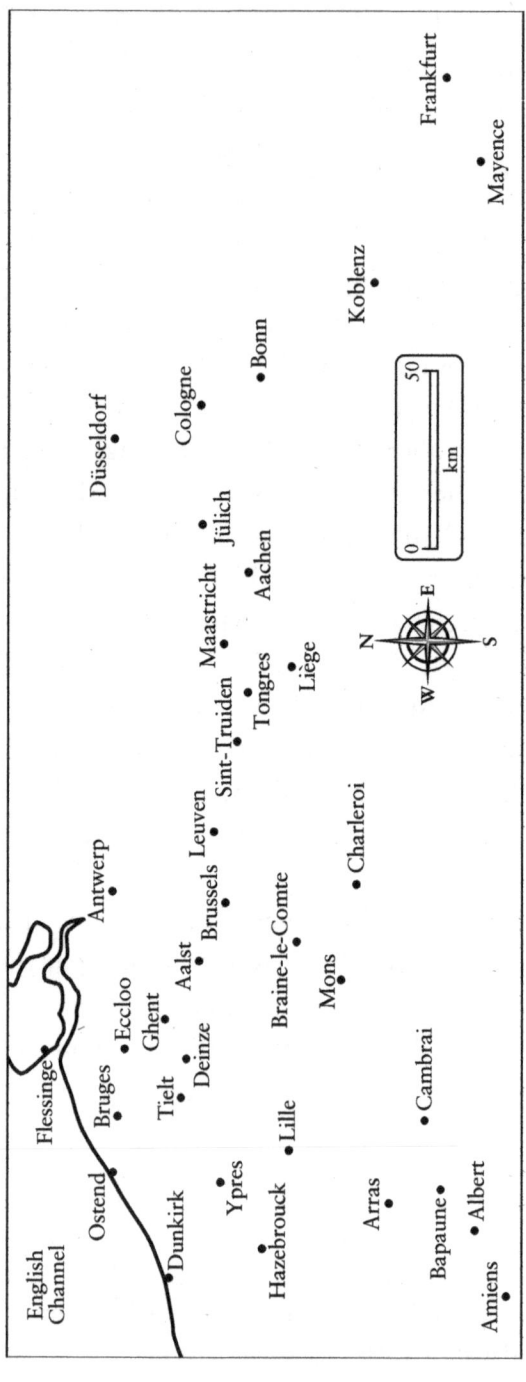

War the order to send a captain to Amiens, to receive conscripts destined for the regiment. *M. le Colonel* Marx decided to entrust me with this mission rather than send a captain to do it and I went to Amiens in my rank of *adjutant sous-officier*. I found there five non-commissioned officers from the depot which were under my orders, and I remained there for eight days to receive the hundred and fifty recruits that I led to Maëstricht, passing through Albert, Bapaume, Cambrai, Valenciennes, Mons, Braine-le-Comte, Brussels, Louvain, Saint-Trond and Tongres.

To lead these recruits to the regiment it was necessary to employ the greatest care and use no threats of punishment. It was necessary to persuade them, to encourage them, give them pay every day and be careful that the *brigadiers* paid very exactly the men of their squads and above all, not to make them pay to drink with them as happens so often. The commander of the detachment must march with the recruits throughout the journey, talk with them and promise them everything they ask for. My good Picards often asked me how long they would be in the regiment before they became non-commissioned officers, etc., etc. I gave positive responses to all their requests and I only had two deserters.

I remained in Maëstricht from the 3rd February 1804 until the 11th March, and I then left to join the regiment at Bruges. During this time, it often changed its cantonments, at Eccloo, Ypres, Hazebrouck, Ostend and finally it was in barracks at Dunkerque from the 14th August to the 3rd September 1805.

The Netherlands was generally unhealthy, particularly for those who were not born there; the regiment had many sick at Bruges. Eccloo, which is situated between this town and Gand, is healthier. Ostende is better than Bruges, but going towards Flessingue, where the regiment furnished detachments every five days, the air became so unhealthy that our detachments returned with most of their men struck with fever, despite the distributions of eau-de-vie[21] and vinegar given to the troop each day. At Dunkirque the regiment had no one sick, there they had distributions of wine, vinegar and eau-de-vie.

Six months after the arrival of the regiment on the coast, we embarked a hundred and fifty hussars on *prames* [a type of boat] with officers drawn from the depot to command them. These men were armed and equipped and, on the same boats were also embarked a hundred and fifty complete harnesses to be distributed after the unloading of the army in England to mount English horses.

The mounted squadrons were to be embarked at the moment of departure of the expedition. We had already embarked and disembarked several times a certain number of horses on all the transport boats to practise men and horses. The army was fully prepared to make an expedition to England when it received the order to march on the Rhine. It had stretched all along the coast of Holland as far as Bayonne. The principal forces were concentrated in the camps of Ostende and Boulogne; when the emperor joined the army his imperial headquarters was established in this last town.

---

[21] A cheap form of brandy.

Chapter 4

The Austerlitz Campaign of 1805

The war of the Third Coalition began in 1805; the coalition consisting of Austria, Britain, Russia, and nominally, Sweden. The French army was poised to invade Britain, but the defeat of the French and Spanish fleets at Trafalgar and the threat of invasion from a resurgent Austria, forced Napoleon to renounce his planned invasion. The Grand-Armée *was launched in an astonishing march towards the east to meet the threat of Austria, whose army was commanded by the Archduke Ferdinand, later to be supported by the Russian army of Kutusov.*

*Davout's troops took no part in the manoeuvre that surrounded the Austrians under Mack at Ulm (26*th *October), but protected Napoleon's rear by screening Munich. After his success at Ulm, Napoleon marched east against Vienna, attempting to prevent Kutusov's Russians joining the Austrians. On this march, Davout found himself providing flank protection on the right (south) of the army, thus avoiding the manoeuvring of the main body commanded by Napoleon against the retreating Russians and fragmented Austrians. On the 8*th *December, Davout's corps encountered Merveldt's 10,000 Austrians at Maria-Zell and heavily defeated them. Called to join the emperor near Vienna, Davout decided to pursue the demoralised Austrians with just a hundred hussars, whose advance-guard, consisting of only twenty men of the 7*th *Hussars, was commanded by Curély. In the following actions, Curély, leading his detachment of just twenty hussars, captured three hundred Austrian infantrymen and then charged an Austrian cavalry regiment of five hundred men! This action* *earned him two invitations to supper with Marshal Davout, but Curély, a lion in the face of the enemy, was too timid to accept an invitation to eat with a marshal of France!*

The 7th Hussars took no part in the famous battle of Austerlitz, during which Curély served away from the regiment on a long reconnaissance. He re-joined after the battle when Davout concentrated his corps to take part in the pursuit. An armistice was concluded soon after.

Curély's fine conduct during the campaign was well rewarded. On the 14th March 1806 he was to be awarded the **Légion d'Honneur** *for this campaign and on the 8th January 1806, aged 32, he was commissioned as a* **sous-lieutenant** *(second lieutenant).*

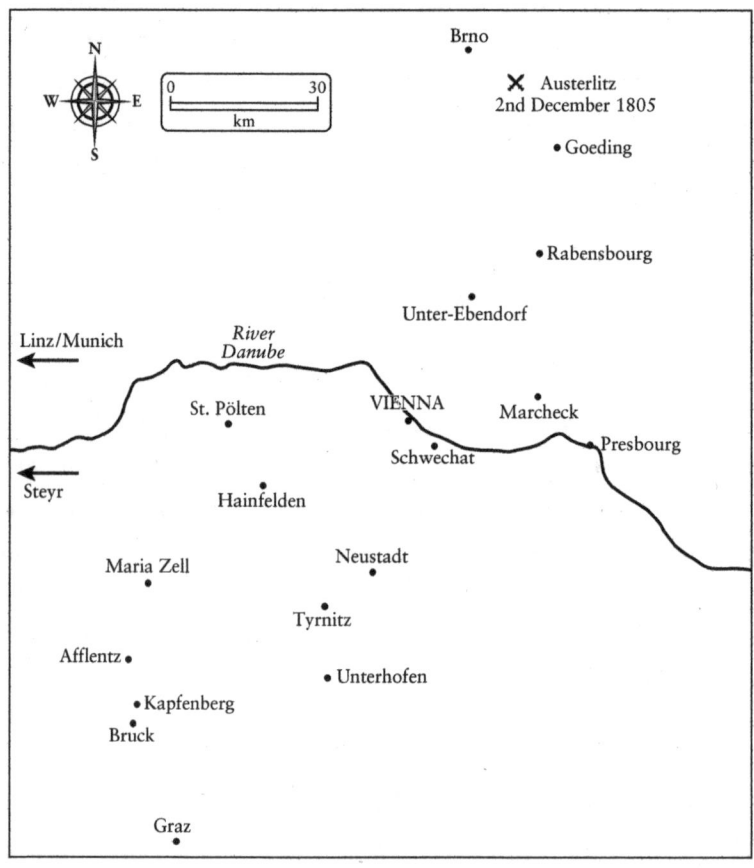

The army, the finest in the world, set off on its march on the 2nd November 1805, by all roads, to move on the Rhine. The regiment passed by Cassel, Bailleul, Lille, Tournay (stopover), Ath, Mons, Binche, Charleroy (stopover), Namur, Ciney, Marche-en-Famène, Saint-Hubert, Neufchâteau (stopover). I left the column at Neufchâteau on the 17th, to go to see my father, without doubting it would be for the last time, for I had the misfortune to lose him on the 2nd December following. After having passed three days with him, I re-joined the regiment at Sarrebrück on the 24th September. It passed through Deux-Ponts [Zweibrücken] and Kaiserslautern, from where it doubled the leg to go to Grünstadt. Finally, on the 28th, the army corps of Marshal Davout, of which the regiment was a part, crossed the Rhine at Mannheim on the 1st October. It then crossed the Neckar and, on the 8th October, part of the infantry crossed the Danube on rafts, while the cavalry, the artillery and the rest of the infantry crossed the river over the bridge at Neubourg.

The army corps moved on Munich to prevent the Austrian reinforcements and the first Russian troops marching to the support of the Austrian army that the emperor had forced to retire into the town of Ulm, after having beaten it in several engagements. This army, commanded by Mac [sic], laid down its arms on the 26th October [at Ulm] and was led as prisoners into France. The emperor then advanced with all his troops and, as the enemy had burnt the bridge over the Inn at Mühldorf, Marshal Davout repaired it quickly. The infantry and cavalry crossed there, the cavalrymen crossing on foot, leading their horses by the bridle. We crossed the Traun at Lembach [Lambach] on the 2nd November, the Ens at Steyer [Steyr] on the 6th. Near Maria-Zell on the 10th November, Marshal Davout's corps struck the Austrian corps of Field Marshal Meerfeld, beat it and took 3,000 to 4,000 men and a quantity of cannon.

The next day he moved on the capital of Austria, but a hundred men chosen from amongst the 7th Hussars and commanded by *chef d'escadrons* Méda, were charged with the pursuit of Meerfeld's corps which was retiring on Bruck; I was chosen personally by the *chef d'escadron* to form his advance guard, with twenty non-commissioned officers and hussars of my choice. Early in the morning of the same day, the detachment started its march. I had been ordered to charge all out when I met the enemy. After having made a great number of prisoners during the day, I finished by entering their camp at ten o'clock in the evening. I had taken all their posts and I threw the camp into the greatest disorder by a rapid charge with my handful of men shouting wildly. The commandant had remained a league to the rear to gather up all the prisoners. The next day, the 8th, the detachment started its march in the early hours and, a league before arriving at Afflenz, I captured more than three hundred infantry with my twenty men. I continued my advance when, in a very sunken lane which only allowed a frontage of five men, my small detachment was suddenly charged by the regiment of Meerfeld Uhlans, five hundred strong. There was no middle way; it was necessary to be audacious to be victorious by not leaving my sunken lane. This is what I told myself; in the position that I find myself in, I have twenty men with me; ten thousand men could not force me to retire, since they could only fight on a front of five like us. So, instead of turning back in view of this troop, which was coming towards us at the gallop, I said to my hussars, "You are all the bravest soldiers of the regiment; charge and break through the enemy." I left at the gallop. The shock was hard and the fight lasted nearly ten minutes, head-on, man to man, until the enemy, noticing the commandant's detachment which had arrived, believed that it was the head of a considerable column and, turning about, started his retreat. I pursued it into the town of Afflenz and made many prisoners, while the *chef d'escadron* held on the height to the rear with his eighty men. If, at the sight of this column, I had retreated with my twenty men and left the sunken lane, the hundred men of the detachment would all have been captured, since the rest of the regiment had followed Marshal Davout and was eight or ten leagues from us.

During the fight in the sunken lane where the two heads of column sabred each other man to man, the blade of my sabre was broken in striking at the face of an uhlan. I only had the time to take the sabre from a hussar who was at my side and who, turning to the rear, was immediately replaced by his *serre-file*[22]. When the detachment re-joined the regiment, the *chef d'escadron* made his report to the colonel, with whom I had not yet made war, "This devil Curély," he wrote, "he is good everywhere!" I received the cross of honour [the cross of the *Légion d'Honneur*] for this action.

The enemy having abandoned the small town of Afflenz, which is surrounded by walls, the detachment slept in the place the same evening; we closed the gates and put a good guard on each during the night; the hussars of the guard remaining on foot with their horses close by.

An isolated corps of 30,000 Austrians came to pass through the town. Finding the gates closed and guarded by men who received them with carbine shots, they passed by and continued on their way; we took it for an alert.

The next day, the detachment left again very early and marched on Kapfenberg. On the route to Vienna and Bruck Meerfeld's corps had evacuated Bruck and retired on the Austrian Army of Italy. Finding itself beaten there [Bruck] by the main body of the French army, which had marched long days by the road from Saint-Polten to Vienna, it could have been forced to lay down its arms at the exit to the mountains, as it had Marshal Davout's corps behind it and the main army in front of it. But it manoeuvred wisely and retired towards Italy.

---

[22] Literally the 'file-tightener' or 'file-closer'; i.e., the man in the rank immediately behind.

The detachment having mounted, the *chef d'escadron* strongly reprimanded an officer, M. Legendre, because several men of his sub-division had drunk several bottles of wine, and he finished by instructing him to leave the detachment immediately to re-join the regiment. The officer obeyed straight away. I then requested the *chef d'escadron* if I could speak to him alone. I said to him, "How can you want this officer to re-join the regiment, which is perhaps twenty leagues from here? He will be murdered by the locals, and this will throw on you all the hate of such an event. Do you want me to go and find him?" "Yes!" he replied. I did this and certainly saved the life of this officer. I later had occasion to render him the same service a second time.

The detachment having arrived at Kapfenberg, the *chef d'escadron* pushed reconnaissances on Bruck and beyond, as well as on the road to Vienna. We only encountered some stragglers, but we captured a convoy of twenty to twenty-five vehicles moving from Vienna to the Austrian Army of Italy. These vehicles were filled with muskets, musketoons, lances, horseshoes and nails, boots and uniforms for the troops. We took the best teams to follow us in two vehicles that we filled with boots, horseshoes and nails. We uselessly tried to sell the rest of the convoy to the locals; we had to burn it because it would otherwise have fallen back into the hands of the enemy.

The mission of the *chef d'escadron* being complete, he planned to retire and join the army with his two precious vehicles. I had proposed to him to follow the best and shortest route from Bruck to Vienna via Neustadt; he preferred to take one that was more difficult and longer, but at the same time the most secure, and we re-took the route along which we had come. We slept successively at Afflenz, Unterhofen, Maria-Zell, Tyrnitz, Hainfelden, Garru, Schwöchat, two leagues from Vienna, on the road from Presbourg, and finally to Vienna on the 17th November. The detachment had received the order to march on this capital because the inhabitants were holding hostile demonstrations against the French troops which occupied it, but on our arrival, all was in order. We remained there until the evening of the 19th. The *chef d'escadron* hastened to have the boots taken on the Bruck road given to Marshal Davout, the horseshoes and nails being kept for the regiment. At the same time, he addressed his report to the marshal, in which he spoke well of me. The marshal was good enough to invite me twice to dinner and both times I was too timid to dare to accept his invitation despite all the urging of the *chef d'escadron*. The marshal, being content with the conduct of our detachment, again sent *chef d'escadron* Méda as a partisan [with his detachment] to observe the part of Hungary which bordered the March, or Morawa, river. On the 19th, the detachment slept at Kagaron; on the 20th and 21st it marched during the night, only taking a few hours rest during the day, and passing by Marcheck, Asdorff, etc.

In the night of the 21st to 22nd November, a very dark night, I was charged with the rear guard, which meant that I marched at the rear of the detachment to ensure no one was left behind and to remain alone from time to time at some distance, to listen for anyone following us. The *chef d'escadron* marched at the head and stopped very often on his side, to listen for any enemy in front of him. But it happened that, in a halt of this type, which was very long, the commander started his march again without having me warned. After some time, tired of waiting at the rear, I wanted to go to the front to reassure myself that they had not set off and you can imagine my surprise when I found there were only fifteen men with me, of which the two at the front were asleep on their horses and had not followed the movement of the column! It should be said in passing, the commander of a column, when he sets off at night, should send officers from the headquarters along the column to ensure everyone follows on.

As for myself, I immediately took over and, instead of remaining in the rear, I put myself at the head of my fifteen men. I marched thus for a long time in the plains of Moravia and finally found a large village. I went to the mayor's house after having spoken to my men. I took care to ask after my detachment, persuaded that the inhabitants would give me some news of them if they had any. I immediately arranged lodgings for twelve hundred hussars, which were to arrive three or four hours after us. At the same time, we took a house in which to refresh men and horses, carbines loaded on the table and four armed men guarding the horses while at the same time, listening out for the least sound. Four hours having passed, I noticed that the inhabitants began to doubt the arrival of the troops that I had announced. As dawn broke, I mounted my fifteen men, took a mounted guide, and left the village where I had been secure with so few men. There, not seeing any indication of the way that the commander had followed, I contemplated retiring on Vienna, for there was no great security crossing the vast plains of Moravia with fifteen men and this without anywhere to head for. I recalled that the day before yesterday, seeing the *chef d'escadron*, who had gone off on his own to consult his map, I approached him to ask what country we went to travel over and he had replied to me, "No one is to know except me." But whilst he was saying this, I noticed at the end of his finger was the name Rabensbourg; this was all I had seen and learnt. I immediately took my map and saw that I was not far from this point. I questioned my guide and he replied that we were only four leagues away. I ordered him to lead us there, promising him a good reward and at the same time warning him that if he let me down I would have him shot. I had judged correctly. After having travelled a league, I noticed in the distance the *chef d'escadron* with his detachment, heading in the same direction as me. I immediately made a reconnaissance, as did he on his side, and we were soon reunited to our great mutual satisfaction.

Indeed, we went to sleep at Rabensbourg, and then the next day at Noendorf and then at Luntenbourg, from where we pushed, the three following days, reconnaissances on Goeding and different points. We recognised a significant movement in the Russian army which, indeed, was marching on Austerlitz.

On the 28th November, the detachment made a retrograde march, crossing the Danube on a pontoon bridge at Presbourg on the 29th and re-joining the regiment at Schwöchat on the 30th, which set off, crossing the Danube at Vienna on the 1st December to go to Austerlitz by forced marches, sleeping the same day at Unter-Ebendorf, on the 2nd at Dunavitz and learning in the morning of the 3rd of the victory of Austerlitz. During the 2nd it [the regiment] only had to repulse a few parties of cavalry which were attempting to turn the army's right to seize the main road from Vienna to Brunn; it slept the same day at Satschan and marched on the 4th to Nicolschitz, near Goeding. This day we skirmished here and there and, towards evening, we learnt of the armistice concluded between the Emperor Napoleon and the Austrian Emperor. Hostilities ceased everywhere; the regiment stopped at Nicolschitz and the next day it slept at Teinitz from where, after a rest of two days, it re-took the road to Hungary, re-crossed the Danube on the pontoon bridge at Rohrau to return to Bruck, where it remained until the 6th January 1806. On the 1st January, we re-took the old calendar and abandoned the republican calendar.

At this period, we started to evacuate the hereditary states of Austria, conforming with the treaty of Presbourg. The regiment moved first to Gmünden, close to the lake of this name and, after a month's rest (from the 22nd January to the 22nd February), it left for Pöttmes, close to Neubourg, where it arrived on the 11th March, and was passed in review on the 19th by Marshal Davout, close to the tomb of the celebrated La Tour d'Auvergne, the first grenadier of France. We set off again on the 24th to go to Rensberg. It was only in this cantonment, where we passed the whole month of May and half of June, that I finally received my brevet of the *Légion d'Honneur*.

I received at the same time, my nomination as *sous-lieutenant*[23] at the choice of the government, and I was placed in this rank in the élite company. My brevet of the *Légion d'Honneur* was dated the 14th May 1806 and my nomination as *sous-lieutenant* the 8th January of the same year.

I had been adjutant for nearly four years. It is a position that demands the greatest activity; it is necessary to be familiar with all parts of the service and in particular, all manoeuvres. The *adjutant-sous-officier*, having dealings with all the personnel of the regiment, to perfectly know the spirit of each so that their reports do not result in continual punishment; that he is sober, discreet, and knows all that is happening in the regiment. It is necessary for him to have the integrity to resist the occasions that his position gives him to plunder without anyone's knowledge. It is in the exercise of these functions that I drew the majority of what I knew of the military art. I learnt during peace all that which it is necessary for the commander of a regiment, and during war I have had all the opportunities to learn to move, not only a regiment, but a brigade and even a division, by the different orders which continually passed under my eyes. Besides the functions of *adjutant-sous-officier* that I filled in the regiment, since our arrival in Bruges until the moment when I left the 7th Hussars, I was responsible for all the accounting of clothing, of great and small equipment, of armament and of harness, of the purchase and making of all the effects necessary for the war squadrons. I held a register in duplicate of everything each company held and, every three months, as far as circumstances allowed, I did a survey by company of all that each of them had received and lost during this amount of time.

Colonel Marx, who appointed me *sous-lieutenant* after the government, often said to me, "I will keep you as *adjutant sous-*

---

[23] Literally 'under lieutenant', but the modern British equivalent of second lieutenant, or ensign in the cavalry of the time.

officier for a long time because I have need of you, but immediately that you are *sous-lieutenant*, I will quickly make you *adjutant-major*." What he promised me was soon realised, but under not his orders; he obtained his retirement before this happened, as I will explain when the time comes.

Chapter 5

The Campaign of 1806 Against Prussia

The Treaty of Pressburg had effectively ended the Third Coalition without Prussia having made any contribution to the war. However, it was only now, after the humiliating defeat of Austria and Russia at Austerlitz, that Prussia declared war on France. The war was to see the double French victory at Jena and Auerstadt in October 1806.

In this campaign, Curély's 7*th* Hussars were brigaded with the 5*th* Hussars under command of General Lasalle, one of the French army's most celebrated light cavalry commanders. His regiment would distinguish itself at the actions of Zehdenick and Prenzlow, and particularly at the taking of Stettin, although it was to take no part in the two great battles.

Having been recently commissioned, Curély was placed in the regiment's compagnie d'élite *(the élite company)*, a post of some importance and a recognition of his bravery and experience. This company, manned by the most experienced and capable soldiers, was inevitably given the most dangerous and demanding missions as well as serving as an example to the rest of the regiment.

Two days before the battle of Jena *(on the 12*th* October)* a detachment was pushed forward towards Leipzig consisting of only fifty hussars. Twenty-five were drawn from each of the 5*th* and 7*th* Hussars commanded by Captain (later general) Piré of the 7*th*. A second lieutenant of the 5*th* commanded the twenty-five of this regiment and Curély those of the 7*th*. Arriving in darkness they remained formed on one of the squares of Leipzig through the whole night, sending patrols along all the roads, whilst at the town hall Piré bluffed the town council by demanding rations and money for a much larger force. The three-thousand-man garrison had fled at the news of the arrival of the French. As day dawned, the city began to stir and realising the weakness of the force that occupied it, Piré's men had no option but to leave. The detachment re-joined the brigade having apparently covered 35 leagues (about 140 kilometres) in twenty-four hours.

On the 14th October, the brigade, following the orders they had received, marched quietly between the two battles (Jena and Auerstadt), without taking part in either. Curély claims to have been able to hear the roar of cannon on both sides. However, the brigade was able to take their revenge for missing the battles in the pursuit of the Prussian army, an ideal role for light cavalry. For the brigade, the pursuit lasted from the 15th October until the 7th November and took it through Erfurt, Berlin and as far as Stettin (now in modern Poland). From the beginning of the campaign, the cavalry reserve, of which the brigade was a part, had captured 72,000 men, including 1,000 officers, 77 standards, 509 cannons, and 18,454 horses. In twenty-eight days, it had covered an average of 42 kilometres a day and on certain days had covered double this distance.

Curély was once more to distinguish himself: on the 26th October, at Zehdenick, he passed through the Prussian cavalry and on the 27th, at Prenzlow, on a night reconnaissance with twenty-five men, he identified the route of Prince Hohenlohe (the commander of the left wing of the Prussian army). This information was given to Lasalle and Murat who used it to capture the enemy column after a cavalry combat which forced them to surrender. The trust that Lasalle had in Curély is shown by him being ordered to remain in command of the town of Demmin to receive two detachments of the brigade which had been sent to Stralsund. He remained there until after the surrender of Blücher at Lübeck when he was ordered to retire to Berlin where he arrived five days before the brigade. The brigade was then sent forwards towards Poland, pursuing the remains of the Prussian army, and Curély was present at the surrender of Stettin on the 30*th* October.

Blücher's surrender at Lübeck effectively marked the end of the Prussian Campaign and the beginning of the Polish Campaign. The advance guards of Davout, Lannes and Augereau were sent forward to the Vistula, arriving on the 5*th* December. In the fourteen days rest that they were now able to take, Curély was to oversee the maintenance of the uniforms, armament, equipment and harness of the regiment; a responsibility that became his on his appointment as adjutant. He obviously carried out these duties competently and having already proved himself in battle and on campaign, Colonel Marx was to comment, 'This devil Curély is good at everything.'

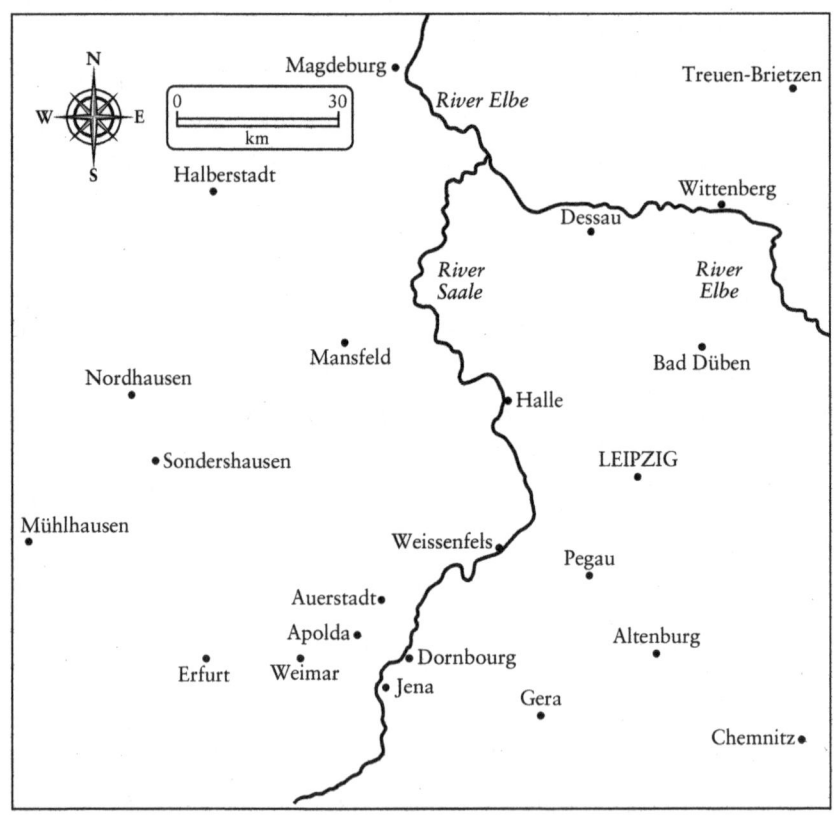

War with Prussia was decided on; on the 26th September 1806, the regiment left its cantonments in Mosbach, seven leagues from Heidelberg, and slept the same day at Adölsheim, then passing by Boxberg, Rothambourg, Mülheim, Fornach, near Nuremberg, Turm, near Forchheim, Bamberg, Hayen and arriving in the evening of the 7th October at Wissenbrun, near Cronach. We marched all through the night to reach Sallbourg on the 8th; this day we encountered the Saxon advance guard, with which we skirmished a little. On the 9th, the regiment was at Tanna, and on the 10th at Auma, where General Lasalle concentrated his brigade, composed of the 5th and 7th Hussars. On the 11th, the army marched on Gera; during this day, the élite company, of which I was a part, was sent on the road to Leipsick [Leipzig][24] on which we took more than two hundred equipages belonging to the Saxon army. The next day, the 12th, a reconnaissance of two hundred cavalry from the two regiments was pushed as far as Pegau. It was commanded by *chef d'escadron* Mathis, of the 7th, who had been ordered to push forward on Leipsick. Twenty-five men from each regiment were chosen for this expedition. I was nominated to command those of the 7th, Captain Piré, who was also of the 7th, to command the whole, and an officer of the 5th to command the twenty-five men of his own regiment. This detachment of fifty hussars, under the orders of Captain Piré (today lieutenant-general), left Pegau as night fell and arrived at the gate of Liepsick at 11.30pm. On the way we had found a Saxon soldier who gave us information from which we really profited. He informed us that the town was surrounded by a wall, in which the entry gates were simple, that there were two infantry battalions with a strength of 1,200 men and nearly four hundred dragoons, that the gate by which we proposed to enter had a post of twenty five men with two sentries, one outside

---

[24] The French equivalent of "*Qui vive*" or "who goes there?"

and the other in front of the guard house which was right next to the gate, and finally, that the town was full of strangers of all kinds.

After a short deliberation by the three officers of the detachment, it was agreed that on entering the town we would announce the arrival of the emperor with his army, that we needed lodgings for him, his suite and all the headquarters, adding that the army would camp outside the town and that we had to arrange immediately 500,000 rations of bread, forage, oats, etc... Convinced that this announcement, made in the middle of the night, would cause widespread disorder and that they would all try to save themselves in flight, we started to execute our plan straight away.

Arriving at the gate, we knocked; the Saxon sentry shouted, "*Verda?*" One of our German hussars replied in his language, "Saxon hussars." Where have you come from? Where are you going?" asked the *sous-officier* of the post. Our hussar replied, "We have come from the army, and we have come to guard the town during the confusion, because it is said that those pigs the French are approaching." Then a gate opened; at the same moment, the sentry was seized by the neck, twenty-five hussars dismounted as fast as lightning, entered the guard house and made prisoners all those they found in there (it is good to observe that the post was commanded by an officer, but that this officer had been asleep in his bed). On the *place d'armes* there was another post of twenty-five grenadiers, which was also disarmed. We left at the gate of entry a *brigadier* and four of the most determined hussars with the order to die there rather than allow the enemy to re-take the post and we immediately ran to the post of grenadiers who were disarmed without a shot being fired. The captain, escorted by four hussars, then went straight to the town hall, demanded the magistrates, and explained to them the object of his mission. Me, I took command of the detachment and I held myself mid-way between the town hall and the gate by which we had entered. The rumour was now spreading through all quarters of the town that the French had arrived, even with the emperor, etc. Immediately, infantry, cavalry, merchants, traders took flight and we saw all that which fear produces in such a case. It was a frightful hubbub and, however, neither men nor women were touched by our hussars, for our detachment remained in formation, in the greatest order. I kept sending a patrol composed of a *sous-officier* and four hussars to watch everything that was happening. Each time that one of these patrols returned, the *sous-officier* said to me, laughing, "They are saving themselves! Cavalry, infantry, vehicles, everyone is mixed up..."

It was already 4am, and my captain, still with the magistrates, had still not returned. From time to time however, he sent to tell me that the lodgings and rations were going well, but I should be ready for the arrival of the emperor, to lead him to his lodgings. Finally, it was five o'clock and day was starting to dawn, and my captain had still not returned. I read on the faces of several townspeople who were watching us, that they had not fallen for our trick, and it appeared to me not to be prudent to await daylight in the town. I sent a *sous-officier* to tell the captain that the emperor had arrived and wanted to speak to him immediately. Although he had not completed his mission, he arrived straight away. I pointed out to him some gatherings that were starting to form. He said to me, "Leave! It is time." We left the town at walking pace, but as soon as we were out of sight, we broke into a trot and three leagues from Leipsick we made a halt for a quarter of an hour. Finally, half a league from Pegau, where the detachment awaited us, we were able to refresh the men and horses which had not eaten for twelve hours.

Chef d'escadron Méda, who commanded another part that was also directed on Leipsick, but via the route of Halle, arrived before the gate designated under this name about an hour after our exit from the town by the Pegau gate. The population, realising what had happened, the cavalry retraced their steps and commander Méda was vigorously charged, but he lost no one.

During this time, the emperor manoeuvred to attack the Prussian army. *Chef d'escadron* Mathis had received the order to re-join the part of the army that was at Weissenfels. Immediately that he had re-joined he set off again to arrive in the evening in this town where we found the regiment.

The detachment of commander Mathis had left Gera on the 12th to go to Pegau, where he arrived in the evening. After refreshment, he and the fifty men of Captain Piré left for Leipsick where they arrived the same evening at 11.30pm. They had thus covered twenty large leagues during the day of the 12th; they had remained mounted all night of the 12th to 13th and, without unsaddling, they left again for Leipsick as I have said, on the 13th at 5am to go to sleep early at Weissenfels, having made fifteen good leagues on this second day.

The next day, the 14th, the day of battle, the army corps of Bernadotte and Prince Murat's cavalry reserve, of which we were a part, was at Weissenfels and the surrounding area, went to Dornbourg before daybreak and remained there until towards 3pm without firing a shot, while we could hear to our left the cannonade of Jena, and to our right, that of Auerstadt. Finally, at 3pm, we set off; we crossed the Saale, climbed the hills, and marched far onto the plain in the direction of Weimar, but saw nothing. Thus passed this famous battle, at which two numerous corps took no part.

The next day, the 15th, all the cavalry set off before dawn heading for Weimar and Erfurt. Lasalle's brigade formed the advance guard and found the roads covered in fugitives and vehicles. It passed the night close to Erfurt and started its march again on the 16th, finding only fugitives on the road. This day the brigade slept far ahead of Erfurt. On the 17th, General Lasalle was ordered to scout the march of Blücher's army corps which was retiring in good order in the direction of Sondershausen and having attacked the rear of the Prussian column with his scouts, he was forced to make a retrograde movement which was nearly disastrous to him. The enemy had 20,000 infantry and 5,000 cavalry; the brigade had only six to eight hundred men. Lasalle made his retreat in good order and did not lose a man, but he was blamed by the emperor and put on the orders of the army for having fled from the Prussians. When he knew of this order, he wanted to blow out his brains; he was prevented, and he went to speak to the emperor. The latter listened to him and when Lasalle discussed the facts as they were, Napoleon said to him, "I have been misled, be calm and continue to serve me as you have until now." General Lasalle was one of the bravest in the French army, with a sound *coup d'oeil* and was careful when it was necessary.

On the 17th we slept near Mulhausen, on the 18th at Sondershausen, the 19th near Halberstadt, the 20th four leagues from Magdebourg, the 21st between Magdebourg and Dessau, on the 22nd near Dessau, the 23rd at Truen-Brietzen after having crossed the Elbe at Dessau, and the 24th at Charlottenbourg passing Potsdam. During the night of the 24th to 25th, I was ordered, with twenty-five hussars, to escort the French general[25] who was to summon Spandau to surrender. On the 25th we went to Oranienbourg, passing close to Berlin. On the 26th, the brigade set off very early in the morning and at Zehdenick, encountered the black hussars and dragoons of the Queen of Prussia. The brigade crossed the bridge over the small river which passed through Zehdenick, then formed into line on the plain and attacked the Queen's dragoons who were in line in front of a wood. The enemy line was pierced by the élite company of the 7th, of which I was a part as *sous-lieutenant*, which forced the rest of the line to break up. A moment after this charge, I noticed a well-mounted Prussian officer and resolved to capture him. During the pursuit, I gave him two thrusts of my point in his kidneys, at the same time saying to him, "surrender." He did not reply; then I gave my horse some spur and arriving level with him on his left, I struck

---

[25] General Victor who was then the chief-of-staff of Lannes' corps.

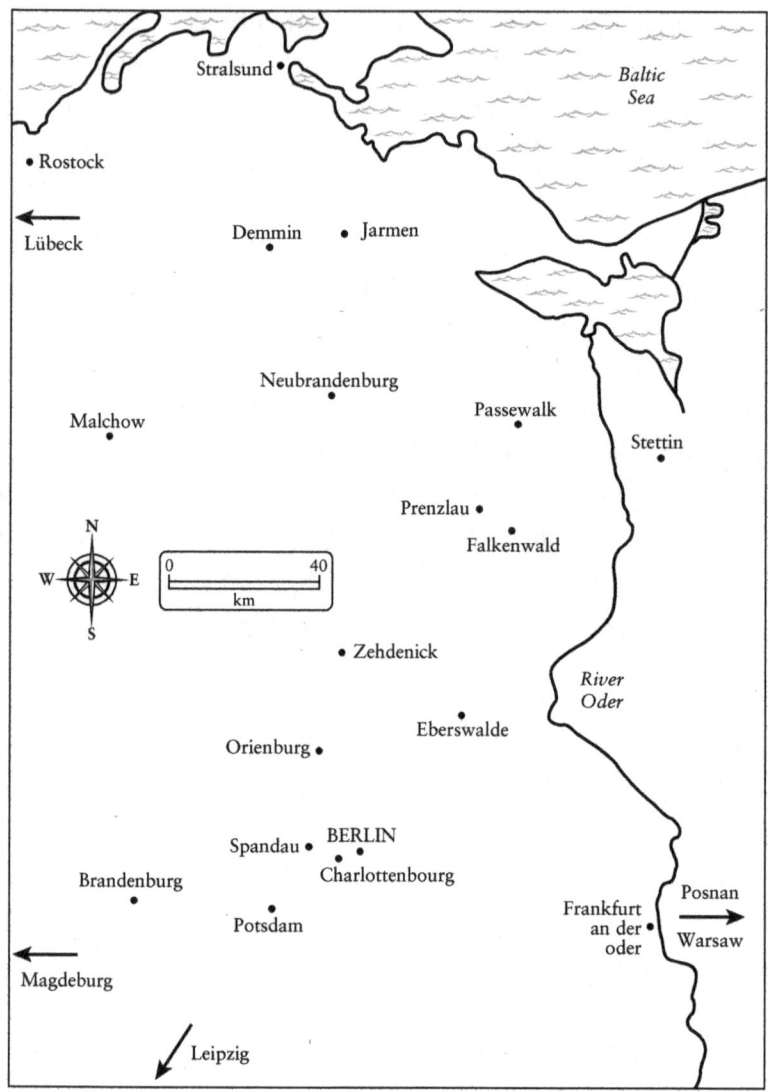

a reverse blow, which cut his nose down onto his lower jaw. This time he surrendered, but as I had passed through the enemy line when pursuing my officer along the main road which passed through the wood, I found myself behind three hundred enemy dragoons. I took care to hand over my prisoner, still mounted, to one of my hussars, who was still near me and who I made go into the wood. The dragoons, fleeing in the greatest disorder, passed by me and several threw sabre blows at me, that I parried and which I returned at my ease. We pursued the dragoons until beyond the wood, but at this moment, fresh troops, and noticeably the black hussars, who had not yet been engaged, charged us and pushed us back into the middle of the wood. Then appeared the division of dragoons commanded by General Grouchy, who took the charge, pursued this cavalry for a long distance and captured two to three hundred men.

The next day, we set off early in pursuit of the enemy. I was the advance-guard with twenty-five hussars and was ordered to do a reconnaissance of Prenzlow. The brigade had remained three leagues in the rear of this town. I approached the gates; it was still not dark, and I noticed to my left on the main road, a strong column which was heading for this town. I could easily tell that it was not one of ours; it was, in fact, Hohenlohe's Prussian corps and I immediately retired. A village in which I was going to pass was occupied by troops; night had come, but from the sounds and the language I quickly realised that they were Prussians. I made a detour to by-pass the village without being noticed and re-joined my route and I arrived at the brigade where I immediately made my report to the colonel, then to General Lasalle. The latter informed the Grand Duke of Berg [Murat], who was a little to the rear with the main body of the cavalry. On the account that I had given of my reconnaissance, all the cavalry set off before dawn, heading for Prenzlow. Lasalle's brigade was first to arrive before this town and found the Prussians retreating along the main road, their head of column having already passed Prenzlow heading for Stettin. Lasalle's sudden attack forced them to put their artillery into battery and to stop their movement to present a defensive front to us ahead of the town, which gave the Grand Duke the time to come up with all his cavalry. On the Prince's arrival, more than half the enemy column had already passed

Prenzlow; the rear of the column was in the town or on the main road to its rear. Immediately, Murat ordered all his cavalry to charge, and we entered Prenzlow all mixed up with the Prussians. All those who had not passed the town were taken, cannons, caissons, infantry, and cavalry. The gate of the town was obstructed with dead Frenchmen and Prussians. The 7th Hussars lost there, amongst others, one of its bravest soldiers.

The Prussian troop that had left Prenzlow heading for Stettin had taken up position on a height six hundred paces from the town, of which it had closed the gate behind it, and prepared to defend itself well. The Grand Duke of Berg had the gate broken down and sent a negotiator to the enemy to summon them to surrender. The Prussians stripped the negotiator, fired on the trumpeter, and sent them back on foot. It is worthy of note that, during this time and of the capitulation, he did not have a musket shot fired. Prince Murat, seeing his negotiator return in such a state, became terribly angry and sent a new negotiator with a summons to the Prince de Hohenlohe for all of what remained of his army corps to lay down their arms immediately, otherwise everyone would be put to the sword. The Prussian general was intimidated and capitulated; all were taken, apart from the general and his equipages. The French cavalry alone made the Prussians lay down their arms; an infantry regiment only arrived at when the Prussians filed out.

It is worth observing that this enemy army corps had a strength of sixteen to seventeen thousand men and included part of the Royal Guard, that for four days lacked bread from its fatherland, that this troop had not been paid for a long time, that the infantry were not lodged and, without the power to collect rations, marched day and night because of the poor combinations of their generals so that the soldiers, always unhappy, were badly disposed to do their duty. Would it not have been better to demand requisitions on the whole country across which this army passed to nourish it, than to leave it in shortage in the middle of abundance and to abandon to the enemy all the resources of a country rich and intact? Bad luck to the sovereigns who, to spare their country, leave their soldiers to die of hunger! For the people, war is the greatest plague of the world, I agree. So, monarchs, if you love your people, do not make war, but if you are forced to do it, do it with the whole nation, with all the resources of your country. Take it to the enemy's territory, and after three months force them to make peace.

The day of the 29th was still more extraordinary. General Lasalle moved with his brigade, followed by a caisson of cartridges, onto the heights near Stettin; the artillery of the place sent us several shots and forced the brigade to retire behind a curtain of heights to get shelter from the balls. The caisson was sent round and round the heights to make the enemy think that we had artillery with us; the caisson also received several artillery discharges. Night approached, the general sent two officers into Stettin as negotiators, to summon the Prussian governor to hand over the place to the French and he retired with his two regiments a league to the rear to pass the night there. Towards 2am on the 30th October, the negotiators sent to signal the capitulation of the place to General Lasalle. The garrison, with a strength of 6,000 men, were to lay down their arms on the glacis at 8am. The general immediately informed the *duc de Berg* [Murat] of this capitulation, and requesting he immediately send some infantry and cavalry that could arrive before Stettin before 8am at the latest to be there for when the Prussians marched out. He then went with his brigade to the gate of the town where he established himself at dawn. At 7am the gates were handed over and occupied by the two élite companies of the regiments of hussars. It was 8am, and the Prussian garrison was ready to march out while we had not a single gun or infantryman. At 8.30, a regiment arrived with two guns and whilst they formed up in line, the garrison marched out and laid their arms on the glacis before this regiment and the two regiments of hussars. Only half the garrison had thus laid down their arms when the Prussians noticed the small number of French. Part of those who had left the place took their arms up, but the capitulation had laid down that the muskets should have false flints of wood, instead of flints and the Prussian general had scrupulously executed this article. We did not give his soldiers time to replace them; they were immediately charged by the two regiments of hussars, who dispersed them in the plain. We pressed the exit of the rest of the garrison so that towards 11 o'clock the town was completely empty of Prussian troops.

Six thousand men were made prisoners or dispersed; the place had a hundred guns in battery, but the gate of the Oder and the crossing of this river were entirely free. One would have assumed that there was a practicable breach in the rampart to allow an army to march in, but in this case, the garrison would have been able to cross on to the right bank of the Oder and retreat on Colberg, or Dantzick etc... Such was the ineptitude and the fright of some of the Prussian generals during this period.

The Grand Duke of Berg arrived towards midday with part of his cavalry and some infantry. He put the infantry into Stettin and with his cavalry he left immediately to march either on Lübeck where General Blücher was, or to encounter this general, for he could go to Stralsund to occupy that place or attempt to return on Stettin, not knowing that this place was occupied by the French. We passed by Falkenwald on the 30th, Uckermünde on the 31st, Jarmen on the 1st November and Demmin on the 2nd.

From there, the Grand Duke of Berg continued his march on Lübeck in long days with all the troops under his orders. As for me, I was assigned by the prince to take command of Demmin to maintain order, to collect up the stragglers, to keep open communications and to observe Stralsund, a town belonging to the Swedes, with whom we were also at war. Two detachments, one of the 5th [Hussars] the other of the 7th, had been directed on Stralsund; they came to join me on the evening of the 4th November and on the 5th, I received the order to leave the country. I arrived at Berlin on the 15th and I was lodged in the surroundings with my detachment, awaiting the regiment which was returning from Lübeck. The brigade was passed in review on the square of the Château de Berlin on the 21st and left the same day for Poland, passing by Francfort-sur-l'Oder, Meseritz, Posen, Sempolnow etc...

On the 5th December, it had gone to Lowicz, close to Warsaw and cantoned at Gorcé on the 6th, on the left bank of the Vistula, where it stayed for seven days. I went to pass part of this time in Warsaw itself, to have some repairs to armaments and to buy some things indispensable for starting a new campaign.

Chapter 6

The Campaign of 1807 in Poland

*E*ven after the stunning French victories and pursuit of the Prussians in 1806, a large force of Prussian troops refused to surrender and marched east to join a Russian army that was marching to confront Napoleon. Anticipating a challenging campaign, Napoleon strengthened his army. In December the French army advanced into Poland and later defeated the Russians in the tough battles at Eylau and Friedland in 1807. The war was ended by the Treaty of Tilsit.

On the 30th December 1806, Colonel Marx was promoted to général de brigade *and was replaced as commanding officer of the 7th Hussars by Colonel Colbert. As we shall see, this change of command was to see a further upturn in Curély's fortunes. Lasalle's brigade, in which the 7th Hussars served, was a part of the Reserve Cavalry Corps commanded by the celebrated cavalry commander and Napoleon's brother-in-law, Marshal Murat.*

The Russian advance guard, commanded by Bennigsen, had advanced to the line of the Vistula river, but much of the Russian army was still not concentrated and, hoping to join forces with Buxhoden and Kamenski, he fell back to the northeast as Napoleon advanced, leaving the French to occupy Warsaw. Lestocq, commanding the remaining Prussian troops, lay some distance to the northwest of Bennigsen and fell back in concert with him. Kamenski, assuming command of all the Russian forces, attempted to throw the French back across the Vistula, but without success and upon which he resigned his command. Napoleon ordered Marshals Augereau, Murat and Davout against Golymin. At this town on the 26th December

1806 the marshals were confronted by the corps of General Golitsyn. Lasalle's brigade were the troops leading the French advance but were driven back by Russian cavalry. As more French troops arrived, Golitsyn, aided by the terrain, was able to withdraw.

The engagement of Lasalle's brigade at the battle of Golymin became a classic to study for French cavalry officers, but not for the right reasons. Lasalle's brigade received the order to charge the Russian artillery; it moved off, but one of the officers (who remains anonymous), without doubt wanting to rectify the brigade's alignment, shouted 'stop!'. This order was repeated along the whole line, and suddenly the entire brigade, apart from the élite company of the 7th Hussars, turned at the gallop. It took half an hour to rally it and return it to where it had started, where Lasalle, furious, held it there in line under the enemy's fire until the middle of the night. According to Curély, the two regimental colonels (Marx was still in command of the 7th Hussars at this point) were promoted to général de brigade for their previous services but were also retired from active service.

On the 27th December, Curély was sent to Napoleon with an escort of twenty-five hussars to give him an account of the action at Golymin. It was the first time he had spoken to his emperor, and apparently he spoke with more frankness than courtesy. Hardly had Curély finished his account than Napoleon galloped off, indicating to him where he would find his brigade. On arrival, he found a new colonel had arrived, Édouard Colbert, who was later to command a division of cavalry of the Imperial Guard in 1814 and the Red Lancers of the Guard at Waterloo. Curély found himself with a mentor who was to help him advance more rapidly through the ranks than he had been able to do thus far in his career.

After the actions at Pultusk and Golymin, the French went into winter quarters. However, unexpectedly attacked by the Russians, Napoleon tried to draw Benningsen into a trap. However, his plans having fallen into the possession of the Russians after they had captured a staff officer, the Russians escaped, although there were several lively engagements.

Lasalle was now promoted to général de division *and the light cavalry was concentrated into a single division that he commanded. The 5th and 7th Hussars were joined in their brigade by the 11th Chasseurs and were now commanded by Victor de Latour-Maubourg, a renowned and well-respected cavalry commander who was later to become minister of war under the Restoration and governor of Les Invalides.*

On the 4th February, the 7th Hussars made a charge against a force of Cossacks; this was the first time that Colbert led the regiment in action. Colbert wrote of this charge, 'I was under the orders of General Victor de Latour-Maubourg, he ordered the charge, gave and received the first sabre blow; I gave, I think, the second. In the light cavalry it is indispensable that the commanders pay with their person, even the general officers. This charge was successful, as well as others which followed. This fine day nailed and rivetted my epaulettes [as colonel] on my shoulders as I hoped...'

In this charge Curély also hoped to make an impression on his new colonel and he describes how he achieved this. The regulations laid down that once the charge was sounded, everyone charged on their own account, the bravest and best mounted arriving first on the enemy and Curély used this to bring himself to Colbert's notice. He clearly succeeded and soon after was entrusted with a dangerous mission, forming the very advance guard of Ney's corps as they pursued Lestocq's Prussians to prevent them joining the Russians at the battle of Eylau, which was fought on the 8th February 1807. Although successfully engaging the Prussian rear-guard, they were unable to stop the main body making a significant intervention at Eylau, in which Curély took no other part.

The brigade of which the 7th Hussars was a part received a new commander in March 1807; this was General Pajol who fought with distinction throughout the Napoleonic Wars including the 1815 campaign in which he commanded a cavalry corps. The brigade continued to serve in Lasalle's division.

Moving into winter quarters, Napoleon believed the campaign was over until the weather improved, but the Russian army under command of General Bennigsen unexpectedly advanced against him. However, as Bennigsen hesitated, Napoleon launched a counter-offensive forcing the Russians back. In the pursuit that followed, Curély was constantly in action, in particular at the entrenched camp at Heilsberg on the 10th June where he was conspicuous, and the Russians finally stood to face the French at Friedland on the 14th June. The battle was a significant French victory, but Pajol's brigade took no part; they were detached with Murat to attack Konigsberg where Lestocq's Prussians had taken refuge. The day after Friedland, they were sent to cut off the Russian withdrawal from Friedland. For several successive days the 7th Hussars were engaged with the Russian rear-guard during which Colbert was wounded, though not seriously. On the 19th June, by which time the brigade had reached the river Nieman, an armistice was agreed. This eventually led to the treaty which was signed between Napoleon and Czar Alexander at Tilsit.

Curély's promotions had been slow up to 1807 but in this year, he entered the period in which he advanced most rapidly. Having been commissioned as a sous-lieutenant on the 8th January 1806, he was promoted lieutenant on the 27th March 1807, without leaving the élite company, adjutant-major on the following 8th May, and captain on the 8th June. Wounded on the 9th June at Guttstadt, he was reported for his brilliant conduct at Heilsberg the following day. It seems clear that Colonel Colbert had realised his value and was determined to promote him to the appropriate rank that had previously been denied to him.

During the next twenty months, until the war against Austria in 1809, the brigade was cantoned in Poland, then Prussia, and finally in Westphalia. During these times of relative peace, Curély was to spend some time as commandant of various towns and given a number of important missions.

The brigade crossed the Vistula on the 15th December at Warsaw, remained at Gradffski on the 21st, then moved forwards on the 22nd and crossed the Bug on the 23rd, despite the resistance of the Russians. We killed men and horses and took some prisoners. We continued our march on the 24th and in the evening as we bivouacked, we encountered the enemy. On the 25th, the brigade came under heavy artillery fire after having crossed a long and narrow pond; it lost several men and horses and was forced to retreat. It arrived before Golymin on the 26th December towards 10am and found, about a quarter of a league below this village, cuirassiers of the Russian Guard and dragoons, forming a total of about 1,000 men with eight or ten guns in battery, all deployed in a plain with their left anchored on a wood. The Russian army, coming from Pultusk, deployed up the road which passed through Golymin to go to Machow; the tracks were terrible, principally for the French army, which only had back tracks available to it. My view was that the aim of the French army was to bar the route to Golymin to the Russians, to throw them into the marshes of the Orezyc river which flowed to their right, and to force them to lay down their arms; one or the other could have been achieved, at least in part, if the two generals commanding on this point[26] had agreed.

Lasalle's brigade waited for the Grand-Duke's troops for three hours; they arrived very slowly, with very few infantry and a single artillery piece which, not able to get through the line, fired from the enemy's flank without hitting it. To the left of Murat's corps was placed Marshal Augereau with almost all his infantry, which formed in square and *en masse* in the middle of the plain, a cannon's range from the road on which the Russians passed, who presented their left flank to us. Murat had thrown what little infantry that was available to him into the wood which was on the right of his army

---

[26] Murat and Augereau.

corps and to the Russian left. Towards 2pm, the attack was ordered; our line of cavalry had its right supported on a wood. Lasalle's brigade formed the extreme left and was to charge the Russian artillery. Hardly had this brigade gone twenty paces forwards to charge when we heard shouted, "Halt! Halt!" and the shout was repeated along the whole line.

The enemy did not fire a single cannon shot and yet the two regiments turned about and retreated; they could only be rallied after half an hour. An inconceivable thing! There was neither a cavalryman nor an infantryman in front of our brigade; there was in truth eight or ten guns, which may not have had the time to fire if the charge had been quick, which in all cases would certainly have taken place after the first volley. The cavalry which was to our right did not stop its movement; it knocked down the enemy and captured some men and horses as well as some standards.

It is proven, and what I come to recount has been demonstrated repeatedly, that when a line of cavalry has started a charge, it should never be stopped in its movement; to the contrary! In general, one should charge as quickly as possible to overthrow the enemy line, break it and throw it back into the second line and so on, to put your adversary in the greatest disorder that you can.

Immediately that the brigade was rallied, General Lasalle found the élite company of the 7th Hussars, which had remained alone and without running the least danger on the ground, otherwise abandoned in disorder. Then the general led his two regiments under the enemy cannon, and they remained there until midnight without moving.

To give an idea of the loss that this brigade suffered from the artillery fire as punishment for its retrograde movement, it suffices for me to say that the general, who remained at the front, had two horses killed under him. Men and horses fell at every moment, no one moved, and not a murmur was heard.

If Marshal Augereau had led his infantry into the wood which was on our right, and if the other corps had manoeuvred in concert, the enemy would have been cut off and lost half his army, whilst he would have left us everything that he could not have dragged away. The fighting ceased towards 1am.

At dawn on the 27th, I was commanded to go to Ciecanow with twenty-five hussars to take the news to the emperor. He marched with Soult's corps to cut off the enemy from Machow, but the poor state of the roads obliged him to stop this corps at Ciecanow and he went himself with his guard cavalry to Golymin in the very early morning.

I met him about halfway; he questioned me on the affair of the day before and I replied to him, perhaps with too much frankness, that things could have gone better. "How?" he said to me. "Yes, Sire," I replied, "we took a lot of the enemy, but we could have taken more." "Did you take cannons, prisoners?" he responded. I replied, "Many cannons were abandoned by the enemy on the main road, and myself, on the way to meet you, I have taken three hundred Russian stragglers." "Ah! I get it. Well, go and re-join your brigade at Machow; it will arrive there before you." Thereupon, he left at the gallop. It was the first time I spoke to the emperor.

As he had ordered it, and after refreshing my men and horses in a good village, I was able to re-join the brigade at Machow; but Colonel Schwartz of the 5th Hussars and Colonel Marx of the 7th, who were both already a bit old, no longer commanded their regiments; they were retired as *généraux de brigade* and both went to rest; it was agreed that the punishment was soft.

The next day, the 28th, the brigade received two colonels; the 7th had Colonel Colbert, to whom I was to owe all my promotion up to *chef d'escadron*. We slept in front of Machow; the enemy continued his retreat and we followed him from afar to observe his march.

On the 12th January 1807, after several days of alternating marches and stops, the enemy was far off; we received the order to take cantonments on the Vistula. The regiment thus fell back as far as Voschyzgin, where it stayed from the 19th to the 28th; during this time, I went to Plockon on the Vistula to have arms repaired and to see to the various necessities of the service for which, as I have already said, I was responsible.

However, the Russian and Prussian armies had concentrated and executed an advance on the lower Vistula to beat the army corps of Marshal Bernadotte, who was cantoned next to Elbing. At this news, the emperor was obliged to give up our cantonments and make long days with the intention of taking the enemy's army in the rear. The brigade was then commanded by General Latour-Maubourg, today lieutenant general and governor of Invalides after having been minister of war. As to General Lasalle, he had been nominated as *général de division*, and the 5th and 7th Hussars were part of his division. The brigade set off on its journey passing by Drobin on the 29th, Mlawa on the 30th, Neidenbourg on the 1st February, between Passenheim and Allenstein on the 2nd and it arrived to bivouac on the 3rd near Allenstein. We passed the night on the heights in two feet of snow and without fires in extraordinary cold. The Russians had captured the officer charged with carrying to Bernadotte the order to retreat to draw the enemy onto the Vistula and allow the emperor to attack it in the rear. Having thus recognised the trap that awaited it, they quickly fell back and did not dare to oppose the emperor's march. Early in the morning on the 4th, we found part of the Russian army waiting for us beyond the river Alle; it was beaten and chased from position to position. This day, in a charge the brigade made against Cossacks, I tried to overtake my colonel in passing close to him, to attract his attention; I was happy enough to succeed.

It was the first affair in which the new colonel commanded the regiment, and it was always good, in such a case, to be noticed advantageously. Immediately after the charge, the colonel, who was with Generals Lasalle and Latour-Maubourg, called for me, and in front of these two generals, he said to me that if I overtook him again in a charge, he would have me arrested. I was content with the compliment... We pursued the enemy all day and, in another charge which took place before evening, I was happy enough to save M. Legendre from the hands of the enemy, the same officer that I had prevented Commandant Méda from sending away from our expedition on Afflentz. His horse had fallen, he was alone and about to be surrounded; I prevented the enemy cavalry from approaching him while he remounted his horse. The brigade, exhausted, slept the same evening at Valtersdorf. We fought all day on the 5th whilst advancing, and we pushed as far as Herzogwalen. On the 6th we slept at Wormditt and on the next day, the 7th, Lasalle's division was put under the orders of Marshal Ney, charged with cutting the retreat of the Prussians who were retiring in all haste on the main road from Mehlsack by Eichholz to go to Eylau. Marshal Ney, leaving Wormditt, took the direction of Kreutzbourg by a back road. After leaving Landsberg to our right, we continued to march until nightfall. The village where we were to sleep was occupied by the enemy; our advance-guard made vain efforts to dislodge them, and we could hardly see anything. "Curély," Colonel Colbert said to me, "take twenty-five men from the élite company and go and ambush the enemy; do as you wish, but it is necessary that the village is free when I arrive there." Thereupon, I left at the trot as quickly as the darkness and terrain allowed. I managed to turn the village and entered at the gallop; I then had the colonel informed, who had not yet arrived. The enemy had taken refuge in the houses and had stopped firing; all were taken by the hussars who spread into the houses at the arrival of the division.

The next day, the 8th, the day of the battle of Eylau, I commanded an advance guard of forty hussars. The army corps set off before daybreak. I took the direction given and, at the first village, I encountered Prussian posts. I took one party and gave chase to others. Towards 9am, I noticed the Prussian army, which was only 15 or 16,000 men, defiling before me on the main road and presenting me with their right flank. I straight away informed General Lasalle, who immediately marched after me, as well as Marshal Ney who followed with the infantry and, awaiting the arrival of these troops, I attacked the enemy with my forty hussars. I repulsed the cavalry that was opposed to me and almost struck the column, which was forced to oppose me with infantry and six guns. Whilst this was going on, the marshal deployed his troops to attack the enemy; all was ready about eleven o'clock. The Prussian attacks were beaten and they were cut off. The rear of their column was thrown onto Kreutzbourg, the head marching in haste on Eylau to take part in the battle, of which we could hear the cannonade clearly. It snowed, the weather was terrible and immediately the Prussian army had been cut in two, the marshal left in the area of the fight a brigade of infantry to observe the part of the column, which was retiring on Kreutzbourg, moving with the rest of his army corps in the pursuit of that which marched on Eylau. I thus continued with my advance guard, having received the order to follow the enemy as closely as possible, which I did. Arriving in view of Eylau, I noticed the enemy setting fire to a bridge over which we would have to pass. I charged straight away, routed them, and had the fire extinguished by my hussars, helped by several locals who were close to hand.

If this bridge had been burnt, the army corps of Marshal Ney would not have arrived in time to take part in the battle and would not have threatened the right and rear of the enemy towards evening as he was able to do. This is how things happened: Marshal Ney had advanced a brigade of infantry with some hussars as far as a village close to the right and rear of the Russian army. Towards 10pm, this brigade was attacked by the Russian reserve, which had been allowed to arrive at close range and which, after a fire fight of more than an hour, suffered so badly that it took flight.

I was with the advance guard on this day, as I have said, and therefore provided the *grand'garde* at night. We remained mounted almost all night. Towards 2am, I had a fire made, lay down and was asleep in an instant. When I got up, I was so stiff that I had to be helped up. A little movement got rid of this stiffness and put an end to the indisposition caused by the excessively cold night that had followed the fatigues of the day.

At daybreak, the enemy had disappeared; the cavalry of the Grand Duke of Berg followed it in the direction of Koenigsberg and on the 9th, we slept in bivouac in front of Eylau. On the 10th, we arrived at Villenberg, two leagues from Koenigsberg, where all the cavalry took position on the 11th, and stayed there on the 12th, 13th, 14th and 15th. There we lacked everything, we did not even have potatoes and no forage for our horses. The enemy being in presence, we remained mounted all the nights, and we had several alerts by day. The regiment received seven or eight young men from the École Militaire that the emperor had sent as *sous-lieutenants* and who, on a trial basis, we made to mount guard with twenty-five men, but gave them an experienced lieutenant or *sous-lieutenant* to guide them; they found the work very hard.

The troops lacking everything, the emperor retired the army behind the Passarge and Alle to live, and on the 17th we crossed, near Eylau, the ground on which the battle had taken place on the 8th. I saw there a wounded Russian who was still not dead; he had made a fire and was surrounded by the bodies of seven or eight of his comrades.

We retired via Landsberg, Wormditt, Guttstadt, Wartenbourg and Peterswalde. Before daybreak on the 3rd March, we deployed to attack the enemy, who had followed us and held very close to the line that we wanted to occupy. I was designated by the colonel to command the forty hussars charged with forming the advance guard for the infantry which, in this situation, was to march first; the Cossacks were surprised at Glottau. We continued our march and encountered their infantry that we beat close to Guttstadt. At this moment, I had two hussars killed by balls. When the crossing of the river had been forced by the infantry, I pursued the Cossacks to well beyond Peterwalde. Always skirmishing, I thus gained much ground and very quickly. The Cossacks were in full retreat. I noticed behind a wood a column of more than three hundred cavalry. There was no time to lose to scout it, and I thought it necessary to go there personally; I thus broke into a gallop followed by two hussars and in approaching I saw that they were horses in hand, that is to say, the second or third mounts of cavalry and infantry officers, led by soldiers or servants with a weak escort. I took with my two hussars eight of those which had the best appearance and quickly retired. I re-joined the regiment very shortly after. I gave to the hussars the contents of the large portmanteaux taken on the horses. I kept one of these for myself and the two hussars that had accompanied me sold the seven others for their own profit.

The brigade, having suffered much during the campaign, was sent to Elbing to re-fit. It was commanded by General Pajol. The headquarters of the regiments were placed in Elbing itself, the companies in the surrounding villages and farms. The élite company of the 7th was at Oberswalden. We remained in these cantonments from the 26th March until the 5th June 1807. Almost all the cavalry of the army was in the area of Elbing to a greater or lesser distance. It was the best part of all Prussia; the land is below sea level, the houses are separated by four, five or six hundred paces and situated on a straight line, a wide road bordered on each side with a large and deep ditch over which there was a bridge opposite each house. Despite this precaution, the roads were always bad during winter; this country is cut by numerous streams leading, close to Frische-Haff, to a kind of gulf in which the water is kept by mills by means of machines of wood which take it from the streams.

All the cavalry was perfectly reformed; the men that had remained in the rear had re-joined, the small and big depots had sent men and horses to the regiments. The emperor passed it in review on the plain between Elbing and Pomehrund. He found it as fine as it was numerous. The clothing, armament, all had been returned to the best state.

It was in this cantonment that Colonel Colbert nominated me, on the 26th March 1807, lieutenant in the *compagnie d'élite* and, the following 8th May, *adjutant-major*.

Marshal Ney's army corps, which occupied the most advanced line at Guttstadt and surrounding area, was attacked by the enemy in the first days of June. The emperor ordered the cantonments raised and the fine resistance offered by Marshal Ney to the whole Russian army gave time for the troops in the rear to arrive. We left Elbing on the 6th June to sleep the same day near Preuss-Holland, and on the 7th at Mohrungen. On the 8th we encountered the enemy close to the Passarge. As we knew he came to destroy the bridge, I was sent to find a ford. The infantry who were beyond the river fired a battalion volley at me, from which happily I was only struck by a single ball which struck my sword belt obliquely, and I was left with a heavy bruise on which the doctor made some light incisions. We crossed the river and pursued the enemy with our swords in his kidneys as far as Deppen. On the 9th, we continued the pursuit, and the regiment made several fine charges, in one of which I was lightly wounded in the left arm by a Cossack lance; I returned it with interest. This day we stopped at Alkirch, near Guttstadt, and the next day, the 10th, we marched on Heilsberg. The enemy retired into an entrenched camp situated on the left bank of the Alle and touching Heilsberg. He was vigorously pushed up to this camp; the cavalry and the 7th Hussars in particular made some very fine charges. The fighting only finished very late in the night and we slept right at the foot of the entrenchments. The next day, the two armies observed each other without a musket shot being fired. Marshal Davout made a movement coming down the left bank of the Alle, which convinced the Russians to abandon their entrenched camp and, in the night of the 11th to 12th, they crossed the Alle at Heilsberg to go to Friedland by the right bank of this river. The emperor set off in their pursuit and on the 12th, the army bivouacked almost halfway between Heilsberg and Bartenstein, then on the 13th level with Bartstein and Schippenbeil. The celebrated battle of Friedland took place on the 14th; all the troops achieved prodigies. On the 15th, we pursued the Russians, and the cavalry swam the Prégel near Wehlau; on the 16th, we pushed always forwards, skirmishing; the advance guard bivouacked near Billa on the 17th and on the 18th pushed them to within three leagues of Tilsit, still always skirmishing. My horse was wounded by an arrow shot by a Kalmouk. I had been watching these cavalrymen with curiosity; they were a poor troop.

On this day, Russian negotiators arrived at our advance guard carrying peace proposals.

The armistice was declared on the 19th, and the brigade, after having passed through Tilsit, went to sleep at Ragnitz on the Niemen. It soon went into more extended cantonments whilst the peace negotiations took place at Tilsit, and on the 21st July, after peace was concluded, the regiment was sent into cantonments at Ortelbourg. After remaining there for a fortnight, on the 17th August it received the order to move to the frontiers of Austria, passing through Poland.

Between Pultusk and Sierock, we crossed our old battlefields, then by Warsaw, in a fortnight (of which one day was a day of rest) we went to Radomsk, a small town where we remained from the 1st September to the 7th October. Here I commanded the place. The regiment was then cantoned until the 8th November at Koniecpol and surrounding area, on the river Pilika which separated Poland from Austria. I was still commandant of the place. The regiment left this cantonment to re-enter Prussia, crossing Silesia via Czenstochau, Oppeln, Brieg, Breslau, where we crossed the Oder, Glogau, Driesen and Friedeberg, where we arrived on the 27th November to canton in this town and the surrounding country until the 20th February 1808; that is to say for three and a half months. General Pajol was still commanding the brigade. The regiment started off again to then return to Higher-Silesia, taking almost the same route and arrived at Glowitz on the 11th March. The headquarters and the 1st Squadron were lodged in this town, the 2nd, 3rd and 4th Squadrons at Peiskretscham and Tost. We remained there until the 11th July, that is to say four months, and left there to go to Ratibor. I received from Marshal Davout, on the recommendation of Colonel Colbert, a commission of commandant of the place and was paid as such to command Ratibor.

The regiment remained in this town and the surrounding area from the 13th July until the 18th November 1808. Colonel Colbert had the advantage of being able to concentrate his regiment to carry out some manoeuvre training so that the regiment was able to pass rightly for the best trained in the army.

On the 19th November, the regiment left Higher-Silesia to go to Westphalia, crossing all Silesia. I was designated by Colonel Colbert, in passing through Neisse, to hand back this fortress to the Prussians; the French not having left a cannon and the arsenal was completely empty. We then passed through Reichenbach, Schweidnitz, Jauer, Goldberg, Görlitz, Bautzen, Meissen, Leipsick, Halle..., and we arrived at Aschenleben in Westphalia on the 12th December, to remain there until the 13th March 1809; three full months.

Since the Peace of Tilsit, the greater number of French troops had left for Spain; there only remained in Prussia the corps of Marshal Davout, who in the month of March 1809, was about

50,000 men strong. The Austrians made new preparations for war against France; Marshal Davout received the order to leave Prussia and to move with his army corps to Ratisbon. Consequently, the regiment sent its main equipages to France and set off for Austria on the 14th March 1809.

Chapter 7

The Campaign of 1809 in Austria

*I*n March 1809 Pajol's brigade was sent to the frontiers of Bohemia and was to become part of Montbrun's light cavalry division. Colbert was now promoted to général de brigade *and left the regiment. It was usual that when promoted to general rank, the newly promoted officer chose his aides de camp from his own unit, whose officers, their abilities and loyalty, were well known to him. Colbert chose Captain Curély and* sous-lieutenant *de Brack.*

Whilst de Brack accepted this sign of favour as an opportunity to enhance his career prospects, the rather more modest Curély was reluctant to leave the family that his comrades in the 7th Hussars had become to him and with whom he had fought alongside on many battlefields. He had also grown up in the army with disdain for the privileges of the staff and their accelerated promotion, and accepted the honour that Colbert bestowed upon him with evident reluctance. However, both officers continued to serve with the regiment until the arrival of their formal appointment.

The role of Montbrun's division in the coming campaign was to be of great importance. Austria's preparation for war forced Napoleon to hurry back from his campaign in Spain, despite feeling he was on the point of destroying the small British army that was under the command of General Moore. The commitment of the main French army to the peninsula forced Napoleon to raise a new army for the coming campaign that relied far more than usual on large numbers of recently trained conscripts. However, at its core was the very experienced and renowned 3rd Corps (still commanded by Marshal Davout) which was then under the name of the Army of the Rhine. This was deployed on the left bank of the Danube, close to Ingolstadt, whilst another corps, under the command of Marshal Masséna, concentrated at Augsburg and a third, under command of Marshal Lannes, formed in the rear. Troops from Bavaria, which was being directly threatened by Austria, and Württemberg, also fought with Napoleon.

On the 10th April 1809, General Pajol, who commanded the French outposts, received from the Austrian commander-in-chief, the Archduke Charles, a declaration of war. Marshal Berthier, Napoleon's chief-of-staff, gave the initial orders until Napoleon arrived, hastened the French movements and gave them more focus.

Montbrun's cavalry was attached to Davout's corps which was ordered to concentrate at Ratisbonne and to move up the right bank of the Danube as far as Abensberg. In this flanking march, away from the main body of the army, there were several important engagements and Montbrun's division, with two battalions of the 7th léger [light] Regiment was ordered to protect the vulnerable left flank (the right was protected by the Danube). This early part of the campaign saw fighting around Landshut and Ratisbonne which included the battles of Abensberg (a clear French victory) and Eckmühl [Eggmühl]. Davout's and Lefebvre's corps were isolated around Eckmühl and the Archduke Charles hoped to destroy them. The initial Austrian attack was held up by Montbrun's division and with French reinforcements on the way, Davout attacked and after bitter fighting defeated the Austrians. The 7th Hussars made several charges.

After the battle, Montbrun's division found itself on the Austrian line of retreat and penetrated into Ratisbonne in pursuit the next day. The 7th Hussars were first to enter the town at the same moment that Lannes seized the Straubing gate. Curély took a leading part in skirmishing with the Austrian cavalry that provided their rear-guard. As Napoleon directed his march on Vienna, Davout's corps were ordered to pursue the defeated Austrian army on the right bank of the Danube, with Montbrun's division *providing the advance-guard. As the regiment reached Cham, de Brack and Curély received their letters of service as aides de camp to General Colbert. After a painful farewell to their old regiment, in which Curély had served for sixteen years, they moved to join their new brigade. Colbert was then at Vienna; his brigade consisted of the 7th and 20th Chasseurs-à-Cheval and the 9th Hussars and was attached to the corps of Marshal Lannes. The brigade had the nickname of the Infernal Brigade. The two officers joined it the day before the battle of Essling (which was fought on the 21st and 22nd May), waiting some time before the small town of Ebersdorf [Kaiser-Ebersdorf] for its turn to cross the pontoon bridge that crossed the Danube south of Vienna. When its turn arrived only Colbert, his two aides de camp and the first squadron of the 9th Hussars had crossed onto the island of Lobau when the bridge was broken for the third time, leaving the rest of the brigade on the home bank. Curély was sent to give the bad news to Napoleon. The emperor ordered Colbert's brigade to remain in reserve and the three officers remained on the island for the next few days until they were able to return to the brigade. Once more concentrated, but having missed the battle of Aspern-Essling, Colbert was ordered to scout the routes along which Prince Eugene's army was coming from Italy to join Napoleon after their victory over the Archduke John.*

During this duty, Curély was involved in an action which was described by de Brack,

'In 1809, Captain Curély, an aide de camp with me to General Edouard Colbert, was tasked to reconnoitre the march of the Austrian army, which was retiring, but which turned to face our Army of Italy. At the head of a hundred cavalrymen, he advanced ten leagues (about 40 kilometres) from our division, turned the Austrian army, and sneaked so secretly on their rear that when night was drawing in, he found himself hidden in a wood three quarters of a league in the rear of the village in which the general headquarters of the archduke [John] was established. A large, dusty plain separated him from this village. Two or three Hungarian marauders who he had stopped gave him useful information.

A great number of cows were returning from the fields and were heading to the village, passing close to his hiding place; he seized the cow herders and made them bring the herd into the wood until it got dark, then set them off again, placing his men on foot in the middle of them, leading their horses by the bridle; he headed towards the village in the protection of the thick cloud of dust that was raised. Thus, he penetrated to the village square where with his own hand he blew out the brains of one of the guards of the archduke. At this signal, his cavaliers remounted and profiting by the enemy's surprise left the village and the next day re-joined Colbert's brigade without having lost a single man or horse.'

It will be seen that Curély only covers this event very briefly in his memoirs. Thanks to the information he returned with, two days later, General Colbert was able to make a junction with Prince Eugene and the Army of Italy.

Colbert's brigade joined Prince Eugene and fought with the Army of Italy against Archduke John's forces at Karako (where Curély was wounded), Papa, and finally at the battle of Raab (14th June). Although outnumbered at this latter battle, the Austrian forces were generally of poor quality and although they occupied a strong position, Eugene won an overwhelming victory and was able to join Napoleon.

The fighting around Raab was significant for Curély as despite his heroics, as we shall hear, he was to fall foul of General Montbrun and be denied reward for his actions. We cannot be sure if Curély's apparent criticism of Montbrun's qualities as a tactical commander stem from this incident, as Montbrun seems to have been widely admired in the army, or whether it reflects his own wounded pride. However, much to his relief, soon afterwards the brigade left Montbrun's division and came under command of Marshal Oudinot. Thus, in the heat of the battle on the first day of the battle of Wagram (5th July) he was to receive his next wound and was forced to watch the fighting of the second day from the window of his temporary hospital room in the village of Hözendorf. Colbert was also wounded in this battle and was lucky to survive, having been shot in *the head at point blank range. De Brack states that 'this ball entered close to his right ear and exited close to his left ear'! The ball had apparently passed round the head under the skin without penetrating his skull.*

Whilst Curély's wound ensured he took no further part in this campaign, he was still to benefit from his service during it. Both Colbert and Curély re-joined the brigade in time to participate in its review by Napoleon. Victorious campaigns were inevitably followed by rewards and promotions for those who had distinguished themselves. During the review, General Colbert presented Curély to the Emperor and requested the rank of chef d'escadron (squadron leader) in the 20th Chasseurs. This was granted and meant that Curély would remain with the brigade in his new appointment. The brigade remained in cantonments in Austria and then Germany until the 22nd March 1810 when its final duty before being dissolved was to escort the Empress Marie-Louise to Paris and a marriage to Napoleon. Curély was to command two squadrons of the 20th Chasseurs in escorting her from Kehl across the Rhine to the palace of Strasbourg. The regiment was then sent into garrison at Nantes to be a part of the armée des côtes de l'Océan where Curély remained from May 1810 until February 1811. During this time, he married Mademoiselle Giraud, daughter of the port commander. Curély soon became a father of a daughter whose godfather was General Colbert, but he was not present at the birth as he had already departed on his next adventure.

All Marshal Davout's army corps, cantoned in Prussia and Westphalia, started their march for the frontiers of Bohemia, approaching the Danube. As we were at Bayreuth on the 20th March, Colonel Colbert, who had been nominated as *général de brigade*, left the regiment; as he left the regiment, he asked me if I wanted to be one of his *aides de camp*. I asked him to give me a little time for reflection, thinking that aides de camp were not very respected in the armies. I listened to the advice of my friends; several advised me to remain with the regiment and one of them said, "The honest man is respected and esteemed everywhere; leave with the general, you

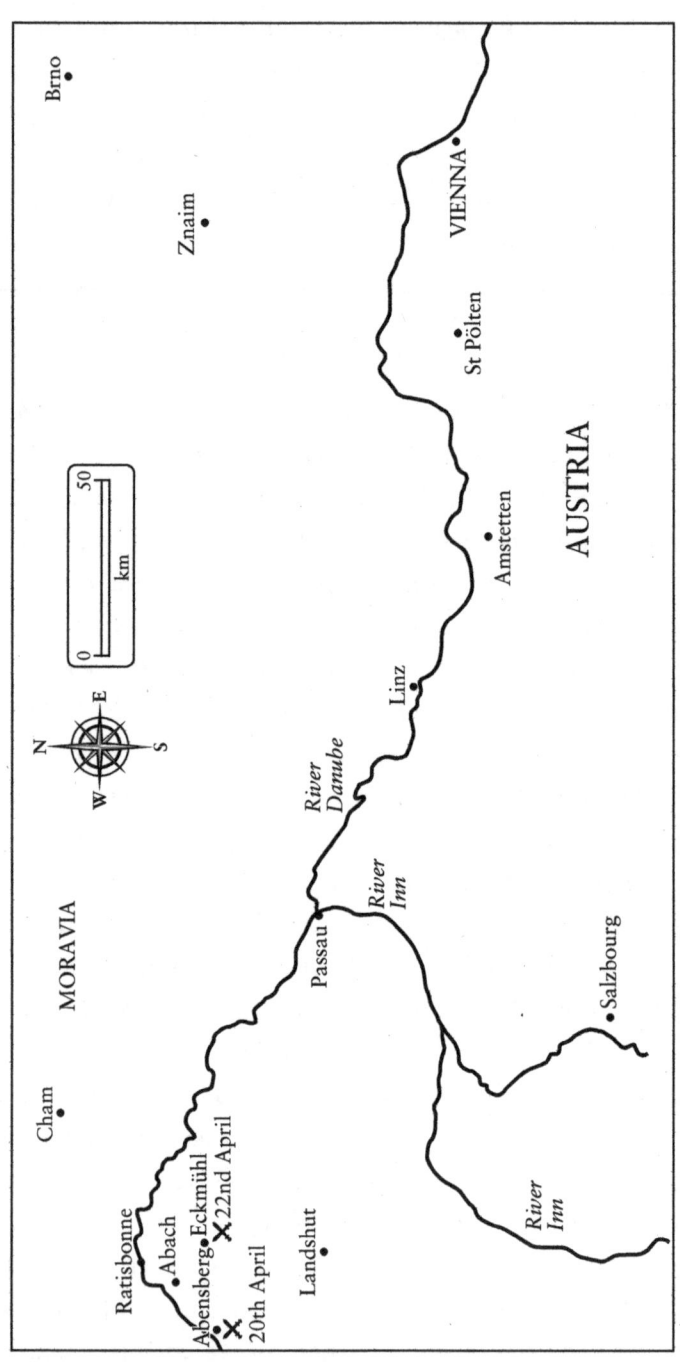

will make your way." The advice of this friend decided me to accept; the general requested to have as *aides de camp*, M. de Brack, *sous-lieutenant*, and me, then left to join his new brigade. We remained at the regiment, M. de Brack and I, until the arrival of our [formal] nomination. The regiment continued its march as far as Regenstorff, which we reached on the 11th April. A retreat on Ratisbonne [Ratisbon] was decided on; hostilities had not commenced, but the Austrians marched on this town. On the 17th we crossed the Danube. A regiment of infantry was left at Ratisbonne to defend the bridge over the Danube, the French making a movement during the 18th and taking position at Abach. Here they were attacked on the 19th and gave up ground without notable loss. Montbrun's division, of which we were a part, remained in position whilst the other troops followed Marshal Davout. The enemy having abandoned Abach, General Montbrun entered there on the 20th and remained bivouacked on the 21st and 22nd. Before dawn on the 23rd he moved on Ratisbonne. The enemy was beaten at Eckmühl [Eggmühl] and retreated on this town. General Montbrun's cavalry charged the fugitives several times and killed or captured many of them. On the evening of this affair, I could not move my right arm I had made so many sabre blows during the day; I also received five or six bruises from sabre blows which were not effective, and my horse was lightly wounded by a sabre blow to the head.

The emperor had Ratisbonne taken by escalade; we used ladders against the walls of the town to get over them and made 7 or 8,000 prisoners. The French infantry regiment, the 65th, that had been left in this town when we retreated, had been made prisoner by the enemy. We found their flags re-entering Ratisbonne, where the inhabitants had behaved poorly towards the French. The emperor was wounded by a ball from the ramparts. The enemy, retiring to the left bank of the Danube, burnt all the houses around the bridge to prevent the French from pursuing them; the town suffered much.

The emperor moved straight on Vienna on the 24th; a weak army corps, of which we were a part, was launched in pursuit of the enemy who were retiring into Bohemia. The regiment found itself at Oberdorf, on the extreme frontier of Bohemia, when M. de Brack and I received our commissions as aides de camp to General Colbert. We left the regiment after having said our goodbyes to all the old comrades with whom I had served with for fifteen years. I did not leave without a heavy heart. I will observe here that often, by an excess of attachment to the regiment in which one has served for a long time, it is hard to decide to leave it. Without doubt it is an excusable error, but it is proved that the officer who abandons the line to serve in a headquarters often obtains a great advancement that he would certainly not have obtained remaining in his regiment, where seniority has rights and so merit does not always prevail. Merit often excites some jealousy in the regiments but always finishes by breaking through.

We joined General Colbert near Vienna on the 10th May. Colbert's brigade, composed of the 7th and 20th Chasseurs and the 9th Hussars, marched on Ebersdorf to cross the Danube; it slept in the wood near this town on the 20th. It filed over on the large bridge over the Danube on foot, the men holding their horses by the bridle, at the moment when the bridge was broken by a mill that the enemy sent down the middle of the river (these watermills are based on a kind of solid boat, held by an anchor; they are placed in the current of the river which makes them work). A squadron of the 9th Hussars, which were at the head of the brigade, found themselves with the general and his aides de camp on the left bank of the Danube, the other squadrons of the 9th Hussars, the 7th and 20th Chasseurs remained on the right bank. I was sent by General Colbert to the emperor to inform him of the accident which had happened and to ask for his orders. The emperor replied to me, "That the general should continue his march and move into reserve with his squadron. As to

The Campaign of 1809 in Austria 93

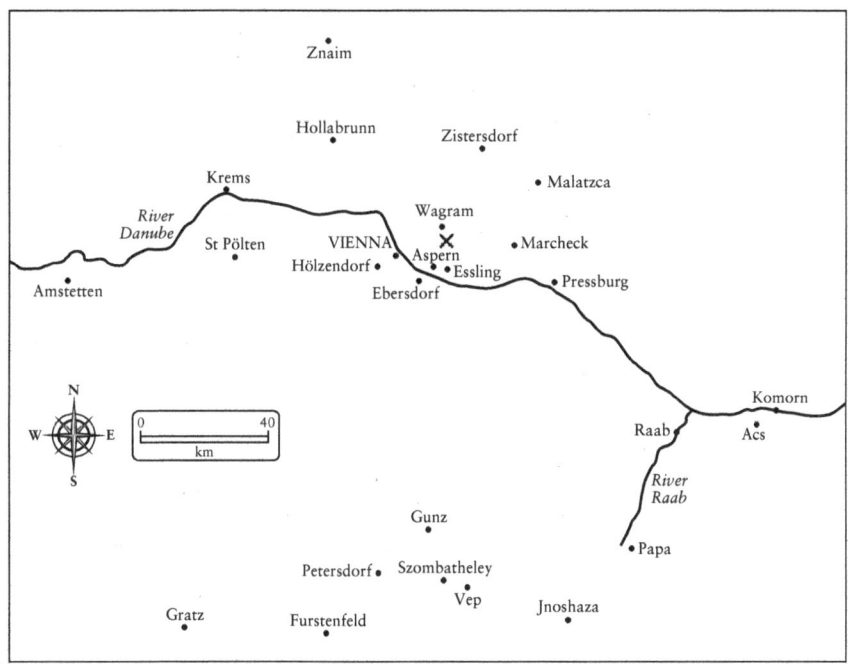

the rest of the brigade, I will give its orders." This was the second time that I spoke to the emperor. The army was only partly across onto the left bank of the river. Marshal Davout's corps, the artillery park, etc., remained on the right bank. The bridge was only repaired after four days. General Colbert moved forwards with his squadron of hussars, but an instant after, our troops were forced to give ground because ammunition was short. We fought until the evening, and we retired during the night onto the island of Lobau, formed by an arm of the Danube. General Colbert provided the extreme rear guard. After having re-crossed the bridge established over the small arm, it was broken and the whole of the part of the army that had fought found itself contained on the island of Lobau without rations or forage. The Danube was swollen, and it could only be crossed with difficulty in boats. The first night that the troops passed on the island, the infantry ate several cavalry horses, notably that of an officer whose horse had escaped. The officer, looking for it the next morning, found only the hide with the saddle and bridle by the side. General Colbert, accompanied by his aides de camp, crossed the Danube in a boat by order of the emperor to re-take command of his brigade and went with it towards Hungary.

Colbert's brigade, entering Hungary, was ordered to distribute Napoleon's proclamations to the Hungarians which tried to persuade the population to abandon the Emperor of Austria's cause, but these proclamations had no effect; the inhabitants refused them, and the Hungarian insurrection continued.

The Austrian Army of Italy, which had been beaten by the Viceroy of Italy, was in full retreat; I was sent by General Colbert with fifty men from the élite company of the 9th Hussars from Gunz, where the brigade was located, to Furstenfeld, to find out where this army had reached. I saw that its rear guard was at Furstenfeld and that it was continuing its retreat down the Raab on Papa. I covered forty leagues to go and return in two nights and a day, only stopping to refresh the horses. I left on the 4th as night fell and had returned at dawn on the 6th. On the journey I made several prisoners and passed through the enemy army in a country where there was no affection for the French. On my return, I wanted to take a guide at Petersdorf, where I had stopped on the way; it was then midnight. This village was full of Austrian troops; suddenly a fusillade of shots came from all the windows and the main body of my men awaited me close to a bridge which was at the entry to the village over a small river that ran into the Raab. In the village I took a road to the right and at the gallop, abandoning my prisoners. After a quarter of an hour, I halted and listened; no one pursued me. I had the roll called and was very happy to see that I had not lost a man or a horse, and that there was not even anyone wounded. It is best, when one marches as partisans or when making a long reconnaissance, to not return by the same route. Here is an example... Immediately the roll had been called, I took a route across the fields to re-join the road I had left. I again crossed the river with no trouble, and I arrived at Gunz with my troop very tired, but with my mission complete. The brigade started its march two hours after my arrival, to contact the enemy on his march. It slept at Kreuz on the 6th, near Vép on the 7th and the 8th, 9th and 10th at Jnoshaza. The light troops of the *Grand Armée* had been sent in pursuit of the Austrian Army of Italy; they awaited the arrival of the Viceroy with his army. This prince breakfasted with General Colbert on the 11th. The 9th Hussars, commanded by Colonel Gauthrin, vigorously attacked the enemy cavalry at Karako and made some prisoners. In one of the charges in this affair, I was wounded by a sabre blow to my left cheek and my horse also received a sabre blow to the lower lip. We bivouacked in front of Karako and, on the 12th, we pursued the enemy beyond Papa, taking many prisoners from him, always in cavalry combats. On this day, in the area where Colbert's brigade was located, we could clearly see Montbrun's division which included the 7th Hussars. I expressed the desire to General Colbert to go to see my old comrades, and he allowed me to go. *Sous-lieutenant* Hulot, who was serving the general, came with me and we took a mounted chasseur to follow us. On the way we found a small river which forced us to make a detour, and, on this detour, we found ourselves facing two Hungarian squadrons of the new levée, through the middle of which it was necessary for us to pass to get to the 7th Hussars or we would have to turn back. I took the first option; I seized the chasseur's carbine and advanced to close range. I killed a horse with my first shot and a man with my second; the two squadrons retreated, and we passed on. I saw my old friends again with pleasure.

The next day, the 13th, we marched on Papa on the Raab. On this day there were several more cavalry combats, unwisely engaged by General Montbrun. The 20th Chasseurs Regiment pointlessly lost fifty men killed by the enemy's balls; we bivouacked facing them. The Viceroy's French army concentrated during the night and towards ten o'clock in the morning of the 14th, the battle of Raab took place. The Viceroy overthrew the enemy at all points. On this day, General Montbrun had Colbert's brigade under his orders, besides his own division. Charged with driving in the enemy's extreme right by turning it with seven regiments of light cavalry, General Montbrun passed along a very narrow road with marshes on each side. These protected the Hungarian Insurrection, which was composed of the new *levées*, and who were very difficult to dislodge. Again he succeeded in getting Colbert's brigade pointlessly cannonaded. The cavalry that was opposed to us should have lost half their men; we should have taken all their guns and then moved onto their infantry who started to retreat in the greatest disorder and made them prisoners. Instead of this, there was no one taken from the enemy because of the presumption of the general, who wanted, it was said, to take the Archduke John, commander of the Austrian army, who was not taken. In this battle, charging at the head of the 9th Hussars to force the passage between the marshes, I had the occasion to sabre all at leisure. After the crossing of the defile, a drunk Hungarian hussar, pistol in hand, had passed through our line. He was coming back from behind towards my side; I went to meet him, and I split his head open with a sabre blow. His horse did not stop but carried the hussar almost back to his own lines where he was taken by the French skirmishers. For myself, I sprained my wrist with the force with which I had struck the sabre blow. The next day, General Montbrun's cavalry was ordered to go to Acs, a league and a half from Komorn, a fortress located on the left bank of the Danube with an entrenched camp on the right bank where the enemy army had concentrated. Colbert's brigade again had the misfortune to find itself under the orders of General Montbrun.

Arriving at Acs and after having scouted the terrain, Colbert's brigade was deployed to the advance posts; the three regiments each on a different point. The 7th Chasseurs at the bridge on the main road that led to Komorn; the 20th in the gardens opposite the bridge of a mill which also led to Komorn and the 9th Hussars to the right of the village in the plain. We maintained this position until the 30th June. The Viceroy's army retired into the area around Raab.

During this fortnight, the cavalry often made strong reconnaissances on Komorn and the surrounding area. For his part, the enemy pushed several against us. On the 21st, two hundred enemy hussars marched on Acs; the sun was down, but it was still light enough to see them. Someone came quickly to warn General Montbrun who was at dinner with his generals, the headquarters, and the aides de camp in the fine château of Acs, which belonged to M. d'Esterhazy. We immediately mounted. General Colbert sent me to the 7th Chasseurs; de Brack, his other aide de camp, was sent to the 20th Chasseurs and the general went in person to the 9th Hussars. I left at the gallop and after having passed our advance posts, I recognised the Hungarian hussars which were quietly retiring. As I returned, I encountered General Montbrun who had come to see what was happening; he was accompanied by one of his generals of brigade and an escort of twelve or fifteen men. I informed him of what I had seen, assuring him that the enemy was retiring very peacefully and that we could let him go without anxiety. He did not want this and ordered me to take a guard of twenty-five men from the 20th who were lodged nearby and to charge the enemy, which is what I did. We sabred the enemy's left, but his right, seeing how few were in their pursuit, turned bridle and charged us in our turn as well as General Montbrun who, with his suite, were just to our rear. He was charged so impetuously by the Hungarian hussars, that were all directed on him, that he was obliged to retire by the small mill road. The two generals lost their hats and the general of brigade also left an epaulette behind. Night having arrived, we could see almost nothing. The enemy, galloping close to General Montbrun, entered the village; the general, the 20th Chasseurs and the 9th Hussars, all of Montbrun's division, retired in haste into the plain, a good half a league from Acs. During this rout of General Montbrun, seeing no one pursuing me, I took refuge with the 7th Chasseurs who had remained quietly guarding the principal point. I then listened to all the racket that was taking place in the village; the enemy were behind us. I quickly informed Major Labiffe, who commanded the 7th Regiment, of what had happened, and I advised him to guard the exit of the bridge with his élite company to prevent the enemy from leaving the village, and to face Komorn with the rest of his regiment. He did this and, indeed, several Hungarian hussars that appeared as they left were taken prisoner. The noise having ceased in the village, we listened for a long time and heard nothing. Finally, I requested M. Labiffe to give me a few men to scour the village; I found no one there, not even a local as they were all hiding. I returned close to M. Labiffe and I asked him again to remain in position because it was presumed that the enemy had gone to the mill and that General Montbrun had surrounded them to the rear of the village. I then left to look for this general. After having run around and listened well, I heard some noise in the plain, went in that direction and found General Montbrun with his six regiments. I informed him of all that had happened; he replied to me, "Ah!...I will make my report after what you have come to tell me and without doubt it will be right." However, on my saying the enemy had retired and that the 7th Chasseurs had not abandoned its position for a moment, he determined to re-take the post that he had left. Indeed, all was quiet for the rest of the night... As we were returning, it was then midnight, I had not noticed that two hats of our generals were missing. General Montbrun said to me, "Curély, you were involved in the affair and know the roads around the village, please do me the favour of going with General X... and my aide de camp to search for our hats and a general's epaulette, that we lost in the fray." I went there and led these two sirs to all the points where the general had gone. We found the epaulette, but the two hats had been carried off by the Hungarian hussars and the next day they were carried in triumph through the town of Komorn.

The next day after dinner, General Colbert, Colonel Gauthrin and I, walked in the courtyard of the château. General Montbrun, seeing all three of us laughing from the windows of his room, thought that it was the history of the hats which was making us laugh. He reproached General Colbert, who answered him well, but from that moment on I had the misfortune of displeasing him. He gave proof of this to Colonel Gauthrin who, after the battle of Wagram, found himself commanding the brigade in the absence of General Colbert who had been wounded by a ball to the head in this famous battle. Colonel Gauthrin, in his quality of commanding the brigade, had proposed rewards asked for by the emperor and had put me in the return to receive the cross of *Officier de la Légion d'Honneur*; but, this return needed the signature of General Montbrun who, seeing my name, struck it out and said to Colonel Gauthrin, "Curély has no need of my support to be *Officier de la Légion d'Honneur*."

The army of the Viceroy of Italy set off on its march on the 1st July to join the emperor and effect the crossing of the Danube close to Vienna. In the morning of the 5th we crossed the bridge constructed by the Emperor's orders at the same place as it was broken on our first passage. The *Grande-Armée* crossed onto the left bank of the Danube through the night of the 4th to 5th, and we entered the line towards 4pm. We left General Montbrun with pleasure to go to be under the orders of General Oudinot, who attacked the village of Wagram. It was nearly 7pm when I was struck in the left knee by a ball, which flattened against the bone and round the kneecap. I went to the ambulance established in the plain to the rear and the ball was easily extracted. I was then obliged to pass the night of the 5th to the 6th in bivouac, and in the morning, I was put with great pain onto a horse. I suffered much and my servant led me thus to the bridge where I found a brigadier of the 7th Hussars named Ocqui. This brave old comrade, with whom I had served for a long time, was leading some rations for his regiment in several vehicles. He hurried to empty one and reloaded it into the others and gave it to me. I was then led to Hölzendorf, a village situated on a height a little less than two leagues from Vienna and where there is found a château belonging to the Emperor of Austria. I arrived there towards midday on the 6th. From my window, I could clearly see the fighting between the two armies and my joy was extreme when I noticed the retrograde movement of the Austrians, well indicated by the smoke of cannons and musketry. The same evening, I learned with the greatest pleasure the news which spread about the outcome of the battle.

I remained in this village until the 21st July, where I was treated by a Portuguese surgeon. During this time, an armistice was concluded and the peace of Schoenbrunn followed. General Colbert, who had been wounded at the battle of Wagram during the 6th July, charging at the head of the brigade against the Austrian squares, had gone to Vienna for treatment. When he knew where I was, he made me move close to him and we remained in Vienna until the 11th August. The general was healed, my wound was getting better, so I left with the general for Marcheck on the 12th. We crossed the battlefield where the air was so polluted that we could not put our noses out of the vehicle. He found the brigade lodged around Marcheck and re-took command. We remained there until the 7th September, and we left on the 8th to go to canton at Malatzca in Hungary and the surrounding area. On the 21st, the emperor passed General Colbert's brigade in review, who nominated me to be *chef d'escadron* in the 20th Chasseurs as reward for the services I had rendered and the wounds I had received. I then left my brave General Colbert to go to join the 20th Chasseurs at Zistersdorf, where it remained cantoned until the 2nd November. Peace concluded, it started its march to evacuate the Hereditary States, passing via Vienna, Saint-Pölten, Traun, Wels, Lintz, Munich, Memmingen and Rastadt. Besides making some long stops, it finally crossed the Rhine on the 22nd February to reenter France and remain thirty two days in the area of Strasbourg. During these thirty-two days, Colbert's brigade was disposed in a manner to escort, from the Rhine to Luneville, the Empress Marie-Louise, who came from Vienna to Paris. I commanded the two squadrons of the 20th Chasseurs which crossed the Rhine on the 25th March to receive her and I escorted her as far as the palace at Strasbourg. After her departure, I received the order to leave and on the 26th, I slept at Saverne with my two squadrons, then at Sarrebourg, Blâmont and Lunéville, where the regiment remained together until the 9th April. I profited from this time to go to finish up some family affairs at Aillers and I re-joined on the 9th at Nancy, the regiment having received the order to leave for Orléans. It was there on the 26th and remained there until the 2nd May, being sent to Nantes where I arrived on the 16th May 1810 to remain there until the 22nd February 1811. It was in this town, my dear children, that I married your mother.

Chapter 8

His Campaign in Spain

In July 1810, two squadrons (the 3rd and 4th) of the 20th Chasseurs had been sent to Spain to become part of the 9th Corps of the Army of Spain that was commanded by General Drouet d'Erlon. In February 1811, Curély was also ordered to Spain with the 2nd Squadron, not to join the other two squadrons of the regiment but to become an independent squadron in the small Army of Catalonia. When the order arrived, being in temporary command of the regiment, he took it upon himself to bring this squadron up to strength with the worst of the men in the regiment and then to mould them into good soldiers.

The squadron left Nantes on the 22nd February and arrived in Spain after a march of thirty seven days. It came under the command of General Gareau who had much fighting experience during the Revolutionary Wars but had done little fighting since. It was not long before Curély was in action against the Spanish. On the 16th June he was ordered to join the 7th Army Corps of Marshal Macdonald which was then employed in the blockade of Figuières. For the next four months whilst it was on this duty, the squadron was to suffer greatly from the heat and a lack of rations; more than 60 chasseurs became ill, probably with malaria which was rife at that time. Curély took a great interest in the health and welfare of his men and thanks to his care only two of these men died in hospital. After an honourable defence, Figuières surrendered on the 19th August having tied down the 7th Corps from the beginning of April and prevented it from contributing to Suchet's attack on Tarragona which he was finally able to capture without the help of Macdonald.

From October 1811 to January 1812, Curély's squadron was responsible for collecting rations from around the province. This was a difficult and dangerous duty; long marches across a country infested with bands of guerrillas.

Finally, at the beginning of 1812, General Decaen, successor to Macdonald, sent Lamarque's division, of which Curély was a part, to relieve the garrison of Terragona which was blockaded by a force of British and Spanish troops. Curély's squadron took part in the action at Altafulla, where 10,000 Spanish faced 8,000 Frenchmen. The French cavalry played a decisive role in the fighting which is described by Curély. In his report of the action, General Decaen wrote,

'The enemy, broken at all points, attempted however, to reform on a height outside the village of Sagonte. General Hamelinaye, of Lamarque's division, was ordered to attack by the left, whilst with Espert's brigade, General Lamarque marched to attack from the front. In this attack, chef d'escadron Curély, of the 20th Chasseur Regiment, with his squadron and one of the 29th Chasseurs, made a brilliant charge against more than 400 cuirassiers and hussars of Saint-Narcisse, of which a great number were sabred. A hundred horses and sixty prisoners were taken by the chasseurs.*

'…2,000 men taken, killed or wounded and all the enemy's artillery captured, are the trophies of the combat of Altafulla, where all the troops competed with each other in ardour and courage.'

After this battle, General Decaen recommended Curély for the Officer's Cross of the Légion d'Honneur, *but he did not receive it.*

Just a few days after the action at Altafulla, Curély's squadron was ordered to move to Bonn to take part in the invasion of Russia. His short time in what was a comparative sideshow in Spain had not given him much of an opportunity to shine. He had not taken part in any significant engagements, not really fought against the British or faced a very capable mounted enemy. He was probably relieved to be leaving Spain but was blissfully unaware of the massive challenges that lay ahead.

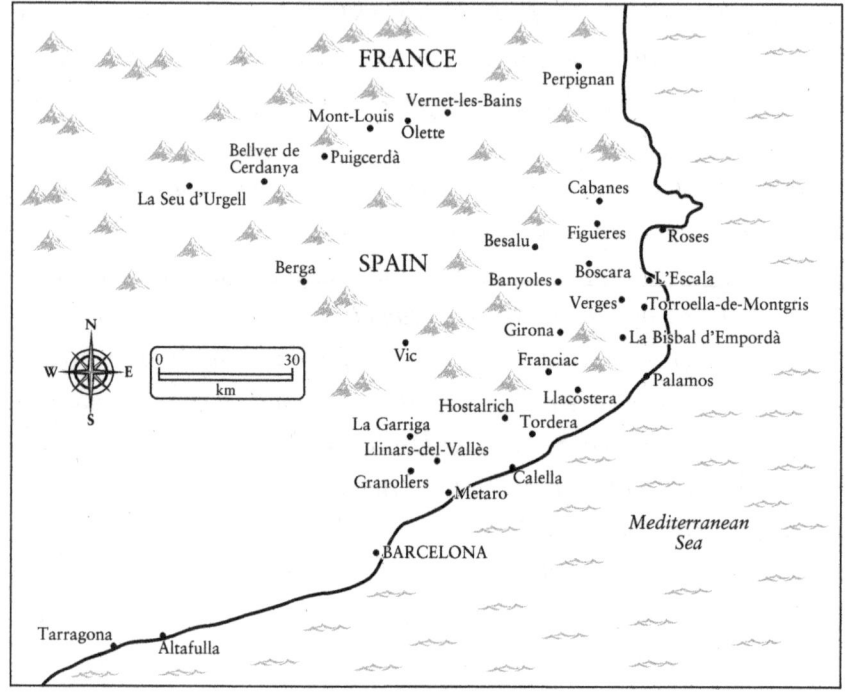

At the moment that I received the order from the minister to leave with the 2nd Squadron to go to Spain, the colonel was on leave, and I commanded the regiment. The order laid down that the two companies forming the 2nd Squadron should be made up to an effective strength of two hundred men. I chose in the companies that were remaining, to complete those who were to depart, all those that are called the 'poor heads' or more generally the 'poor subjects.' I was persuaded that, led with much clemency and firmness, they would be good soldiers. I was not deceived in my expectation; after having punished one or two very severely, I made all the others excellent subjects, docile and giving above all, an example of the most perfect subordination.

I left Nantes on the 22nd February 1811, with the two hundred chasseurs under my orders, well mounted, equipped and armed as

I desired. I found the French army at Bellver de Cerdagne [Bellver de Cerdanya], in front of Puycerda [Puigcerda].

I arrived in Spain after thirty-seven days marching (of which seven were rest days), without having left a man or a horse in the rear. Every day I passed the men and horses in review to assure myself that the turnout and specially to identify the horses which were starting to get injured by the saddle; the remedy in this case consists in correcting the saddle, for the injuries of this kind are only those occasioned by a lack of care. In this fashion, I did not have an injured horse. On my arrival in Cardagne, I was put under the orders of General Garreau, who was charged with the investment of the forts of Urgel. The day before we were to start our march to begin the investment, the general was informed of the surprise of the place of Figuières by the Spanish (this place was also called the fort of San-Fernando) and received at the same time the order to send to Figuières almost all his infantry. When I heard a portion of the troops were given the order to go to Figuières and that of which I was a part were ordered to remain in Cardagne, I marked my discontent very highly before the general's aide de camp, who did not hesitate to report it to him. I hoped that by going before Figuières I would have more opportunity to fight the enemy than remaining isolated in a small corner surrounded by mountains. It was necessary to obey and remain, but I had turned General Garreau against me; I should not have complained so much or better still, kept quiet.

The troops destined for Figuières having departed, General Garreau retreated and, on the 14th April, we entered Montlouis. Very early on the 15th, the general, having learnt that three hundred Spanish soldiers had come to raise contributions at Puycerda, had me leave with a hundred cavalry of my squadron to go and fight them, and he followed me with his infantry. I took the lead and made three leagues at the trot and, arriving close to Puycerda, I saw the Spanish leaving and climbing the mountain of San-Martino. I had them followed by a dozen chasseurs under the orders of an officer and, with the rest of my troop, I turned the mountain, that I knew well, at the *grand trot*. I arrived as the Spanish crossed the peak that hid me from their view. I found them formed up in perfect order; I had them charged without wasting a moment and they were broken. Seventy-five of them that had thrown themselves into a farm, surrendered as prisoners; all the rest were sabred and killed; we took several mules that were with them. I brought back the prisoners to General Garreau, who appeared very satisfied and made his report on this affair in the following terms:

> Three hundred Spanish who levied a contribution at Puycerda were attacked by a hundred men of the 20th Chasseurs who took seventy-five prisoners; the rest were sabred and killed.

This report was very truthful, but only lacked my name; the general had not forgotten my words and the wound was too fresh. He had no part in this success which was down to me alone, for he was a league and a half to the rear with his infantry when I attacked the Spanish.

In the evening, all returned to Montlouis. I was lodged with my two hundred chasseurs in the citadel, where there were passable stables with rooms for the men above. I was the governor of this citadel; every evening the keys were brought to me, and someone came to pick them up in the morning. We remained there quietly until the 22nd and, after the orders that the general sent me, I left with my squadron on the 23rd to go to Figuières. But I received a counter-order halfway there and was obliged to return to Montlouis, where I arrived on the 26th and where I remained until the 16th June. On the 21st May, I had been struck by a violent rheumatism which made it impossible to be cured at Montlouis. General Garreau was informed who was at the waters of Vernet. He had been told to go there and had the goodness to have a room prepared for me and offering his table to me which I accepted. I thus departed on the 17th June; I slept the same day at Olette and at Vernet on the 18th. The general did everything he had promised, and more; I will always remember how good to me he was. The waters of Vernet made me suffer much; they only needed to touch me to cause me the most violent pains. I was pulled from my bed to the baths on a chair, then a mattress of covers and a blanket was brought to me, to put me at the entrance to the bath, because I could not stand the trip from my bed. Finally, after having remained at Vernet for twenty-five days, I thought I was strong enough to re-join my squadron which, in my absence, had received the order to go to Figuières. Because of my sufferings, all my hair had fallen out and, to bring it back, I had to shave my head. I left Vernet on the 12th July and on the 16th, found my squadron cantoned at Cabanes, from where it did service before the fortress of Figuières, which was blockaded by the French army under the orders of Marshal Macdonald. The squadron remained in this cantonment until the 30th September, the time at which the Spanish garrison of San-Fernando surrendered to the discretion of the marshal.

Nothing remarkable happened during this blockade; the enemy made a single attempt to break through our lines two days before they surrendered, but failed, and, after having suffered considerable losses, returned to the fort. Sometime previously, the Spanish had forced seven to eight hundred French prisoners to leave the place, as useless mouths to feed. That is to say the garrison, composed of all the army's depots, that they had captured when they surprised and took the fort; these prisoners were thrown out of the gates and, hardly were they out, than the Spanish fired on them with canister to make them get away from the place quicker. I cannot remember more than a day, where I was going to the house of Marshal Macdonald (I went there often, but never without being invited), as he returned from a tour of the advanced posts, he said to me as he dismounted, "Duty is being done badly, I found a sentry asleep; he is now sleeping the sleep of eternity." I could not think for a second that he had put his sword through his body, for the marshal, despite the exact discipline that reigned in the troops under his orders, was extremely genial and affable. But such is the unfortunate necessity that finds a general-in-chief make examples! Marshal Macdonald had the goodness to send me twenty-five bottles of Bordeaux for the 15th August, the day of fête for the Emperor Napoleon...

Since the arrival of the squadron at Cabanes until our departure for Russia, the horses only lived on straw taken from the countryside and oats that had come from France, sometimes however, local barley, corn from Turkey and the Carab [Carob] tree, a kind of pea species with black bark, produced by a tree that is called by the same name of Carab. At Cabanes, my chasseurs all fell sick one after the other; I sometimes had as many as sixty unavailable at the same time. This epidemic was caused by the heat of the climate and by the fruits that the soldiers ate. As I did not have a surgeon attached to my squadron, I decided to treat them myself after having consulted the doctor-in-chief. I could not send them to the hospital where they would have laid on straw heaped up on each other, very poorly nourished, still poorly cared for and from where, when they left, they would be directed to France, so the result would soon have been that I had two hundred horses and not a single man. Here is how I did it: immediately that the sickness was declared, I purged them with jalap[27]; then I made them take quinine in wine; finally, I made them drink as much wine as possible. By this means I managed to keep all my men, except two that I could not remedy and who I sent to hospital where they died.

---

[27] Jalap is a purgative drug obtained generally from the tuberous roots of a Mexican climbing plant.

During September, at the moment when the rations started to run out for the Spanish in San-Fernando, we noticed some English sails on the sea, by the side of the fortress of Roses. A disembarkation of the English was feared, to make a diversion and disengage the garrison of San-Fernando, and I was sent with some infantry as far as Perclada, but the sails disappeared, and we returned to our cantonments.

The squadron left Cabanes on the 1st October to go to Torroella-de-Montgris, where it remained until the 28th. The epidemic ended, and I had no more than twenty sick who were getting better bit by bit. The second day after our arrival at Torroella, I received the order to send reconnaissance patrols of ten to twelve men commanded by a *sous-officier*, out to two or three leagues into the country. Wanting to know the country myself before sending patrols, I left with the first of the reconnaissances composed of a *maréchal des logis* and eleven chasseurs. I travelled quietly through five or six villages which had been designated to me. I arrived thus at a last village, situated on the mountain and surrounded by walls. I took all the precautions necessary in such a case and, approaching, I saw several inhabitants flee who were in the fields. I advanced with caution towards the gate and again noticed some women who seemed frightened. I remained outside with my detachment and I sent the *maréchal des logis*, accompanied by a chasseur, to arrange some lodgings and to tell the *alcade* (the mayor) to come and speak to me. My intention was not to go into the village, but I needed to speak to the *alcade*; it was therefore necessary to send someone to tell him to come, and I directed the *maréchal des logis* to arrange the lodgings in order to persuade the enemy, if he was in the village, that I was going to enter and thus prevent them from taking the *maréchal des logis* due to a lack of a richer prize. The *alcade* arrived, I questioned him a lot and I asked him particularly if the enemy were in the village. He replied 'no' and that no one had seen them for a long time, that I could enter in all security and that I would be well received as all the French troops were who came there. When the conversation was over, I said to the *alcade* that I was very upset not to be able, for the moment, to accept his invitation, that I had to leave, but that I would return another time. The *alcade* left me abruptly. I then set off quietly to head back. Hardly had we covered fifty paces than I noticed more than two hundred *miquelets*[28] who left the village running towards us. The country was mountainous and cut by hedges so I took the *grand trot* with my patrol, and we received their fire at long range, so that I had neither men nor horses wounded. Arriving at Toroella, I informed the colonel of infantry who commanded this place of what had happened. He ordered me to immediately take with me a hundred chasseurs and a battalion of his regiment, to go to take the *alcade*, to punish the inhabitants and to chase the enemy off if they were still there. At my arrival, the *miquelets* had disappeared. I refreshed the troop, took the *alcade* and I returned to the colonel, who sent him to headquarters with my report. If I had entered the village, the *miquelets* would have seized the gates and we would all have been taken or killed. One cannot be too careful on these sorts of reconnnaissances and especially in Spain.

On the 29th October, the squadron left Torroella to go to raise 'ordinary' contributions on the country side that was controlled by the French. With the column there was a kind of taxman; we slept first at Vergés, then at Bisbal on the 30th. Entering this town, we were fired at. I passed through the town at a gallop but saw no troop either inside or outside; the inhabitants said they had seen nothing but they were in the houses. We marched on until the 5th November by Palamos, la Bisbal, Girone Banolas, Besalú and Bascarú, where we remained until the 28th.

---

[28] Guerrillas.

We left again on the 29th to escort a convoy of merchandise, wheat, flour, beef etc., destined for the garrison of Barcelona. On this day we slept at Girone, where the convoy was concentrated and the next day we set off. The escort was composed of four to five thousand men.

We slept at Franciade on the 30th, Hostalrich on the 1st December and Llinas on the 2nd. Leaving Llinas at 3am, we found the route barred by 25,000 *miquelets*, country people and Spanish soldiers. All were broken and chased off; the convoy passed without losing a gain of wheat. We had in the service of France, a company of Spanish *miquelets* who always marched with us; but our new friends liked us no better than the enemy *miquelets*. The convoy continued its march on Barcelona and we found at Granoellers, opposite Garriga, the garrison which had come before us. It received the convoy and went peacefully into Barcelona. The enemy, who had rubbed shoulders with us on our right, formed up before us again at Garriga in the evening. The infantry was already skirmishing with them when I came up to charge them; they immediately retreated. We slept at Granoelles on the 4th and 5th, and the next day the convoy escort turned back without being threatened by the enemy. After having made a circuit to raise the contributions, we returned to la Bisbal and remained there until the 16th.

The country of Hostalrich to Granoelles is a country of mountains and woods. The road is often cut by streams; there is even a place where, over half a league long, the road, in a thick wood, crosses the stream thirty times, which is called 'the road of the thirty steps.' It was a very dangerous passage for stragglers.

From la Bisbal, we went to make a stay of seventeen days at Llacóstera, then we went by Tordera to Calella, a small town by the seashore where, for twenty-four hours, the English cannonaded the town and the troops that were there. We concentrated the small army at Hostalrich on the 19th January 1812; it took bread for eight days and the cavalry received oats for four days. The next day, the 20th, the army set off to go to relieve the garrison of Tarragone. The Spanish were close to this place on the land and the English bombarded it from the sea. At this period, the army of Catalonia was commanded by Lieutenant-General Decaen; the part of the army that marched to raise the siege of Taragone had a strength of five to six thousand men under the command of Lieutenant General Lamarque. For myself, I was under the immediate orders of *général de brigade* Hamelinaye. On the 21st we slept under the walls of Barcelona. As we arrived before this town, the garrison came out for the same object as us and advanced a half-march in order to deceive the enemy as to our numbers. Before dawn on the 24th, Lamarque's division joined the garrison of Barcelona before Altafulla, where the enemy had come to confront us and had occupied a very advantageous position. They were 10,000 strong and thought they were only going to fight the garrison of Barcelona, which was only 3,000 strong. This garrison was commanded by Lieutenant-General Maurice Mathieu who, at our arrival, took command of all the concentrated troops. The garrison had its left on the sea with Altafulla in front of it, Lamarque's division occupied the right, and with my squadron I was the extreme right. The attack started on the position of Altafulla, which was taken by the garrison of Barcelona; at the same time, the 3rd *léger*, of Lamarque's division attacked the enemy by his left and rear. In less than an hour, he was dislodged from his position with the loss of two or three guns. Then they rallied in a new position and, with infantry, established themselves a little to the rear and left of the village of Saguita, on a height from where we could observe the small plain of this name, in which the Spanish cavalry was formed in line ahead of the village. I received the order to charge with my squadron and a squadron of the 29th Chasseurs that was placed under my command. I immediately descended the heights and crossed a very difficult ravine; I then formed my troop on the march and, at a hundred paces had the charge sounded. We entered the enemy cavalry. The mêlée did not last long, but it was hard, and the enemy took flight; each sabre blow of my chasseurs threw a Spaniard to the ground. We could not have charged with more boldness and fearlessness. We pursued this cavalry still sabring them, and we made them pass through the village of Saguita in the greatest disorder. The Spanish infantry, which was in line behind the village, seeing their cavalry in this confusion and seeing that it too would be struck shortly, took flight in such a fashion that their line broke up as quick as lightning and in less than five minutes we could only see a few cavalry, who stopped a quarter of a league from the village between two woods into which his infantry had thrown themselves. I wanted to go to see for myself why this cavalry had stopped; I took with me my three officers, four chasseurs and a trumpeter. It was all that remained with me: the other chasseurs were holding the prisoners and horses. I approached with my eight men, the Spanish cavalry were about thirty; I did not want to attack them, fearing a trap, but in advancing with my small troop behind a very thick hedge, I noticed ten paces from us a man stretched out as if he was dead. I said to one of my officers, M. Guillaume, to go and see if this man was still alive; he went around him two or three times without dismounting and returned to me to say that he had on a soldier's greatcoat, under which he could see a jacket with a small stripe made of silk and that he was certainly a sergeant. As we did not much respect the Spanish, prisoners or not, we left him. The Spanish cavalry did not move, neither advancing nor retiring. I fell back to Saguita to rally my troop and give them a rest. In this charge I did not have a man or a horse wounded, and I was the only one to have received a sabre blow on my shako. At the height of this mêlée, I saw a Spanish officer who defended himself against one of my chasseurs; I said to him, "Take this "officer." "He will not surrender," replied the chasseur. Then I struck the face of this officer with a big sabre blow, and I said to the chasseur in moving away, "This is how you take them! Bring him."

My chasseurs took more than a hundred Spanish horses, but unfortunately, they were nearly all mangy and I was not able to take any into my squadron for fear of contagion; they were all sold cheaply to the infantry. My squadron took six cavalry officers, many cavalrymen, and still more Spanish infantrymen. The next day, at Walls, I learnt that Baron d'Éroles, a Spanish general-in-chief, had been thrown from his horse and taken by French cavalry; that the latter left him on the battlefield without realising who he was because he was wearing a soldier's greatcoat during the battle. At this account I recognised my man, and I reproached myself for the lack of scrutiny with which I had displayed in these circumstances, but it was too late.

Immediately after the affair finished, I was complimented by the generals on the charges I had made, and they all told me that I would not be lacking in citations of distinction in the general-in-chief's report. Indeed, the report of General Decaen to the Minister of War, dated from Girone on the 31st January 1813 and inserted in the *Moniteur* of the 11th February, expressed thus in my regard;

> The enemy, broken at all points, tried however, to again reform on a high mountain beyond the village of Saguita. General Hamelinaye, of Lamarque's division, was charged with attacking again by his left, whilst with Espert's brigade, composed of the 42nd Regiment and the 4th Battalion of the 16th *de ligne*, General Lamarque marched to attack the front. In this attack, *chef d'escadron* Curély, of the 20th Regiment of Chasseurs, with his squadron and a squadron of the 29th Chasseurs, made a brilliant charge against more than four hundred cuirassiers and hussars of Saint-Narcisse, of which a great number were sabred. A hundred horses and sixty prisoners were collected up by the chasseurs.

The enemy, broken at all points, was put to flight and in such a rout that at least half threw away their arms.

Not a man of this army corps escaped which a few days previously had boasted of taking Tarragone. The mountains and deep ravines had favoured the debris of fugitives, pursued all day and the next day in different directions. It was so dispersed that one had only seen bands of fugitives which announced that all was lost.

Two thousand men were taken, killed or wounded and all the enemy's artillery was taken; such were the trophies of the combat of Altafulla, where all the troops had rivalled each other in ardour and courage.

I confirm and take as witness all the individuals who were present at the attack on Saguita, that my cavalry alone was engaged and that the French infantry did not fire a musket shot.

General Decaen, in sending his report to the Minister of War, had put me on a return to receive the cross of the *Légion d'Honneur*, that I had had since 1806, whereas he should have put for me to receive the cross of Officer in this order; I lost for a second time the opportunity to be nominated Officer.

When my troop had rested and recovered at Saguita, it was put in pursuit of the enemy and moved on Walls, where it slept on the 24th. We encountered no vestige of the Spanish army. Arriving close to Walls, where this army had passed and where we still saw some traces, I asked a local man who was working the ground if he had not seen the Spanish pass; he replied 'no', and, despite all the terrible threats that I used he was insistent that he had seen nothing.

Lamarque's division was ordered to move to Mattaro and arrived there on the 29th, remaining there until the 2nd February. During our route next to the sea, we were cannonaded by English vessels and arriving at Mattaro we had to evict 2,000 guerrillas. The day after our arrival in this town, the soldiers learnt that in a big house situated by the side of the sea there was a store of sugar belonging to the English. They immediately ran to the store and pillaged it. The English, who were on the sea watching the pillage, approached with three vessels and cannonaded the pillagers, as well as the town, for three days. I saw there, a French infantryman carrying a sack of sugar, knocked to the ground by a ball that had bounced next to him; he casually got up, put the sack of sugar on his back and retired as if nothing had happened.

The division frequently changed position, leaving Mattaro and returning there. In all these changes, on arrival it was necessary to clear out the enemy who occupied it. Several times I was ordered to surprise them. For this the general gave me one or two battalions with my cavalry, but I could never do it; the Spanish troops always left their post a good hour or hour and a half before my arrival and retired into the mountains, so they were well served by the people of the country. On the 21st March, being at Hostalrich, I received the order to go to Girone with my squadron. I left the next day, the 22nd, and slept in the town that evening. I made, with my officers, a visit to General Decaen.

After having made the most flattering praise of the squadron I commanded, the General expressed all the regrets to see us leave and gave me the order from the Minister of War which directed me to go to Bonn, on the Rhine, with my squadron, where the depot of the regiment was located. There we were to renew our clothing and change the poor horses, in a word, to entirely re-equip the squadron and, from there, to leave to join the Army of Russia. General Decaen had the kindness to order that I was to be paid, in passing through Perpignon, all that which was due to my squadron. He also had paid a particular payment accorded by the emperor, on Spanish contributions, to the commanders of the Army of Spain, a payment fixed at three hundred Francs per month. I received only 1,200 Francs for four months, the eight other months are still owed to me.

During the year that I passed in Catalonia, the troops received exactly their rations; bread was never lacking, sometimes we were given dried cod for two days instead of meat. I can confirm that my squadron were never permitted to take a morsel of bread from the house of the inhabitants; I received no complaints. The government provided wood, which was weighed; the greatest order reigned in the small army of Catalonia. I never ate with a Spaniard nor accepted from one of them even a glass of water. The officers ate with me, a chasseur made our soup, and an officer was responsible for watching over the servant. Wine was not expensive; sugar, coffee, chocolate were all in abundance and cheap. Our servant cost us nearly twenty *sols* per head per day, not including the rations provided by the government.

When the squadron learnt of its departure for Bonn and from there to Russia, there was a general exclamation of joy. The troop hoped to be better over there than they were here, as there were changes every day. I did not want to trouble their happiness for an instant by telling them what Russia would be like, for I already knew some things and it was easy to predict that a mass of 500,000 men would not have all the amenities that my chasseurs promised each other, having only seen Germany.

For my own account, I was very pleased to leave Spain, not because we could have been better elsewhere, but because I found myself isolated and far from the eye of the master. In this respect, without doubt, I left with more pleasure than my chasseurs.

Chapter 9

1812, the Campaign of Russia

*A**t the end of 1811, the 20ᵗʰ Chasseurs had two squadrons at the depot in Bonn (the 1ˢᵗ and 5ᵗʰ), Curély's 2ⁿᵈ Squadron in Spain and the 3ʳᵈ and 4ᵗʰ Squadrons reforming after the original squadrons bearing these numbers had been incorporated into the 13ᵗʰ Chasseurs in Spain. By the 1ˢᵗ May, the regiment had been ordered to concentrate in Berlin, but the 2ⁿᵈ Squadron, under command of Curély, given the distance it had to travel from Spain, was not to join the regiment until the 21ˢᵗ August, when it arrived in front of Polotsk, deep into Russia. The march from Spain to Polotsk was to take him and his men a total of 115 days marching and 38 days of rest. At an average of 30 km a stage, this makes a total of 3,450 kms! From Mayence [Mainz], he took command of detachments of other regiments that were being sent to reinforce their regiments in Russia, adding another 305 men to the 220 of his own regiment. These men were formed into a régiment de marche (a march regiment; a temporary formation put under command of an officer that was responsible for it until the men were able to join their own regiments).*

Throughout the move from Spain to Russia, and throughout the infamous, gruelling campaign that was to follow, Curély's care for the wellbeing, physical and mental, of his men and horses, the maintenance of discipline and battle worthiness loom large in his account. It is evident that as discipline broke down throughout the French army during the terrible retreat, Curély's men stood out from most, and no doubt they realised the value of having such an exceptional officer to command them.

For the campaign in Russia, the 20th Chasseurs (now commanded by Colonel Lagrange) were part of the 6th Light Cavalry Brigade (commanded by General Corbineau), which with the 5th Light Cavalry Brigade made up the corps cavalry of the 2nd Army Corps commanded by Marshal Oudinot. The corps also included two divisions of French infantry and one of Swiss. In total it consisted of 32,000 infantry and 2,400 cavalry. Corbineau's brigade consisted of three regiments, the 20th, along with the 7th Chasseurs (Colonel Saint-Chamans) and 8th Polish Lancers (Colonel Lubienski).

During the initial stages of the invasion, the 2nd Corps was part of the main body of the Grand Army commanded by Napoleon in person, and in early June, before Curély re-joined the regiment, it was in front of Kowno. Due to the fatigues of the march and the lack of rations, by the end of July the French army had already lost 100,000 men of the 400,000 that had crossed the Nieman into Russia; the cavalry, due to the lack of forage, had particularly suffered.

In Napoleon's advance on the city of Smolensk, where the Russians were to concentrate their main army, the 2nd Corps, along with the 6th (made up of Bavarians and commanded by Gouvion-Saint-Cyr), had remained at Polotsk, with the responsibility of protecting Napoleon's left flank against the Russian forces of Wittgenstein. The 2nd Corps therefore took no part in the battle around Smolensk that was fought on the 17th August. Instead, it was to hold the line of the Duna River and fight several desperate actions around Polotsk. By the time Curély re-joined his regiment, the corps cavalry had already lost half its strength; the 20th was in a poor state due to the extreme heat and having been surprised by a regiment of Russian cavalry and forced to flee at the first day of the battle of Polotsk. Curély had to endure the insults of the infantry on his arrival, even though the regiment had redeemed itself during the victory gained the next day. On his arrival, Curély immediately had to take command of the regiment as Colonel Lagrange was sick. The 2nd Corps, now commanded by Saint-Cyr (Oudinot having been seriously wounded on the 17th), generally remained inactive until the 16th October by which time the main army had fought at Borodino (7th September), occupied Moscow and then evacuated it to start its retreat (15th October).

On the 17th October, Wittgenstein took the offensive, supported by a force coming from Finland. Saint-Cyr ordered his cavalry to delay the latter, whilst he faced Wittgenstein. For his own cavalry, Saint-Cyr kept with him just a cuirassier regiment and a small composite force of light cavalry consisting of a squadron from each of the three regiments of Corbineau's brigade (each of 100 men), commanded by Curély.

Curély was to play a major part on the 18th in this second battle of Polotsk, and as his account describes, on the first day, he not only captured some Russian guns (which were subsequently re-captured), but remarkably also took General Wittgenstein prisoner for a short period before he was rescued by his own men. On the second day he took a considerable number of prisoners. Despite what had been a clear French victory, the corps, now commanded by Oudinot once more after Saint-Cyr had been wounded, was forced to retreat towards Lepel.

On the 24th October, Corbineau's brigade was detached to cover the retreat of General Wrede's Bavarian Corps to Wilna. It remained with the Bavarians until the 17th November. However, before it left them, Curély once more had the opportunity to show his ability. He commanded fifty men of his regiment, which, as a part of a rear-guard of 300 cavalry, fought successfully against a force of 1,200 Cossacks and Russian dragoons which Curély describes in his account: his own charge with just these fifty men routing a force of 200 Cossacks.

On the 17th November, Corbineau's brigade were ordered back to the 2nd Corps who were moving towards Minsk. However, in front of them lay the Berezina River and it was here that Curély was to make a vital discovery that was to be fundamental to the escape of the sad remains of the French army from Russia. Curély commanded a hundred men of his regiment leading the advance towards this river to meet up with a Polish *force that was holding the bridge at Borisov. However, the Poles had been attacked and driven off by the Russians and the vital bridge captured. Learning of this, Curély searched for another crossing point and a local peasant revealed there was a ford at the village of Studianka. Corbineau's brigade were able to cross the river at this point. An attempt to seize the bridge at Borisov failed and the Russians destroyed the bridge, apparently leaving the French army cut off from their line of retreat and in danger of being destroyed or forced to surrender by the convergence of three Russian armies. However, thanks to the discovery of the ford at Studianka, it was decided to construct bridges there to get the army across the river.*

The story of the construction of these bridges in terrible conditions is well known and took place while the Russians were deceived by French diversionary manoeuvres. To keep the enemy away from the bridges some of the 20th Chasseurs swam the river each carrying an infantryman with them on their horse. Curély passes over the appalling horrors and chaos at the bridges with little comment; the crossing of the army took place from the morning of the 26th November to the 29th.

After the conspicuous part that Curély had played in the operations of the previous few weeks, he was promised that Napoleon would make him a colonel, but he was to be disappointed. Colonel Lagrange, having acquired a sled, effectively gave up command of the regiment to Curély, and spent his time looking to his own comfort and survival.

Whilst the army crossed at Studianka, the 2nd Corps, of which the 20th Chasseurs remained a part, was used as the advanced-guard and took a prominent role in repulsing the Russian attacks that attempted to prevent the French crossings. Once the army was across, it then became the rearguard, whose mission it was to protect the exhausted army which was trying to reach Wilna. Curély's troops were much pressed by the Russians who, having failed to crush Napoleon's army at the Beresina, were determined to destroy it on its march. In the last few hours before they reached Wilna the regiment were finally relieved from this arduous, but vital, duty. It is only now in Curély's account that he describes in detail the misery of the troops in their retreat. After the successful crossing of the Beresina, Napoleon left the army under the command of Marshal Prince Murat and hastened back to Paris to consolidate his continued reign.

Wilna, which was reached on the 8th and 9th December, contained large magazines and it was finally hoped that the army could be properly supplied and re-organised. It was not to be, discipline appears to have broken down almost completely in most units and the magazines were quickly plundered and many vital supplies wasted. The shambles of a retreat continued on the 10th and on the 12th arrived at Kowno, by which time the Russian pursuit had effectively ended. Of the 400,000 men who had marched into Russia, there were barely 30,000 that were still capable of bearing arms. Of these, the 20th Chasseurs were one of the few units maintaining any unit cohesion; they counted 100 mounted men. On the 29th December, the regiment reached Graudenz on the Vistula; the campaign of Russia was effectively over. Colonel Lagrange, who had made his way back to the depot at Bonn, was able to send a reinforcement that brought Curély's command up to 200 men. The regiment was to be a part of Roussel d'Hurbal's division of Sébastiani's 2nd Reserve Cavalry Corps.

The squadron left Girone on the 23rd March and slept the same day at Cabanes, close to Figuières, then at Boulou on the 24th. When we arrived on French territory near Bellegarde, situated on a height, I called a halt and an about turn; the chasseurs emptied their goat skins as a goodbye to Spain.

We took the road from Perpignon to Bonn in fifty-seven days, in forty-six stages and eleven stop-overs, to Narbonne, Montpellier, Pont-Saint-Ecprit, Valence, Lyon, Châlon-sur-Saône, Langres, Neufchâteau, Metz, Trèves and Polch. We arrived at Bonn on the 21st May and remained there until the 29th. During this journey and in almost all the lodgings, I found mediocre forage, often of the poorest quality and I always refused it. The measures of oats were nearly always too small when they were presented and thus each day I called for the commissioner of war of the place, or, if not

1812, the Campaign of Russia 123

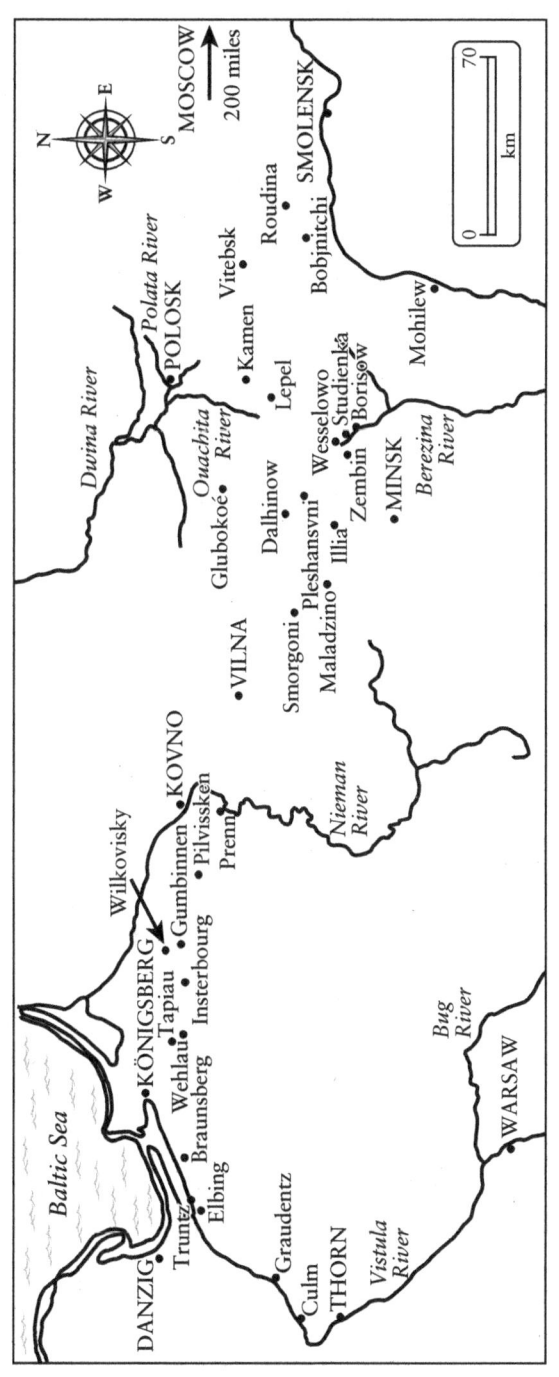

him, the mayor, and broke the false measures in front of him. I drew up a verbal process in four stops, where the fraud was so bad, and I sent the verbal-process to the minister so that the storekeepers would be punished. I do not know if they were, but what I do know well enough is that I was reprimanded for being too severe with the storekeepers. Unheard of! Troops travelling within France could not demand what was owed them without their leader being blamed by the ministry, and however, the emperor would have dismissed a leader who did not do his duty by not giving to his men what was prescribed by law. Even at Bonn, where the depot of the regiment was located commanded by the major, I found the haystacks were not of the required weight. The horses were not receiving straw because it was lacking and the hay was substituted in the proportion of five to ten, so that the ration of ten *livres* of straw each day was replaced by five *livres* of hay; which raised to fifteen *livres* of hay the daily ration; but in fact, the horses received hardly twelve and consequently, never having litter, they slept on the cobbles. Also, some were dying almost every day. Woe to the troops and woe to the country that gives the regiments such leaders!

On my arrival at Bonn, I pressed the major of the regiment to furnish me with all that was necessary for my squadron and to equip the men that I had to take to his depot. It took a thousand pains to obtain what was strictly indispensable. Meanwhile, the quartermaster, instead of giving money, wanted me to account for the full establishment of my chasseurs because he was aware that we were always losing some men and that the excess, or even a part of it, would end up in his pocket. In leaving Nantes, the chasseurs who had come from Spain with me had received their back pay complete, and I had also paid each of my men their full expenses from the cashbox at the depot. At the same time, I also gave them all that which had been withheld in Spain for their expenses of linen and footwear; of course, after assuring myself that they had their complete equipment.

The chasseurs saw me as their father and benefactor although I was only doing my duty. They had, since my entry into the regiment, recognised on several occasions my fairness in their regard, so that, despite the severity with which I punished them when they committed serious faults, they would all have sacrificed their lives for me. I could also lead them anywhere I wanted, and they would always be content. Often in days of misery I heard them say, "If he could make things better for us, he would do it; we must believe that it is impossible for him to do everything." To please me, they were careful to keep their horses healthy and well cared for. The men were always clean, and their arms were in the best state; they would always present themselves in front of me with confidence, even pride. Those whose saddle had injured his horse, himself arranged to come and show me the light injury to his horse and the way he arranged the saddle. My chasseurs never had a dispute with their host. Those who did not provide what was laid down in regulations, the wronged chasseur addressed himself to his chief who immediately rendered justice. In sum, I was the object of general enthusiasm in this regiment, and I never felt more contentment, never more gentle sensations than in the 20th Chasseurs.

When my squadron had been reorganised and brought up to two hundred and twenty men, I left Bonn to go to Russia. My departure was fixed for the 30th May. On the 5th June I arrived in Mayence, where Marshal Kellerman was charged with organising the *régiments de marche*, commanded by senior officers, to be led into Russia. This marshal gave me twenty-two detachments of different cavalry units, to attach to my squadron and form a regiment of five hundred and twenty-five men. I left Mayence on the 7th June, passing by Francfort, Hanau, Erfurt, Hambourg, Leipsick and Wittenberg; on the 26th I arrived in Berlin, where I took several more cavalry detachments who had remained in the rear, to join them to my *régiment de marche*. I left again on the 1st July and arrived at Tilsitt on the 28th and at

Johannsburg on the 31st, having crossed Prussia at its widest point. I found on my way a ruined country. In passing, the emperor's army had consumed everything, forage and food, and I had much pain to maintain my *régiment de marche*. Also, the Prussians wished us, from the bottom of their hearts, all the trouble and misfortune that we suffered from then on. I do not know if it was what they desired, but several told me on the way that the French would not succeed in Russia as they had succeeded everywhere else. On the 1st August, I entered Poland; I crossed the Nieman at Kowno on the 3rd, and passed through Wilna on the 7th. The whole country was as ruined as Prussia by the passage of the army. The country was less devastated from Wilna to Polosk; we found more resources there. At Glubokoé on the 16th August, all the detachments that formed my *régiment de marche* left me to go by Smolensk to the *Grand Armée* and I marched directly with my squadron to Polosk.[29]

I arrived at Seskerky on the 19th and rested there on the 20th. I profited by this stop to get my squadron back into the highest state of cleanliness. I found a mill and ground wheat and baked bread; I distributed enough for four days to my men, and I took the same

---

[29] Curély's squadron had taken 153 days to go from Hostabrich [Hostalric] to Polosk. That is:

Hostabrich to Bonn	49 days march	and	12	rest days.	
Stop at Bonn			8	rest days.	
Bonn to Berlin	23 "	"	"	5 "	"
Stop at Berlin				4 "	"
Berlin to Koenigsberg	20 "	"	"	3 "	"
Stop at Koenigsberg				2 "	"
Koenigsberg to Polosk	23 "	"	"	4 "	"
Total	115 "	"	"	38 "	"

In all 115 days marching, 38 days of rest; at an average of 30 km a stage, this makes a total of 3,450 kms or 860 leagues.

amount on the vehicles. In leaving, I left in this village, situated only four leagues from Polosk, a *maréchal des logis* and four chasseurs whose horses were lame; these were the only ones that I left behind and they were very useful to me.

I left the written order with the *maréchal des logis* to grind wheat and rye and to bake bread that I would send for, and set off early morning on the 21st to join the regiment which was bivouacked before Polosk. My precautions were not wasted, for when I arrived, I found the regiment without bread. I started to have it distributed from what I had brought on the vehicles and informed Colonel Lagrange, who commanded the 20th Chasseurs, of the five men that I had left at Seskerky. As the army lacked bread, I proposed to the colonel to send into this village an officer to oversee the handling, which was done and thus we received bread until the 20th September. At this date my officer and chasseurs were sent from Seskerky by superior orders, but then we did not receive any bread.

Marshal Oudinot's corps was, on my arrival, in position with the Bavarians in front of Polosk on the Dwina. The troops lacked bread, yet the country on the left bank of this river had an abundance of grain. Marshal Oudinot, having been wounded several days previously, had been replaced in command by Marshal Gouvion-Saint-Cyr. The Bavarians were commanded by General Wrede, who was himself placed under the orders of Marshal Saint-Cyr.

On my arrival, everyone found my squadron superb; each man had four spare horseshoes and sixty nails. On the other hand, I found the regiment in the most pitiful state; almost all the horses were without shoes, the clothing and harness were all dilapidated. I asked the colonel to have the horses of the regiment shoed; he replied that he did not have the shoes so I said to him, "Give me the *maréchaux-ferrants* [farriers], and tomorrow you will have shoes and nails." Indeed, I went into the town of Polosk, I found iron, forges and charcoal and, in less than four days, all the horses of the regiment were shod. Four days after my arrival, Colonel Lagrange got a kidney infection and left to rest in Polosk and left me in command of his regiment, the 20th Chasseurs, which, with the 7th, commanded by Colonel de Saint-Chamans and the 8th Polish Lancers commanded by Colonel Lubienski, formed the brigade of General Corbineau. All three had left the headquarters of princes, and all three were young. I do not want to take anything away from their qualities nor their bravery, on the contrary, I had occasion to eulogise M. Saint-Chamans. It is however true that in the affair of the 18th August, three days before my arrival, the 20th Chasseurs had been poorly led. I will not report the details, because I know them only by hearsay and I did not see them, but this much is certain, when they encountered the 20th Chasseurs or men of this regiment, officers or soldiers of the army corps pointed at them. I blushed. One day, some infantry soldiers, seeing me pass with some chasseurs, shouted out loud enough for me to hear them, "There are the ones who run so well." I approached them and said to them, "My friends, I was not there." They did not reply and were a bit ashamed.

Corbineau's brigade remained bivouacked ahead of Polosk, close to la Tuilerie [a redoubt], from the 21st, the day of my arrival, until the 31st. It changed position on the 1st September and was placed below Polosk, close to the Dwina, always on the right bank. It stayed there until the 5th September, but forage was lacking and on the 6th it received the order to leave its bivouac on the Dwina to go and install itself on the banks of the Polota, five leagues from Polosk. Each regiment had its own area to guard and to exploit for its own subsistence. I lodged the 20th as best I could in a hamlet, and I managed to put all the horses under cover. A bivouac is more punishing for the horses than for the men, but we had to guard ourselves tactically and to be constantly alert. The brigade remained in this position until the 20th September, forage was once again exhausted. It was necessary to spread out, the brigade moved further ahead on the Polota and the

20th Chasseurs shared a single Polish style château, called Korleski. This house was isolated and surrounded by a palisade, so I found myself sheltered from an enemy surprise. I thus placed the regiment in the compound and lodged as many horses as I was able, the rest bivouacked. As my magazine of Seskerky no longer existed, I received no more bread; the administration of the army furnished me with none. This is how I made my unit live. I sent the regiment to look for sheaves of rye in the fields and villages which were in front of us but not occupied; I had two thirds threshed' and the straw was for the horses. In the house there was a hand mill and the men relieved each other from hour to hour to grind night and day, and some bakers that I had in the regiment baked the bread. As to meat, this was never lacking, the country was full of cattle. I established a forge in the house, and not only did I keep the shoeing up to date, but I had each chasseur who did not have them, a reserve of four spare horseshoes and sixty nails. Amongst my men there were some cobblers; I bought leather and had them repair our boots. At the same time, I had the repairs done that were most pressing for clothing and harness. We only had a pond for water for the men and horses to drink. I had fermented some oat flour with water in barrels, which gave us a drink that did not taste very good, but was very healthy.

After remaining at Korleski from the 21st September to the 16th October, the regiment left this canton-bivouac in a very good state; men and horses. I was asked, with reason, if all the regiments of the army lived the same. I replied, "no." The light cavalry rarely received bread and at this time received none, so each regiment procured it however it could. The infantry, which remained in the entrenched camp of the 'Swedes', on the right bank of the Dwina and in front of Polosk, received bread now and again, but in such small quantities that the two army corps, that is, the 2nd French Corps commanded successively by Marshals Oudinot and Saint-Cyr, and the Bavarian Corps of M. de Wrede, who on the entry to the campaign were strong, the first of fifty thousand men, the other of thirty thousand, and thus forming an army of eighty thousand men, the two of them together now had no more than eighteen thousand combatants. For, in the different affairs that these two corps had with the enemy army, they had not lost five thousand men, killed or wounded. What had happened to the others? They had died of hunger or deserted to return home.

But we can say, since you were able to feed your regiment, why was the general-in-chief not able to do the same for his army? The question is not difficult to answer. In my opinion, all troops should be able to live in the country that they occupy or which they pass through, whether friendly or enemy. I do not say with a quarter ration or even a half ration; no, with a complete ration. I observe in passing that the men should always be paid every five days, on campaign as in garrison[30], for there is never a country so poor where you cannot find merchants.

The brigade received the order to retire into the camp of Polosk, arriving there in the evening of the 17th. The enemy was marching to attack the camp, whilst another Russian corps, coming from Finland, moved up the left bank of the Dwina to shut up the French army in the town of Polosk. In the evening of the 18th, this army corps was no more than two leagues from Polosk. Marshal Saint-Cyr sent Corbineau's brigade, less three hundred men drawn from all three regiments which were left in the camp under my orders, to reconnoitre it and stop it if possible. It was a colonel who was

---

[30] Never had the troops been so badly paid as under the First Republic and under the First Empire, even at the most brilliant periods of the *Grande-Armée*. One could not think, for example, that at the signing of the Peace of Tilsitt, that is to say at the end of 1807, the pay was behind more than six months (Berthezène). Curély had left the 20th Chasseurs when becoming colonel on the 18th August 1813 and in the month of January 1815, he was still on the pay of *chef d'escadron*.

supposed to command these three hundred men, but I fulfilled this function in the absence of Colonel Lagrange. General Corbineau asked Colonels Saint-Chamans and Lubienski, as well as me, whose turn it was not to march. The two colonels replied that it was not them. "Then it is mine," I then said, and, despite the entreaties of General Corbineau, who knew well that it was not me to remain, he could not persuade these *messieurs*. I said to the general, "It is no inconvenience to me to be left in command of these three hundred men, for, seeing the approach of the enemy, Colonel Lagrange will be obliged to leave Polosk and retake command of his regiment."

The general finally consented to leave me; I bivouacked in the plain in front of the camp, close to the Tuilerie redoubt overnight of the 17th to 18th. I had the order to retire into the camp at dawn. As I was a little late, I was charged by the enemy and pulled back into the camp, which he entered with me and took a gun that I had to abandon but re-took a moment later. I then received the order to send a hundred men of the 7th Chasseurs to the left of the camp, leaving me with just a hundred chasseurs of the 20th, that had come from Spain with me, and a hundred Polish lancers. I deployed in front of the line of entrenchments, on the road leaving the camp. The enemy army did not hesitate to appear at all points and to surround the camp in a semi-circle, the left supported on the Dwina above Polosk, the right also on the Dwina, but below the town. The cavalry engaged along the whole line. Towards midday, the enemy skirmishers having approached from my camp and killed and wounded many men, General Maison gave me the order to repulse these skirmishers. I marched on them with my two hundred men at the walk and in the best order. I repulsed them as far as the enemy line and reaching a small height, I noticed that this line looked unsteady. I then ordered the captain of the Polish lancers to charge two masses of infantry which were to his front, and to my chasseurs of the 20th to charge the guns which were opposite them. At the same time, I sounded the charge. The Russian infantry was broken, knocked over and put to flight by the Poles. All the guns were taken by my chasseurs and the charge passed through the enemy army, the left wing of which was put into the greatest disorder. If our infantry opposed to this wing had advanced, the French would have won a brilliant victory, but with my two hundred men, I was not able to resist more than 1,200 enemy cavalry which charged me a moment later. I had already rallied part of my men close to la Tuilerie, where a French battalion came to take position to support my charge. When the enemy cavalry arrived, I killed with a pistol shot the horse of the first Russian officer who tried to sabre me and I had a chasseur take this officer to the rear, but he was re-taken by his own men. We made a fine resistance at la Tuilerie, supported by our infantry, but at the end we were outflanked, broken and thrown back by the Russian dragoons as far as the middle of our camp. There they were received by a heavy fire which forced them to turn back. We pursued them as far as la Tuilerie, where our infantry had remained, and which fired on them as they passed. They returned to the charge, threw us back again to the middle of our camp, where they were received like the first time and pursued again by us as far as la Tuilerie. This time our infantry had been retired and, an instant after, we were pushed back a third time as far as our camp. Finally, we again pursued the Russian cavalry; they stopped us halfway between their lines and our camp and retired little by little to their side. We did the same to ours and the cannonade started again and lasted until evening.

Most of the prisoners I had taken were rescued and the enemy guns, brought back by our chasseurs, arrived close to our camp but were retaken and all that remained to us were a few caissons which had already been secured. The enemy infantry lost an enormous number of men to the charge of the Poles, and the French battalion which had taken position at the Tuilerie redoubt had inflicted a terrible loss on the Russians. These came to take the redoubt during one of our charges but were always repulsed; the area around was scattered with dead. In this affair, I lost fifty men killed, wounded, or taken, as many chasseurs as lancers. I had two chasseur officers made prisoner; they were too far forward with a few chasseurs during the first charge, and I saw them give chase to all those they found in the rear of the enemy line. *Maréchal des Logis* Denisot, who was one of this group and who was lost after having pursued the enemy at the gallop, found himself disorientated and no longer having any daylight to return to the French army, he was forced to swim across the Dwina above Polosk and cross back over the bridge in that town. I thought he had been killed or at least a prisoner, and I despaired of having lost a well-trained young man who was very brave and for whom I held a particular affection. In one of these charges and when repulsing the enemy, I noticed a *maréchal des logis* of my chasseurs in the middle of the enemy column. I reached him fighting and, seeing that he made no movement, I said to him, "Use your sabre, Garnier." "But I am a prisoner," he replied. At the same moment I killed a dragoon with a pistol shot who wanted to prevent me retaking him, I gave a sabre blow to the face of the one who led him, and I had him take a Russian sabre, but he was forced to retire because his horse was overcome with fatigue. The regiments of Cossacks and dragoons which charged us had more than five hundred men hors de combat. At the end of the charges, their number appeared to me to have been reduced to close to half. We took a great number of cavalry horses.

I was honourably cited in Marshal Saint-Cyr's report to the *prince major-général* [the army chief-of-staff; Berthier], dated the 20th October 1812, a report that I found inserted into the *Journal de l'Empire* of the 30th November of the same year,[31]

---

[31] The 20th Chasseurs had five officers wounded in this fight, of which three died of their wounds.

The battery of la Tuilerie had been taken and retaken three or four times; it was defended by troops of the 8th Division, commanded by General of Division Maison. The defence against the frontal attack does infinite honour to those units charged with its defence, that is to say the 2nd and 37th *de ligne* and the 11th *légère*, as well as two squadrons of the 14th Cuirassiers, commanded by M. Remberg and two squadrons of light cavalry of the 8th Lancers and 20th Chasseurs commanded by *chef d'escadron* Curély, who supported the right of the 8th Division and whose conduct merits the greatest eulogies in all the charges that it received or made against forces so disproportionate to their own.

Marshal Saint-Cyr having been wounded in this affair; Marshal Oudinot retook command of the army. Several days later, the Russian commander-in-chief, Wittgenstein, sent a *parlementaire* [negotiating officer] to the marshal; this officer asked on behalf of the Russian general, for *chef d'escadron* Curély; the marshal replied that I was with the Army. "Well," said the *parlementaire*, "M. de Wittgenstein has charged me to compliment him on his behalf and to tell him that he was very happy to have escaped from his hands."

I did not know that the general-in-chief had charged at the head of his cavalry and that he was the first officer whose horse I had killed when he tried to sabre me. I thought instead that he had been in a group of prisoners taken by my chasseurs and retaken by the enemy.

Early the next day, the 19th, I was complimented by several generals who were good enough to come to find me on the battlefield where I had remained. The enemy retired his left wing during the night of the 18th to 19th and positioned themselves next to a wood behind their first position. The two armies remained quiet during the whole day, each side collecting their wounded which had remained on the battlefield throughout the night. Towards the evening of the

19th, the French army started its retreat and crossed the Dwina on the bridge of boats in Polosk. The enemy noticed our movement and cannonaded the town during our retreat. All the troops had crossed onto the left bank of the Dwina at 2am without loss.

At 5am on the 20th, the Russian corps which had moved up the Dwina was ready to deploy close to the Polosk bridge. Part of the French army was sent to confront him, and I was in this number. We met them marching in the wood and attacked them. They were broken and pursued as far as Bononia, and we took nearly fifteen hundred prisoners. In the afternoon of the 20th, I found my regiment of which Colonel Lagrange had retaken the command. I was feted, embraced, and almost knocked over by people complimenting me.

At the time of my arrival at Polosk, my reputation had preceded me. Some believed it, others, among them the superior officers of the brigade, claimed that it was easy to make a reputation in a small army like that of Spain. However, the unbelievers now came to pay me their compliments.

The brigade slept on the banks of the Ouchatz on the 20th and bivouacked at Roudnia on the 21st; the retreat continued via Arckovka on the 22nd and Bobinitchi on the 23rd. Towards 9am on the 24th, the brigade began its march to cover the retreat of the Bavarian corps commanded by General Wrede, who was retreating in the same direction as the French 2nd Corps, on Lepel. After an hour's march, our rear-guard was vigorously attacked by enemy cavalry. General Corbineau ordered me to go and support it with fifty men of the 20th, but soon I was obliged to replace this rear-guard with my chasseurs as it by-passed and abandoned me. I held the enemy's attacks firmly whilst continuing the retreat. I arrived at a bridge on a marshy stream, almost destroyed by the passage of the brigade; at this moment I was charged by the enemy and I found four or five planks taken up. There was no other way of getting on and it was necessary to cross the stream; hardly had several of my men crossed than the enemy, seeing our embarrassment, fell on us. Those of us that had not crossed the stream stood firm and repulsed the enemy to some distance. In this tricky moment, Captain Hennesson left General Corbineau where he was, came at the grand gallop to disengage me, crossed the bridge with his horse and, with his first sabre blow, cracked the head of a Cossack that was about to thrust his lance at me in such a way that half his head fell onto his right shoulder and the other onto his left shoulder before the body fell. We quickly rushed to the bridge, crossed without loss, and broke it after our crossing. In this position, where we were covered by the stream, General Corbineau held well for more than an hour to give the infantry time to operate its retreat. During this time, the enemy arrived with superior forces and cannonaded us, so we were forced to leave. He then repaired the bridge and put all his cavalry hot on our heels. We then found ourselves standing against a wood, Colonel Saint-Chamans with the 7th Chasseurs and me with my fifty men; the infantry and the cavalry had entered the wood and were passing through quickly. We had against us all the enemy cavalry, accompanied by some guns that fired canister at the 7th. The track which passed through the wood was very straight; to retire by this track in column of twos was to expose us to losing three quarters of our men. I was placed with my fifty men just in front of the defile and had the 7th on my left; I was able to retire without loss, but it was not the same with the 7th. The colonel realised well enough, he came at the gallop to find me and in two words we agreed that with my fifty men I would charge and put to flight more than two hundred Cossacks which were in front of me, that I would then turn quickly to the left to take the enemy main body in the flank which was facing the 7th and that at the same moment, that regiment would charge them from the front. What was said was done. The two hundred Cossacks did not weigh an ounce. I fell on the enemy main body, surprised to see that the 7th had not yet engaged, but it arrived a minute later; the enemy was broken, sabred, put to rout and their guns taken. They returned to the charge but were repulsed. Then a regiment of fresh troops charged in mass; we again held for an instant, but we had to give in. We lost the guns that we had taken, retired on the track through the wood and led off quietly; the enemy respected our audacity.

Colonel Saint-Chamans, who displayed great bravery, was wounded by a lance thrust to the right shoulder. The 7th had a strength of three hundred men, I had fifty; the two of us beat more than 1,200 Russian cavalry, dragoons and Cossacks. The reinforcement that supported them was at least from four to five hundred men. When we were forced to retreat, the enemy thus had more than four men to one. We lost five or six men; the enemy had many wounded, and we killed all his artillery horses since we could not take them with us. In this affair and at the moment that we were approaching the enemy's main body, one of my chasseurs had his horse killed; without hesitating, he got from under his horse, entered the enemy mass with his sabre in his hand, brandishing it right and left, wounding all those that he touched and made himself room, pursuing the enemy on foot as quickly as if he had been mounted. When the enemy retook the charge, he lay on the ground, and in repulsing the enemy for the second time, I saw my chasseur who had got up and cut the hocks of the enemy horses. I pulled this brave man out of the mêlée; he was saved this time but was taken later in the campaign.

We continued our retreat and re-joined the brigade, which had united with the Bavarian corps. We halted a little before evening to refresh the men and horses. General Wrede, having received the order to cover Wilna with his Bavarians, set off towards ten o'clock and, covering his left, took the direction of Pouischna. All night we observed the greatest silence because this counter march could have led us into the enemy army, and we arrived at Pouischna during the 25th. General Corbineau, whose brigade was not part of the Bavarian corps, should have left it when this corps started its movement to cover Wilna, but he had previously been put under the orders of General Wrede to form his advance-guard, and the last order carried to this general not having mentioned him, he thought his duty was to follow the Bavarians. We thus hurried across the plains and woods to right and left between Wilna and Polosk, from the 26th October until the 17th November. Between the 3rd and 4th November we pushed as far as Glubokoé, charged several large guns without carriages on the vehicles which were found in this town and we sent reconnaissances to Wilna. It was on the 4th November that we had the first snow. Finally, after having rested at Valkaotatoué on the 15th, 16th and 17th, General Corbineau, who had received the order to re-join the 2nd Army Corps several times, decided to leave the Bavarians and to set off back.

The brigade slept at Dalhinow on the 18th, in a hamlet on the road from Wilna to Borisow on the 19th, Pleshansvni on the 20th and continued the next day, the 21st, to march on Borisow. I commanded the advance-guard, composed of a hundred cavalry. Arriving two and a half leagues from Borisow, we heard a heavy cannonade. It was the Russian army that had returned from Turkey, which attacked and beat the Polish corps, 6,000 men commanded by Dombrowski, deployed at Borisow to defend the bridge over the Bérésina. General Corbineau halted the brigade and conferred with the three colonels. It was decided that we would immediately go to the left to re-join the Bavarian corps, expecting that the enemy would capture Borisow in front of us and presuming that there were enemy troops behind us and on our right. The general called me and said to me, "Curély, the enemy is in front of us, you can hear the cannon, he is behind us and on our right; we will retire by the left on this road (he showed it to me) and you will provide the rear-guard with your hundred cavalry." Without being surprised by the part he wanted us to take, I said to the general, "We have lost enough time around here, whilst we could be useful elsewhere. With eight hundred sabres we can go anywhere. We should go and join the emperor, and if necessary pass over the enemy at Borisow; I will open the way with my hundred cavalry." "You are right," the general replied, and we continued our march ahead. It was necessary to see the faces of the people that accompanied the general at this decisive moment. Arriving close to Wesselowo, which is on the other side of the Bérésina, it was almost nightfall. The general stopped the brigade off the road in a small plain in the middle of which there was a farm. He had me told to guard all the approaches and that I would answer with my head if the brigade was surprised. I said to the aide de camp who delivered this order, "I will answer for it." The general already appeared as if he regretted taking my advice, he said in front of someone who repeated it to me, that another time he would not follow anyone else's advice. I was content; it was a step in the direction of what I wanted.

An hour later, the general learnt that the Russians were going to seize Borisow with considerable forces (25,000) and that the Poles, chased from this town, retired on the road to Mohilew. At the same time, he learnt that there was, opposite Wesselowo, a ford which crossed the Bérésina; he decided to cross this river and at ten in the evening the brigade was mounted, preceded by a local man who was also mounted and taken from the farm as a guide. The 20th being the head of the column, we crossed, and the horses did not need to swim more than twenty paces. We did not lose a man or a horse. Several friends have informed me since then that at the time of the crossing, men of 'weak heart' embraced each other, said their farewells, drank together, for the last time they said, adding that Curély would be the death of all of them... Unfortunately, there were too many of this type of man. The crossing completed, but all the men with wet legs, General Corbineau set off to reach the road from Borisow to Mohilew. He sent me the order to provide the rear-guard and marched with his guide at the head of his brigade until daybreak. He then stopped in a hamlet of four or five houses in the middle of a wood for men and horses to get their breath back and let them refresh themselves for a moment. When he wanted to recommence the march, he sent to me to provide the advance-guard and sent me a guide. Since the moment he had decided to turn back, he had not spoken to me. Now he sent orders to me, before his habit had been to call for me to give them to me himself. Finally, I took the guide and one hour later we found some Polish soldiers who told us that their corps was a little further on; indeed, an instant later we saw the smoke of bivouac fires. It was only then that General Corbineau came to me; I was always with the advance-guard at the head of my troop. He came up to me and said, "Is it not, Curély, that brave men never die," I replied to him, "No, my general, never!" and the conversation went on to other things.

Finally, we encountered the troops of the 2nd Army Corps, who were the emperor's advance-guard, and as Corbineau's brigade was tired, we were sent to the village of Reschyniscko where we passed the night of the 22nd to 23rd. This same evening, the emperor called for General Corbineau to learn from him where he had crossed the Bérésina and from then it was decided that the army would cross at Wesselowo if the enemy burnt the bridge at Borisow. Early in the morning of the 23rd, Marshal Oudinot's corps, under whose orders Corbineau's brigade had returned, set off for Borisow. It still counted 12,000 combatants, of which 2,000 were cavalry. Four leagues from Borisow, we encountered the enemy who were in front of us. He was vigorously attacked and pushed back as far as the town where a good part of his troops, thrown back to right and left of the road, were able to enter. If our cavalry had charged *à outrance* [all out] into Borisow, it would have prevented the burning of the bridge, the only crossing which remained open to the French army. It was not done; it was not its fault, but, on such an occasion and when it comes to saving an army, we should dare more than we did at this moment. Towards evening, Corbineau's brigade was directed on Wesselowo in pursuit of some enemy troops who had not been able to enter Borisow and who were thrown in this direction. The general had a battalion of infantry to support his brigade. We marched as far as a height close to Wesselowo; it was then nine o'clock in the evening and we could hear the Russians swimming the Bérésina to re-join the main body of their army on the right bank. I asked the general for permission to attack them; he refused me, and the brigade retired into a village to the rear to pass the night. This village offered no resources either for men or horses. The first care of my colonel was to look after himself, leaving us all mounted. Searching for somewhere to place the regiment I noticed a track opening to our right; I had this track followed by an officer accompanied by fifteen men and awaited their return. Soon after the officer returned and said to me, "Two hundred paces from here there is a very large farm where there are a few Russian cavalry, from whom we have taken ten horses. The farm is full of forage." I immediately went there with the 20th and sent an officer to the general to inform him and take his orders in case he wished to give me any. In this farm I found rations of all kinds, more than two hundred sacks of flour and enough *eau-de-vie* for the whole brigade. I had some bread baked and had some flour brought with us. Very early the next day, the 24th, the general sent me the order to depart. I soon arrived at the brigade that was lacking everything and the colonels of the other two regiments sent to the farm to look for flour. Colonel Lagrange, who had remained with the general, said to me on my arrival, "When will I become master of my own regiment? Why have you left without orders, etc." I replied to him, "My colonel, it is the necessity of surviving and to have cover when we can that made me take this decision. For the rest, I have informed the general and you; your men have bread, flour and *eau-de-vie*, your horses have oats; is this a misfortune for anyone?"

The brigade set off and took position at Wesselowo. During the day some infantry arrived, which we hid, and some *pontonniers* [bridging troops], who worked hidden in the houses constructing materials for a trestle bridge. The main body of the army arrived at Borisow, where some *pontonniers* were to work openly to construct the necessary materials for building a bridge, to find the beams and planks etc., to cover it, to make the enemy think that we wanted to cross the river close to this town. We remained quietly at Wesselowo throughout the 25th, our chasseurs making bread with the flour that I had brought with us, and the *pontonniers* worked day and night without break. Early on the 26th, we heard cannon at Borisow; it was a diversionary attack and soon after we saw the emperor arrive at Wesselowo with his headquarters, followed by a column of infantry. At 7am, the enemy who defended the crossing point at Wesselowo left quickly for Borisow and left only a few Cossacks in observation. Immediately the two bridges were erected at the same time; during which a detachment of fifty men of the 20th swam across, each chasseur having an infantryman on the horse's rump, and we deployed this infantry into a small wood to keep off the Cossacks. The *pontonniers* who built the bridge had water up to their necks. It was excessively cold and the Emperor lavished them with encouragement. The troops arrived; infantry, cavalry and artillery, and at 9am one of the two bridges was in a state to allow crossing. Marshal Oudinot's corps crossed first and moved by the main road to Borisow, from where the enemy, warned of our movement, came in all haste. We encountered him halfway; he was beaten and retired while we took position in the woods to the right and left of the road. On the 27th, we skirmished at the advance-posts; during the whole of this day and the 28th, the army filed over the two bridges and took the road to Wilna.

Early in the morning of the 28th, the enemy attacked us vigorously; he was completely beaten. We took a good number of men from him and at night we retired opposite Wesselowo. We heard the cannon on the left bank of the Béresina before evening of the 28th. The *duc de Bellune*'s [Marshal Victor] corps defended the approaches to

Wesselowo and protected the crossing. He was forced to retreat and retired in disorder on the bridges which were broken by the enemy artillery. The French army lost a considerable number of men there who had not been able to cross; vehicles, women, children were exposed to the fire of the enemy cannons: all were there in the most terrible disorder. Whilst the tail of the column filed over, we remained to protect them on the height opposite Wesselowo during the night of the 28th to 29th. It was extraordinarily cold; the wind did not allow a fire to be lit and it was necessary to remain in this position until day. It was the cruellest night that I have passed in my whole life.

During the 27th, I was presented by General Corbineau to Marshal Oudinot, who promised to present me to the emperor the same day to receive the rank of colonel. Indeed, the emperor appeared an hour later and stopped for a moment in front of the 20th Chasseurs, but a despatch which arrived for him at this moment prevented him from seeing the regiment. He left straight away, and I was not presented to him. General Corbineau came to me and said, "Marshal Oudinot has spoken of you to the emperor, he had told him of your affair at Polosk and of General Wittgenstein. The emperor said as he left the marshal, 'Why was he not pointed out?' But you were nominated colonel and you will receive your nomination."

The disasters which followed ensured this nomination was forgotten until the 9th August 1813. Sometime after, General Corbineau was made *général-de-division* and aide de camp to the emperor for the crossing of the Bérésina on the 21st November 1812, at ten o'clock in the evening. Thus, I had fought valiantly at Polosk and I had convinced General Corbineau to cross the Bérésina with his brigade. This crossing, from the information that the general had given the emperor, convinced His Majesty to have the bridges established at Wesselowo; if the ford had not been known of, the emperor and the army strongly risked being taken prisoner... and I was forced to await a more favourable occasion to be made colonel...

On the 29th November 1812, the army having marched off along the road to Wilna, the 2nd Corps, commanded by Marshal Oudinot, formed the rear-guard. The cavalry brigades of Castex[32] and Corbineau forming the extreme rear, slept the same day at Zembin and the 30th at Kamen. Here, Colonel Lagrange procured a sledge and went ahead, leaving me in command of the regiment. The cavalry of the rear-guard, of which we did not cease to be a part, slept between Kamen and Illia on the 1st December, on the 2nd at Illia, the 3rd three hours from Maladzyno, the 4th at Maladzyno, the 5th between Maladzyno and Smorgoni, the 6th at Smorgoni, the 7th between Smorgoni and Wilna, the 8th three leagues from Wilna and on the 9th at Wilna. The Bavarians and some fresh troops relieved us two leagues from Wilna and replaced us as the rear-guard.

During the retreat, from the Bérésina until Wilna, the enemy harassed us every day, not only with Cossacks, but also with artillery and infantry. However, as the cold intensified, the Cossacks that pursued us marched on foot as we did. Every day the army lost a quantity of men; some were no longer able to march, others, having no more rations, preferred being taken rather than to die of hunger. The number of these last was considerable. The few guns that remained to us were abandoned due to a lack of horses which were dying of hunger; the main army burnt most of the houses to keep warm and with the houses, burnt the sick and the men who, unable to follow any longer, had taken refuge there. Often by accident, during the night the fire set light to houses full of soldiers and half of them perished in the flames. The road was scattered with the dead and dying. Some unfortunates, losing their heads with hunger and suffering from the cold, noticing a fire at thirty or forty paces

---

[32] Castex was an ex-colonel of the 20th Chasseurs who went on to join the Grenadiers à Cheval in the Imperial Guard in February 1813 and became *général de division* in November of that year.

stopped, extended their hands to warm themselves as if they were close to the fire and suddenly fell dead. Selfishness was carried to the last extremity. I saw at the rear-guard an infantryman with a pitcher of poor *eau-de-vie* offering, he said, a drink for six Francs, he took an *ecu* from some unfortunate and pulled back the pitcher saying to him, "You are going to die, this will be wasted *eau-de-vie*." I made the unfortunate drink and forced the miserable soldier to hand back his *ecu*. The horse of a superior officer having fallen, the officer was unconscious and thought to be dead, he was immediately stripped and his horse taken away; the officer came round an instant later and found himself naked.

Anyone who did not see this army could have no idea. From ten o'clock in the morning until towards three or four o'clock in the afternoon, it formed a column from seven to ten leagues long on the road across the full width of an ordinary road. Towards three or four o'clock in the afternoon, without any order being given, it disappeared; each individual left the main road to take the back roads that led to villages more or less distant to the left or right up to half a league, sometimes even a league, sleeping there and living as best they could. In less than an hour nobody could be seen on the main road; the most tired remained and entered the villages on this road. Immediately that the rear-guard saw the army dissolve, it halted and took position to prevent, as far as possible, the enemy troubling the rest of these unfortunates. At dawn the next day, he rear-guard set off. After about an hour's march, one saw columns arriving on the road from left and right and, towards ten o'clock, this road was covered with men of which three quarters were unarmed; those who had kept their muskets were not even able to use them as they were in such a poor state. In the column one saw few horses and here and there some sledges. Officers and soldiers were dressed, some in fur-trimmed overcoats, others with a kind of greatcoat made with sheepskin, as worn by the Russians and Poles, others with women's skirts, cloaks etc. The most painful moment for the rear-guard was the approach of evening; the men who, having eaten nothing during the night, had re-started their march in the morning, finding themselves then so exhausted that they stopped, turned round and round two or three times and fell dead; others stopped in groups of one, two or three hundred, telling us quietly that they no longer wanted to march, that they preferred to be sabred rather than continue; neither encouragement nor threats had any result. One finished by leaving them; hardly had we gone a hundred paces than the Cossacks fell on them, put them into ranks, searched them one after another and took everything that they fancied.

At seven in the morning, ten leagues from Wilna, biscuit was distributed to the whole army from this town. On the evening of the 9th, the whole army less the rear-guard was lodged militarily in Wilna and remained there throughout the 9th. All the army's magazines, clothing, equipment, harness, were pillaged. The corps of Oudinot and Victor provided the rear-guard alternately; Marshal Ney commanded it on one day and the *duc de Bellune* on the next. These two corps were reduced to nothing and, on the 4th, leaving Maladzino, there were not two hundred men together. The light cavalry of the two brigades remained alone as the rear-guard and, at the exit of Smorgoni, only the 20th Chasseurs were in a state to offer any resistance to the enemy. From ten regiments that formed these two brigades, five had melted away; only a few officers remained and General Castex was the only general officer present. Arriving at Wilna, I still had a hundred mounted men and almost all the officers.

After having left the rear-guard we continued our way to Wilna and we arrived there early enough to find room there. On my arrival, my host gave me a good soup which I ate with great pleasure but an instant later I felt quite weak; a sweat came over me suddenly and I came round. We found some passable wine at ten francs a bottle;

it was more agreeable to drink than the snow that we had melted in pitchers when we were the rear-guard.

At 3am the next day, the 10th, the *générale* was beaten around the whole town to muster the troops and continue the retreat. I concentrated my hundred men at dawn and set off through the whole army which was climbing the mountain at the exit of Wilna. Never had I seen such confusion, such disorder, such a mix-up. Caissons, which had been left at Wilna at the beginning of the campaign and which had remained in the town throughout, left with the army but they were pillaged half a league from Wilna. Finally, having received the order to go to the Vistula, where all the cavalry regiments were to be concentrated, I passed quickly through the mass of fugitives and slept ten leagues from Wilna on the road to Kowno with General Colbert who I saw again with great pleasure. We had all gathered a few provisions at Wilna and dined together, and, despite the cold, each slept after supper. The little that remained of this supper was to serve as our breakfast, but when we got up, we found nothing; it had been stolen. We left, separated, and on the 11th I slept with my regiment in a village to the left of the road from Wilna to Kowno, seven to eight leagues from this last town. We found bread and forage there and we made soup. There was shelter for all and no duty to perform; one would have thought we had never been better. I left the village in the early hours, passed Kowno, where I took bread for two days and on the 12th, we slept below the town on the left bank of the Niemen. As I marched with my hundred men, without a designated route, being more than twenty-four hours ahead of the army, I took care to ensure my men and horses lived well without overburdening the inhabitants of the places where we stayed.

On the 13th I slept at the château of Prenn, and the following morning having left the château and re-joined the main road, I went along a small column of infantry at the trot, when I heard behind me repeat shouts of 'Curély! Curély!' I could not imagine who this could be. I turned round and noticed my friend Thomas on foot in the middle of the column; his chapeau was pierced all over, the two large 'horns' fell forward and aft; the length of his nose had not prevented it from being frozen. He wore a capuchin cloak and under this the debris of a jacket; under the jacket a shirt of fine black, garnished with white pearls with stripes of mullet on the back; breeches with holes; his boots were worn out up to the ankle and consequently his feet were frozen. Immediately that he noticed me he shouted to me; he needed a horse. Without replying, I rushed to my servant who was on one of my horses and I asked him to give it to me. When he was mounted, he asked me if I was going far to sleep. I replied yes, because it was necessary to make a good journey to put him a little at ease and he wanted each hour to eat. If I passed for a moment at a walk, he shouted at me to trot in order to arrive earlier. Finally, we reached the lodgings; it offered enough resources. My friend entered the bedroom, asked for straw, washed a little, ate for the rest of the day and slept all night. I thus took him to Thorn, and he infuriated me more than a thousand times. On the 14th I slept close to Pilvirsken, between Wilkovisky and Gumbinnen, on the 15th two leagues before Gumbinnen, the 16th between Gunbinnen and Insterbourg, the 17th between Insterbourg and Wehlau, the 18th between Wehlau and Tapiau, the 19th at Goslautern, two leagues from Koenigsberg, the 20th at Drigen, the 21st at the château of Grosklingbeck, the 22nd at Braunsberg, the 23rd close to Truntz, three leagues from Elbing, the 24th at Rosengarten, four leagues under Elbing after having passed this town, on the 25th two leagues from Stein, the 26th at Klein-Nebrau on the Vistula, where I rested on the 27th, 28th and 29th. There I re-joined Generals Castex and Corbineau, who had joined together the debris of their two brigades. General Corbineau wanted me to return to Koenigsberg to be close to the *major-général*, where he said my nomination to the rank of colonel would be. I did not want this and said to him that if my letter of service was there, it would be sent to me where I was. There we had fifteen officers lodged in the same house with all our suite; all the officers were sleeping in the same room on straw. There was a terrible racket every night; our stomachs were still weak, each ate as his appetite dictated and mainly veal meat; when one left, the other came back; we marched on each other and those who had their feet or other part of their body frozen, shouted like the devil unleashed.

We left on the 30th and went to sleep at Graudentz. During the night I received the order to go up as far as five leagues above Graudentz to cross the Vistula on a large bridge that had been thrown across there. Having learnt from the locals that when it was frozen some had crossed on the ice close to Culm, I decided to avoid a detour of ten leagues and crossed on the ice, despite the thaw that had occurred over the last three or four days. I set off on my march and I arrived at the crossing point that was still traced out even though there was a foot of water on top of the ice. I had the regiment's caisson march before me, that I had found at Ebing, and I crossed without mishap with all my troop, but I was blamed and reprimanded by the general.

On the 31st I slept close to Culm on the left bank of the Vistula and on the 1st January 1813 in front of Culm. We continued our route by Schneidemühl, Driesen, Friedeberg, Custrin, Orlvitz close to Berlin and reached the Elbe between Roslau and Dessau on the 27th January, in twenty days march and six rest days. We crossed the Elbe in boats and on the 30th January we arrived at Delitsch. During our march, we formed an army of several bodies of men which were found at Koenigsberg and the surrounding area. This army retired very slowly on Dresden.

Throughout February, the regiment remained at Delitsch; there it was joined by all the small depots and by the men who had been separated, even by the colonel who arrived just in time to leave again with all the men who were dismounted or lame and sent to the depot at Bonn. I had arrived to concentrate two hundred mounted men and I organised them into two companies of which I conserved the command. Of two *chefs d'escadron* that we had with the regiment, one was to return to the depot, and it was me who, as the most senior, found myself directed to go there; but for several reasons, I requested my comrade to go there in my place. He agreed happily and I thus remained with the army and my two hundred men; I was delighted, always hoping that I would be lucky and that I would pick up the rank of colonel.

Chapter 10

The Campaign of 1813 in Germany

*T*he campaign in Germany in 1813 was merely an extension of the Russian campaign of the previous year. It is also known as the War of the Fourth Coalition. In March the coalition consisted of Britain, Russia and Prussia, with Austria joining in August.

Having abandoned his army after the catastrophic retreat from Moscow, Napoleon miraculously raised a new army that was almost as large as the one he had lost. Although full of only partially trained conscripts, he gathered his army in Germany and began a campaign to try and wrestle the initiative away from the new coalition that faced him.

Whilst awaiting the arrival of Napoleon and his new army, the remains of the army that had come from Russia had concentrated around Magdeburg and then manoeuvred on the line of the Elbe to keep the allies at bay. Even after the new campaign properly opened in mid-April, the 20th Chasseurs took only a peripheral role in the early stages and took no part at the first major battle at Lützen (2nd May) and was present, but not engaged, at Bautzen (20-21st May), which, despite both being French victories, were insufficient in themselves to bring the allies to terms. On the 4th June, Napoleon agreed to an armistice that was signed at Pleischwitz and was to last until mid-August.

One of the key reasons Napoleon agreed to this temporary cessation of hostilities was because he was particularly concerned by the weakness of his cavalry arm. During the weeks following the armistice, the regimental commanding officers concentrated on the training of their new recruits. The strength of the 20th Chasseurs had risen to 700 men, but Curély had still to make them fit to fight and applied himself with his usual care to this challenge.

So successful was he in this that General Sébastiani, commander of the 2nd Cavalry Corps of which the regiment was a part (Corbineau's brigade was the 1st of the 4th Division), having inspected the regiment wrote that Curély,

> 'Merits being placed at the head of officers of the arm. His experience, his instruction, his bravery, his zeal for his service to the emperor warrants being rewarded, and I regard it as a duty imposed on myself in the interests of the emperor to request that Curély is nominated as colonel-en-second in his present regiment, M. le colonel Lagrange being very sick in France and unable to campaign.'

However, Curély was not to command the 20th Chasseurs in battle again; before hostilities once more broke out, on the 17th August, he was appointed colonel of the 10th Hussars. The regiment had recently returned from Spain and was a numerically strong regiment (having six squadrons), but one that contained a high proportion of new recruits. His new regiment was part of General Beurmann's light cavalry brigade attached to Marshal Ney's 3rd Army Corps. The brigade was composed of the 10th Hussars and a light dragoon regiment from the small German state of Baden.

The end of the armistice saw the Austrians join the alliance against Napoleon. The French faced three allied armies: The Army of Silesia commanded by Prussian Marshal Blücher, the Grand Army commanded by the Austrian Marshal Schwarzenberg and the Army of the North commanded by the former French marshal Bernadotte, now the crown prince of Sweden. Ney's 3rd Corps, as well as the 5th, 6th, 9th and 2nd Reserve Cavalry Corps, was now part of the Army of the Bober under his own overall command.

Ney's corps faced the Prussians under Marshal Blücher who did not await the formal end of the armistice to advance against the French. Ney, wanting to concentrate his corps, ordered a withdrawal, and soon after taking command of his new regiment, Curély found himself in the thick of the fight. During the withdrawal, having been cut off with two squadrons of his regiment and wounded in the back by a lance thrust, he was taken by the enemy. However, the enemy being dispersed by artillery fire, Curély rushed on foot to re-join his men and was remounted. He stayed with the army as he recovered from his wound but was unable to lead his men. Despite not being fully recovered, he returned just in time to command them at the disastrous battle of Katzbach (26th August), where the army, now commanded by Marshal Macdonald (Ney had been sent to command the French Army of the North; his corps was commanded by General Souham), lost 15,000 men. Despite the catastrophe, the 10th Hussars had not suffered badly and was able to gather up many stragglers in their withdrawal, including a quantity of artillery. Macdonald continued his retreat in constant contact with the enemy and many men and guns were lost, suffering particularly at an action at Löwenberg.

On the day that Macdonald suffered his significant defeat on the Katzbach, Napoleon had gained a decisive victory at Dresden (26th-27th August) against Schwarzenberg's Grand Army. However, this victory was undermined by Macdonald's defeat and the destruction of Vandamme's 1st Corps at Kulm. Napoleon now decided on an advance on Berlin to try and restore the strategic situation.

During this difficult time Curély gives little detail on the regiment's actions as he was still struggling to fully recover from his wound. On the 1st September he was forced to leave the regiment and move to the rear to recover; he was not able to re-join the regiment until the 16th, by which time it had retreated to just east of Dresden.

Although the regiment moved to the north of Dresden to be able to start the advance on Berlin, as the overwhelming numbers of the allies closed in on him and after Ney's defeat at Dennewitz on the 6th September,

Napoleon was forced to renounce this offensive. On his return to the regiment, Curély led it from east of Dresden to north of Leipzig to support Ney after his defeat. During this time, Ney, now once more commanding the 3rd Corps, showed his confidence in Curély, effectively allowing him to ignore the orders of his brigade commander if he deemed it necessary. The 10th Hussars formed part of Ney's advance-guard under command of General Delmas. On the 12th October, Curély once more enhanced his reputation, leading a fine charge at Dessau in which his regiment took more than 450 prisoners.

With three allied armies advancing against him from the north, east and south, Napoleon was forced to concentrate all his forces around Leipzig and prepare to fight what would be the decisive battle of the campaign. The next three days were to determine the outcome of the campaign. At Wachau on the 16th October, Curély fought under the command of the Polish General Poniatowski, disputing the bridge at Dölitz against an Austrian force commanded by General Meerfeld who was attempting to outflank the French right. For the rest of the battle the 10th Hussars became a part of the army reserve under Marshal Ney but did not take a significant part in the battle and withdrew in good order.

On the 18th October, with Ney wounded, Curély came under the orders of Marshal Marmont with whom he made the retreat from Leipzig back towards France. On the 30th October at Hanau, close to Frankfurt, the retreating French army found their route blocked by an Austro-Bavarian army. Both the Austrians and Bavarians had fought for France in Russia, but like all the Confederation of the Rhine nations, predicting the eventual overthrow of Napoleon, had changed sides. The Austro-Bavarians were roughly handled, and the French retreat continued to the Rhine.

From the 1st to the 6th March, I remained cantoned with my two hundred chasseurs at Zörbig. On the 5th, General Belliard came there to pass the cavalry in review. On the 7th, I slept six leagues from Magdebourg and on the 8th we crossed the Saale in boats and approached Magdebourg. General Lauriston passed us in review on

The Campaign of 1813 in Germany 155

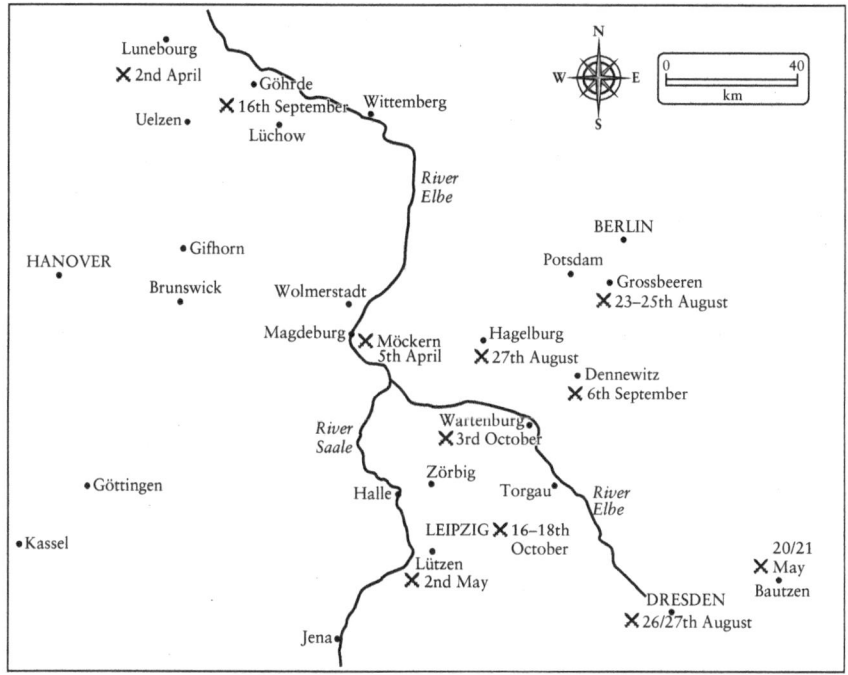

the 10th under the walls of this town in which my two hundred men were lodged on the 11th. I remained there with them until the 4th April. General Corbineau had been promoted to *général de division* and aide de camp to the emperor, and I was under the orders of *général de division* Roussel. General Lauriston commanded all the troops cantoned in the area of Magdebourg. During the time that I passed in this town, General Roussel conducted several cavalry exercises. On one day of manoeuvre, he had me informed that I was to furnish him with two mounted orderlies to follow him on the ground. I chose him the two cleanest, I inspected them and found them so well turned out that, to show how happy I was with them, I gave them an *ecu* of six francs and recommended that they wait on the general well, but instead of waiting on him, they went drinking. The general, arriving at the exercise, told me with humour that he had not found the two orderlies requested by him. I was very surprised and replied to him that I had seen the two men at his door, but returning after the exercise, I wanted to see for myself where these two chasseurs were. I found them still at the inn. Patience escaped me, I drew my sabre and I thrashed them both with big blows with the flat of my blade; I left them and gave orders for them to be put in prison. But towards four o'clock in the afternoon, leaving dinner, I found one of these two men, who was drunk, with a pistol in each hand. I approached him and he marched towards me; arriving close to each other, I saw him make a movement to aim at me with the pistol in his right hand. Immediately, I jumped on him, seized his arm, the shot was fired and burnt my jacket on the right elbow. I struck him straight away and took the other pistol which was still loaded and put it to his throat saying to him, "Ask for mercy or you are dead!" He did this; I led him to my lodgings and sent him to prison; I declared to him that if, in forty-eight hours, he had not deserted, I would have him shot. He deserted.

On the 5th April, the enemy, who had approached the Elbe making demonstrations on the side of Wolmerstadt, troops were sent there of which my regiment were a part and, the enemy having retired, I was forced to remain in this small town by a rheumatism which affected my right knee, while my men followed the divisional commander. I remained at Wolmerstadt until the 12th then went to Brunswick, where hardly had I recovered than I was re-joined by my two hundred chasseurs. We then went together to Gifhorn on the 22nd where we were placed under the orders of General Sébastiani. At this time, the corps of this general had a strength of 17 to 18,000 men, comprised of all the French troops that had collected having made the Russian campaign. The Vice-Roy [Eugene de Beauharnais] was in the area around Magdebourg and on the Saale with the first *ban* [the first call-up of new conscripts], whilst the emperor organised around Weimar the arrival of a new army from the interior of France. General Sébastiani manoeuvred on the lower Elbe and went to Uelzen then Lunebourg where he arrived on the 29th, then remained there on the 30th and 1st May. On the 7th, he learnt while at Luchow, where he had been since the 4th, of the victory of Lützen, and at the same time received the order to join the *Grande-Armée* by forced marches. On the 16th he crossed the Elbe at Wittemberg, where the Saxon garrison made some difficulties in letting us pass [The Saxons were considering changing sides]. On the 21st we formed the extreme left of the French army during the battle of Bautzen, where General Sébastiani's corps was not engaged. Then whilst continuing to manoeuvre, we learnt at Timendorf of the armistice signed on the 4th June. The army was divided into cantonments and the 20th Chasseurs remained, in consequence, cantoned at Seiffersdorf and the area close to Glogau, from the 13th June until the 12th August; that is to say, two months.

I continued to command the 20th Chasseurs which, during these two months, received different detachments which brought its strength up to seven hundred men; the majority were young men that had come from the depot without any military training. During the armistice, I occupied myself with teaching them the handling of arms on foot and mounted; racing and jumping ditches, individual exercises in the pit to make them capable of controlling their horses and to be in control of them when holding their sabre. I then conducted large manoeuvres to get used to moving with order together. I had them doing small scale tactics against each other and I distributed cartridges so that all the chasseurs were capable of skirmishing in their turn. I conducted simulated charges and retreats. In short, the 20th Chasseurs were one of the best trained regiments in the army when hostilities broke out again. Several generals came to see it manoeuvre and all were satisfied. I was delighted myself, and I promised myself that I would do great things with this regiment when we started operations... when I received my nomination as colonel of the 10th Regiment of Hussars. I left the 20th Chasseurs near Liegnitz with much regret. I flatter myself to have carried with me all the regrets of the officers, non-commissioned officers and chasseurs of the regiment. They gave me an irrefutable testimony on my departure.

I left the 20th Chasseurs on the 17th August and joined the 10th Hussars the same day near Leignitz. This regiment had a strength of 1,200 men, although half were young soldiers with no military training. It had come from Spain and was well composed of men and horses. I certainly had a fine command and had been well compensated for my wait. I was received as colonel at the head of the regiment at 4am on the 18th by General de Beurmann who commanded a brigade composed of the 10th Hussars and a regiment of Baden dragoons, which were part of the 3rd Army Corps under the command of Marshal Ney. The marshal, wanting to concentrate his army corps at Haynau, had ordered General de Beurmann to start his retreat early in the morning. The general stopped behind a stream at one thirty as a point of re-assembly, thinking that it would be easy for him to interdict the enemy's crossing. Indeed, the élite company of my regiment defended the bridge, by which they would pass on their own but the enemy cavalry had found a crossing point to our right. It was necessary for us to abandon the bridge and retreat. We immediately had the enemy on our right flank and to our front, harassing us relentlessly. However, the retreat was conducted by echelons and in the best order, and we thus travelled more than a league across a large plain without being broken.

We arrived in view of the French army when General de Beurmann, not wanting to go further back, ordered us to hold firm. At that moment, the Baden dragoons, who held our right, were vigorously attacked by the enemy cavalry and immediately broken. I profited by this movement by charging the enemy in the flank with my two first squadrons and I succeeded in forcing back all those who were in front of me, but when I pursued with the two squadrons that

The Campaign of 1813 in Germany 159

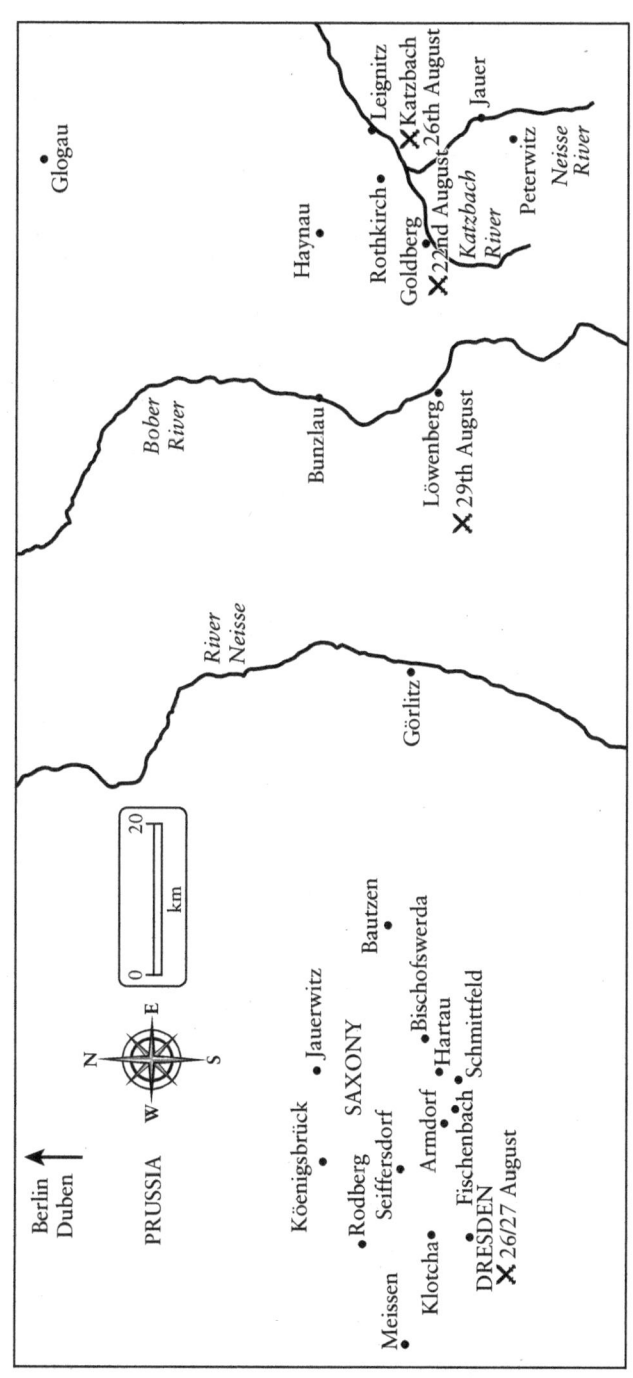

I had charged with, the general retired with the rest of my regiment. The enemy, seeing the Badeners in disorder and the main body of my regiment in retreat, surrounded my two squadrons. We fought hard and nearly all the hussars that were with me got through. At this moment I received a lance thrust in the back from a Cossack while other Cossacks barred my route and finished by throwing me under my horse. I remained on the ground, and as far as I can gather, remained unconscious for five or six minutes. I came to when an enemy officer was striving to get me up; I regained my strength noticing around me about thirty Cossacks or Prussians, lances *'en arrêt'* [held vertically at the rest], forming a perfect square. When I was standing, the enemy officer, I do not know if he was Russian or Prussian, said to me, half in German, half in French, that I was a prisoner and that he would do me no harm. I thanked him from the middle of the circle in which I found myself when at that moment, three or four French cannon balls fell right in the group. The officer who had helped me up had drawn his horse back to mount up, and through the gap that had this had made in the circle, I was able to see my regiment which was at a good cannon's range. The idea of being a prisoner resolved me to try and escape. I did not notice my wound and profited by the gap to flee as fast as my legs would carry me. I did not go far; I was immediately pursued by I don't know how many Cossacks galloping after me and was knocked down by their horses after having received on my shako and jacket several sabre blows which happily did me no harm.

Knocked to the ground on my belly, I expected to die. One of the enemy cavalrymen, I think it was the officer who had got me up, fired a pistol at me from his horse, aiming at my head. I was still wearing my shako which was well fixed in position by the chain that the sabre blows had not dislodged; the ball passed so close to the top of my head that it cut off a large lock of hair that I later found inside my shako. The shot made me make no movement and the enemy, thinking I was dead, and our cannon still firing, did not give them the time to search me. I remained for some time without daring to move, always listening for if there was anyone near me. When I thought I was alone, I slowly turned my head to see for myself; I saw them far enough away not to fear them and I continued my way. Although I fell again, I was not pursued. I got up and headed towards the regiment, when at the same moment I noticed a detachment coming to my aid at a fast gallop. This detachment arrived and I was put on a horse and taken back. From the moment when I was thrown to the ground until when my hussars put me back on a horse, not more than eight minutes had passed.

I was led to the regiment; General Beurmann had his carriage sent to me in which I was laid and taken to the rear. Marshal Ney came along the road to speak to me and to ask how the engagement had gone. I replied to him, "We gave the enemy time to attack us with superior forces and it could have been possible to avoid the check that we had suffered." He replied to me, "The order was to retreat without getting engaged." Indeed, if General Beurmann had retired immediately to the position that I had indicated, I would not have lost thirty men, with an officer killed[33]. For myself, in this engagement I had only to regret my horse as the enemy did not have time to search me. If they had, they would have found on me three thousand francs and a watch. An army that pursues the enemy should give him no respite and attack him every hour, day and night; a retreating army should not leave itself to be attacked as long as it can march.

---

[33] Martinien, who kept a record of French officer casualties by regiment across the Napoleonic Wars, records Curély as wounded. However, the only other officer casualty in the regiment, *sous-lieutenant* de Bruc de Montplaisir, is also recorded as wounded rather than killed as Curély claims.

Although wounded, in the hope of a prompt recovery, I did not want to go far from the army, and I followed the corps headquarters. The army fell back on Bunzlau on the 19th and took position on the left bank of the Bober on the 20th. The emperor arriving with some cavalry, we moved forwards on the 21st and took a few prisoners. On the 22nd, we fell back to draw in the enemy and on the 23rd we attacked him on advantageous terrain near Schmochowitz, but he immediately retreated. The 3rd Corps advanced on Haynau on the 24th, whilst the enemy continued his retreat and took position on a hill near Jauer, behind the Schwartzbach[34] river. The French, always marching forwards, slept near Rothkirch on the 25th. Although my wound was not healed, I re-took command of the regiment, convinced that there would be an engagement. Marshal Ney came to leave us; he was replaced by Marshal Macdonald and the emperor with all his cavalry returned to Dresden. Towards 7am on the 26th, the army set off to attack the Prussians, who were still deployed on the Jauer heights. The 3rd Corps, which was commanded by Souham, held the army's left, occupying the extreme left on the road from Leignitz to Jauer and extending to the right towards Peterwitz. The 5th Corps, commanded by General Lauriston, held the right; the attack in the centre, to which the 11th Infantry Corps and Sébastiani's cavalry corps were committed, were commanded by Marshal Macdonald in person. My regiment was part of the centre. The 5th Corps attacked early in the day and beat the enemy that was before him; the centre was forced to climb the mountain by a very narrow track through a thick wood. Three French battalions and Sébastiani's cavalry corps arrived on the height and formed into line when the enemy attacked in far superior numbers for them to possibly resist. It had rained heavily all morning; the muskets were wet, and the infantry were

---

[34] Better known as the Katzbach, which is often described as a 'torrent' in French histories.

unable to fire. The cavalry was broken and thrown through the woods in the greatest disorder on the narrow track; the infantry were nearly all taken with all General Sébastiani's guns.

At the moment that the French were thrown back, I had started to climb the slope with my regiment and my first squadron was already in the defile. I immediately made the head of the column move to the left and to come to form with me on a small plain on this side of the Schwartzbach, leaving the torrent between the enemy and myself. My plan was to remain in this position to protect our men who, pressed by the enemy, returned in all haste. The enemy did not cross the torrent and I remained there until evening. During this time, the 3rd Corps attacked on its side and was repulsed. Night came; the 5th and 11th Corps retired to the rear very late. I provided the rear-guard with my regiment and passed the rest of the night in a farm two leagues from Goldberg, to cover this town.[35] The rain fell in torrents throughout.

The next morning, the 27th, I had my regiment mount, but found no other person, not even my *général de brigade*, who had left with the Baden Dragoons without telling me where he was going or what I was to do. Finally, I decided to retire on Goldberg. On the way I encountered a company of horse artillery which marched without knowing where it was going, and I ordered the officer who commanded it to march in front of me. I also found several guns and caissons travelling on their own; I collected up all this debris and arrived early at Goldberg where I did not find a single Frenchman in the whole town. Two hours later, Marshal Macdonald arrived with all his headquarters; I hastened to hand over all the artillery that I had gathered up and took his orders. The infantry of the 11th Corps did not wait; we continued the retreat and we marched until

---

[35] The 10th Hussars had one officer wounded on this day, Lieutenant Buchot, who died of his wounds on the 3rd September.

night to take a position in the rear of a small river which drops to Haynau. Hardly had we installed ourselves there than the enemy appeared and attacked us vigorously. We took measures to cut the bridge over which we had passed, but at that same moment the head of the 5th Corps appeared which arrived from our right and was forced to cross over the bridge that we had started to destroy. It was necessary to re-establish it, and this was achieved with much difficulty; however, the 5th Corps crossed without notable loss and at midnight the bridge was definitively broken down.

On the 28th, the 5th and 11th Corps re-started their retreat, heading towards Löwenberg. The Bober, which flows past the foot of this town, was flooded; there were four feet of water over the bridge. Neither a man nor vehicle was able to cross; it was necessary to turn to the right to go to Bunzlau, where the 3rd Corps had crossed and where the other two corps crossed the Bober on the 29th August. The army continued its retreat on the 30th; on the 31st, it was in position to the rear and on the left bank of the Neisse which passes through Görlitz. In this retreat, the French army lost more than sixty guns and caissons in the same proportion, nearly all the equipage wagons and 25,000 men killed, wounded, taken or separated. The battle had been badly engaged; we were not able to get onto the height where the Prussian army was lodged using the defiles which were too narrow. It was necessary to lead with infantry, not with cavalry; it would have been wisest not to have attacked the enemy at all in this position, from which it could see all our movements, whilst we were only able to see anything after having climbed the mountain. General Lauriston alone succeeded in repulsing the enemy on his own point of attack; perhaps it would have been better to have given the 3rd and 11th Corps the same direction as the 5th. Surely the enemy would not have abandoned its position on the mountain for us to attack during this movement. The French army had a strength of 80,000 men and the Prussians, commanded by General Blücher, counted 70,000. It was close to Löwenberg [29th August] that the French suffered the greatest losses; part of the army, the reserve park and the equipages had descended the side closest to this town when the floods barred their passage and forced them to retrograde up the bank which was very steep. The confusion became overwhelming and everything that had come down was abandoned.

Because of so many fatigues, my wound had re-opened; I suffered because I could no longer stay on horseback, and I was allowed to go to Bautzen to recover. I arrived there on the 1st September and remained there until the 8th. The French army was then making a retrograde movement. I was at Hartau on the 9th and Fischenbach on the 10th. Then, my wound being better, I re-joined my regiment on the 16th at Schmittfeld, which was always with the advance-guard and under the orders of General Delmas. We remained there on the 17th and 18th and then at Armdorf from the 19th to 22nd. The army re-taking the advance, on the 23rd, the regiment was ordered to cover Hartau and, on the 24th, Bischofswerda. We then marched all day and all night of the 25th to Rodberg, where we stayed on the 26th and 27th, after having dislodged the enemy. The army then withdrew again and on the 28th we took position at Koenigsbrück, on the road to Dresden, which the army was approaching. On the 29th, we slept at Klotcha, a league and a half from this town, which the 3rd Corps passed through during the 30th to march until after Meissen. On the 1st October I was at Jauerwitz [Kamenz], where I received the order to guard the left bank of the Elbe from Dresden as far as Meissen, with my regiment, two battalions of infantry and six guns. I remained in this position until the 6th. The army then made a new movement, and I slept before Meissen on the 7th, close to Torgau on the 8th and bivouacked close to Duben on the 9th.

The emperor moved on Wittemberg [Wittenberg] on the 10th and we started our march before daylight. Marshal Ney, passing along the column, approached me and said, "Colonel, I think that your

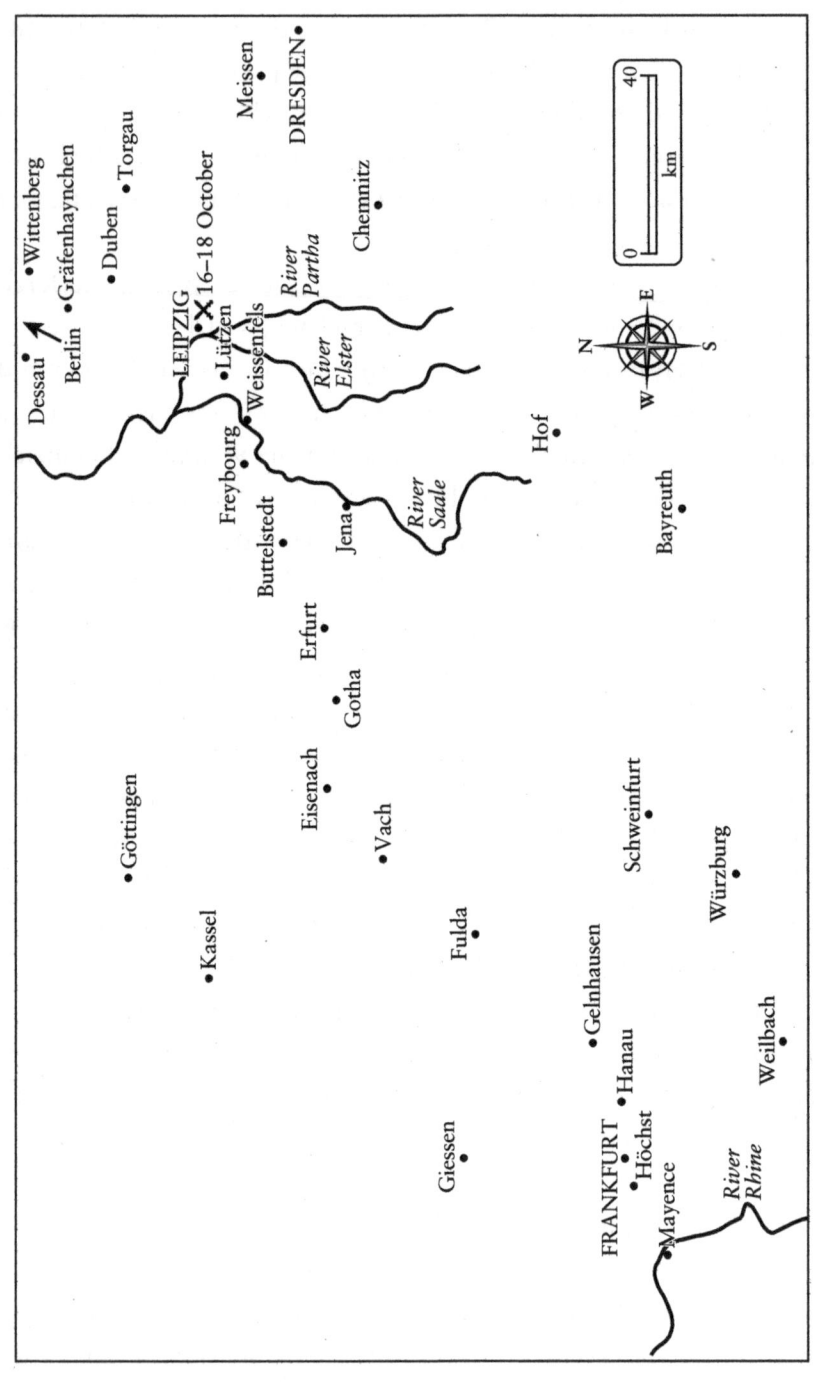

general has become a ***." I replied to him, "I never allow myself to judge my chiefs." As he left, he said, "That is good! When you see something that is bad, do something that is better, I will answer for the rest." This day we bivouacked close to Gräfenhaynchen; on the 10th, the emperor had continued his march on Wittemberg and the division of Delmas, of which I was a part, marched in the direction of Dessau. On the 11th we arrived to within three leagues from this town. The next day, the 12th, in marching ahead, I noticed an enemy column that the emperor had thrown back on Dessau, and which hurried along the road, presenting his left flank to us. I sent to inform the general, who told me to move a squadron forward. I executed the order whilst continuing to march to support this squadron with the rest of my regiment. Arriving two hundred paces from the enemy, I sent to tell the general that it was time to charge, otherwise the enemy would escape us; he replied he would give the order when it was time. On this response, I thought of the words of Marshal Ney and, without waiting, I set my regiment in movement to charge the enemy. Whereupon the general arrived at the gallop and gave the order, "Halt!" I shouted with all my strength, "Forwards! It is me, hussars that you must obey." The general shouted that he would have me shot; then, with contempt, I shouted, "Hussars, do not listen to him." The general did not slow down the charge half a minute; I took with my regiment a hundred and fifty mounted Cossacks and more than three hundred infantry.[36]

On the 13th we stayed close to Dessau which was occupied by the French.

The emperor had crossed the Elbe at Wittemberg and headed for Berlin when he learnt of the defection of the Bavarians and the march of the Russians, Austrians and Prussians on Leipsick. The

---

[36] He does not say here that he had a horse killed under him in this action. The regiment had only one officer wounded; Lieutenant de Dion d'Aumont.

army fell back immediately, and Delmas' division moved three leagues from Dessau during the day of the 14th. On the 15th we continued our march and in the morning of the 16th, we were close to Leipsick, where we rested the horses. At ten o'clock, the battle began; the 10th Hussars moved on Dorlitz towards two o'clock in the afternoon and took part in all the attacks which took place at this point until evening under the command of Prince Poniatowski. The next day, the 17th, the regiment re-joined the 3rd Corps on the Partha; it was not involved in any fighting on this day. The battle of the 18th started early along the whole line and the cannonade continued all day. The 10th Hussars were part of Marshal Ney's reserve. At the desertion of the Saxon army, I moved forwards with my regiment, but the marshal ordered me back into the reserve. We fought here and there with stubbornness on the whole line and the fighting only finished with the daylight. During the night of the 18th/19th, the regiment bivouacked a quarter of a league from Leipsick. At dawn, the whole French army had evacuated its positions in front of the town; I received the order to retire and to take in passing through Leipsick, bread, wine, salt etc. I passed through the town and over the bridges very calmly; it was 10am, and there was stubborn fighting at the Halle and Pegau gates.[37] Once we had left the defile, the brigade commander received the order to scout the right of the road whilst retiring on the town of Lutzen, close to which we bivouacked in the evening of the 19th. The next day, the 20th, the retreat continued; we crossed the Saale at Weissenfels, where the enemy had not had time to destroy the bridge, and the Unstrutt at Freybourg, where the bridge had been destroyed, but was repaired by us. We slept close to this last town. The brigade then arrived near Buttelstedt on the

---

[37] At the battle of Liepzig the 10th Hussars had suffered only a single officer casualty; *chef d'escadron* Mestre-Lacoste, who was wounded, but died of his wounds the next day.

20th and on the 23rd at Erfurt, where distributions of biscuit were made to the whole army and where the enemy surrounded us with light troops. We stayed there until the 23rd and the retreat continued by Gotha on the 24th, Eisenach on the 25th, Vach on the 26th and Gelnhausen on the 29th. The enemy followed us closely and at the same time harassed the flanks of the column. We skirmished every day at some place or other.

On the morning of the 30th we arrived near Hanau, which the Bavarian army occupied and barred our route. It was necessary to beat this new enemy army, which we did completely; it had hardly been eight days since it had made common cause with us; it was chased from Hanau with considerable losses.[38]

The regiment of Baden dragoons, which had formed the brigade with the 10th Hussars, had left the army at Gelnhausen; the major who commanded this regiment came to me to say his goodbyes and I wished him a good journey. It was thus that all the troops of the Confederation of the Rhine successively abandoned the French army. We separated from the Baden dragoons as good friends; they moved off to the left, towards Mannheim. The Saxons and the Wurtemberg cavalry deserted the French army during the battle of the 18th, turning their arms against us[39]; the Bavarians who were facing the Austrians, united with these and went to Hanau with the plan of cornering the French army. The troops of the other small princes of the Confederation left us one after the other. When you are victorious, you have allies; have the least reverse and these allies abandon you. It is the same in society; if you are rich, you have friends; if you occupy a high place in the world, you do not lack

---

[38] The 10th Hussars had a single officer wounded on this day; Lieutenant Bourgeat.

[39] This is certainly true of the Saxon artillery who fired against the French as soon as they crossed the lines. However, the Wurtemberg cavalry did not fight against the French that day.

friends; but if you suffer a reverse of fortune, your friends flee from you; if you lose your position, it is the same; thus is the world!

The Bavarian army having been forced to leave our passage free, the retreat continued on the 31st and we arrived at Frankfurt the same day, close to Höchst on the 1st November and at Weilbach on the 2nd. I crossed the Rhine at Mayence on the 3rd to go and take cantonments at Germersheim, close to the river on the left bank. I still had six hundred mounted men and I was the only colonel to have conserved such a strong regiment. However, I had still lost half my men, including a *chef d'escadron* and several officers killed.[40] During this campaign, the French army had left more than 200,000 men on the right bank of the Rhine.

---

[40] Martinien lists six officer casualties since Curély had taken command; four wounded (including himself) and two wounded and who died of their wounds.

Chapter 11

1814, the Campaign of France

*A*s the 1813 campaign was merely an extension of the 1812 campaign, so the 1814 campaign was an extension of that of 1813. Unusually, this was to be a winter campaign; the allies determined not to give Napoleon the chance to raise new forces as he was able to do the previous year. Apart from a few fortress garrisons, the French army had been thrown out of Germany and most of the Netherlands and had been forced back across the Rhine into France. Of over 300,000 men with which Napoleon had started the 1813 campaign, perhaps only 50 or 60,000 were left. Divisions were the size of regiments, regiments the size of battalions, and the men were in a pitiful state, reduced by hunger, typhus and desertion. France was threatened from the north, the northeast, east and south; the allied armies seemed destined to overwhelm the shattered remains of the French army. Yet despite what seemed to be a hopeless situation, Napoleon was about to deliver what many believe to be his finest campaign.*

In the south, Marshal Soult faced a victorious Wellington who had already crossed into southern France in October 1813. In the east, the mostly Austrian Bohemian Army, commanded by Marshal Schwarzenberg, was to advance from the upper Rhine around Basle. The army facing Curély was the Prussian/Russian Silesian Army advancing from the northeast, crossing the Rhine between Mainz and Koblenz; it was commanded by Marshal Blücher. Two army corps, one Prussian and one Russian, were to liberate the Netherlands and Belgium.

The early part of this chapter gives us some interesting insights into Curély's character before the campaign of 1814 opened. As the French army concentrated in northern France to face the inevitable invasion by the allies, it was struck down by an epidemic of typhus. In describing his treatment of his men who caught this disease, Curély shows the efforts that he went to in their care and we can easily imagine the effect this had on his men. He also shows his modesty and humility in resisting efforts made on his behalf to upgrade the level of his Légion d'Honneur, and his sense of duty as the discussion on Napoleon's future was commonplace through the senior officer corps.

The Bohemian Army crossed the Rhine on the 20th December 1813 and Blücher's Silesian Army on the 1st January 1814. They were faced by only thinly spread French forces that were unable to offer significant resistance or to prevent them crossing.

Marshal Marmont's corps, of which Curély's regiment was a part, consisted of only around 12,000 men which was spread between Landau and Koblenz: a total of over a hundred miles. As he had received reinforcements from the depot, we must assume that his regimental strength was now above the 600 men that remained with him at the end of the previous year.

In no condition to seriously oppose the advance of Blücher's army, the French forces fell back towards Paris without offering determined opposition, awaiting Napoleon to retake command of the army, concentrate it and start executing a campaign plan. Early in the campaign, Curély's regiment skirmished regularly but was not involved in any serious action. For a short time, he even commanded the brigade in the absence of General Buermann and appears to have been quick to take the initiative during this time and to justify his decisions even to Marmont himself.

In mid-January the 10th Hussars were transferred to the division of Gardes d'Honneur. This division was an attempt by Napoleon to rebuild his cavalry force after the disaster in Russia; the men were drawn from the richer families of the empire and were required to pay for their own uniforms and horses. To sweeten the sometimes-bitter pill of service, the new regiments were attached to the Imperial Guard and after a certain amount of time the men were to be commissioned into other cavalry regiments. These regiments were not an unqualified success, many of the dandies that filled their ranks being unable, or unwilling, to adapt to the rigours of campaign. They were soon grossly understrength, and it is certain that the attachment of the 10th Hussars was to address this whilst also giving them an experienced regiment to act as a backbone to the division and to serve as an example to be emulated.

The 10th Hussars were brigaded with the 1st Regiment of Gardes d'Honneur. The brigade was commanded by General Picquet, a contemporary of Curély's, but one whose ascent up the rank ladder had been somewhat quicker, no doubt being helped by having been an aide de camp to Marshal Prince Murat. He was a very experienced and capable commander who, like Curély, had fought in many of the main campaigns of the Revolutionary and Napoleonic Wars. It is very likely that Curély was much relieved from leaving the command of Curto and Buermann, his previous brigade commanders, although he does not say as much.

Picquet's brigade was also under command of Marshal Marmont, and as he fell back, Napoleon was concentrating his army in a bid to confront the allies and halt their advance. On the 29th January, Napoleon fought an inconclusive battle at Brienne and three days later, on the 1st February, the weak French army (about 45,000 men) faced the combined armies of Schwarzenberg and Blücher (together about 85,000 men) at la Rothière. Picquet's brigade had now temporarily come under command of General Gérard who was to protect the French right from the village of Dienville, which stood beside the river Aube, to the village of la Rothière in the French centre.

At this time Picquet's brigade counted 915 men, the 10th Hussars providing the lion's share of this total. Although Napoleon was to suffer a significant defeat, Gérard's infantry heroically held Dienville and the crossing over the Aube in the face of considerable Austrian forces, whilst Curély was entrusted by Napoleon himself with the protection of the French artillery on this flank. A French defeat, the retreat from la

Rothière nearly turned into a disaster with much straggling and desertion, but Curély concentrated on the actions of his regiment. By this time, Napoleon had identified him as a trustworthy and capable officer who commanded an efficient regiment, and Curély seems to have won the emperor's confidence.

The army had time to finally recover from the defeat at la Rothière thanks in part to Curély's holding actions at the bridges of la Guillotière and Laubressel which gave time to the rest of the army to rally. Napoleon now laid his plans for the next phase of the campaign. After their victory at la Rothière, the two allied armies decided to split; Schwarzenberg was to advance on Paris along the line of the Seine, whilst Blücher was to march north and then advance along the main road that ran along the valley of the Marne. This offered Napoleon the opportunity to strike each of them separately, and the French operations from the 9*th* to the 18*th* February have been widely acknowledged as some of his finest manoeuvres, repeatedly striking individual and isolated corps of the two allied armies whilst avoiding being engaged by a concentrated force strong enough to overwhelm his numerically weak army.

Early in February, leaving a small force with Marshals Oudinot and Victor to contain the Bohemian Army of Schwarzenberg, Napoleon marched north to Sezanne to operate against Blücher's stretched out army that marched seemingly oblivious to Napoleon's advance against its flank. Between the 10*th* and 14*th* February Napoleon scored a series of incredible victories at Champaubert, Montmirail, Château-Thierry and Vauchamps against individual corps of Blücher's army. Curély was present at Montmirail on the 11*th*, but took little part in the fighting, but the following day took a significant role in the defeat of the withdrawing Prussians on the road to Château-Thierry which he describes in detail. His actions on this day were fully recognised in Napoleon's report and he was nominated to be général de brigade.

Continuing to command his regiment until his successor arrived, he was part of Marshal Mortier's force that was ordered to pursue the *defeated Prussians while Napoleon turned with the rest of his army to confront Blücher who was hurrying to the support of his defeated corps. This pursuit took Curély to the north and finally a successful raid on Soissons which had been recently evacuated by the allies.*

Having defeated Blücher at Vauchamps (14th February), Napoleon then moved south to confront Schwarzenberg who had pushed back the weak French forces on the Seine. Napoleon now fought a number of successful actions against the Army of Bohemia at Mormont, Nangis and Montereau. Blücher profited from Napoleon's absence to return to the offensive on the Marne, forcing Marshals Marmont and Mortier to retire towards Paris until they were able to hold on the river line at Meaux and defeated Blücher's efforts to cross while Napoleon returned from the Seine to confront him once more.

Having been replaced in command of the 10th Hussars by Colonel Bos, Curély was attached to general headquarters until he was to receive a brigade command. He was at the bloody battle of Craonne where Napoleon was able to achieve a somewhat pyrrhic victory over Blücher, who retired north after the battle to Laon. After Craonne, Curély was to take command of a brigade of very experienced dragoons which Napoleon had drawn from Spain to join the fight in northern France. He led them at the abortive attempt to seize Laon, but immediately after was ordered to give up his brigade to command an ad hoc brigade, the brigade des escadrons réunis.[41] *His divisional commander was General Berckheim.*

With his new command and a battalion of the Young Guard, Curély was to hold the line of the Aisne River, but he was soon recalled to the

---

[41] The 'brigade of gathered squadrons'; these were new formations, mostly made up from new recruits moving forward from their depots and formed into temporary regiments to provide an additional, deployable brigade. They tended to have a short life and the individual squadrons were later sent to join their own regiments.

army. Having been defeated at Laon, Napoleon retreated, but on the way, he captured Reims that had been occupied by a Russo-Prussian corps which he mauled. During his absence in the north, Schwarzenberg's Army of Bohemia had pushed Macdonald's weak forces back along the Seine and Paris was threatened. Napoleon had no option but to leave Marmont and Mortier to attempt to hold up Blücher, while he dashed to support Macdonald.

Once more on the Seine, Napoleon marched against Swarzenberg at Arcis-sur-Aube, whilst Curély was ordered to patrol the Seine above Méry with his light cavalry. As Napoleon's élite heavy cavalry, the Grenadiers-à-Cheval, marched to join Napoleon, they were attacked by superior numbers of allied cavalry. Curély's timely and decisive actions saved the regiment from all being captured or destroyed.[42]

Ordered to march to join Napoleon at Arcis, Curély then received the order to disband his brigade and to send the various squadrons to join their parent regiments. Having done this at Arcis, Curély once more found himself attached to general headquarters without a command.

Having been defeated at Arcis, and desperate to stop the allied advance on Paris, Napoleon decided that instead of marching west and putting himself between them and his capital, he marched east to threaten their lines of communication which he believed would draw them back away from Paris. Unfortunately, Napoleon's gamble failed and the allies, sending only Winzingerode's corps to follow Napoleon, the remainder of the army carried on their march on his capital. Having destroyed Winzingerode's corps, Napoleon was dismayed to find that the Army of Bohemia had continued their march on Paris. Taking most of the cavalry, Napoleon rushed west towards Paris. Curély took no part in the

---

[42] The two regiments (the 1st Regiment was classed as Old Guard and the 2nd as Young Guard) of mounted grenadiers lost no less than 94 men as prisoners in this action with only one killed and one wounded; a very embarrassing loss for such a prestigious regiment.

manoeuvres of this time and followed behind with general headquarters, finally reaching Fontainbleau on the 31st March after the battle for Paris was over and the city occupied by the allies.

On the 2nd April, Curély was given command of a brigade of dragoons in General Roussel d'Hurbal's division. It was with them that he heard of Marmont's defection to the allies, and he was quick to volunteer to hurry towards the capital to see if any of Marmont's troops could be brought back to the army. He was able to turn some back and describes his encounter with some allied officers who tried to stop him; it was they who informed him of Napoleon's abdication.

Curély then narrates the breakup of the army into regimental cantonments and his efforts to stop the inevitable desertions amongst his brigade. Having spent three months on the Loire, he bought a château in northeast France and settled down to an uncertain future.

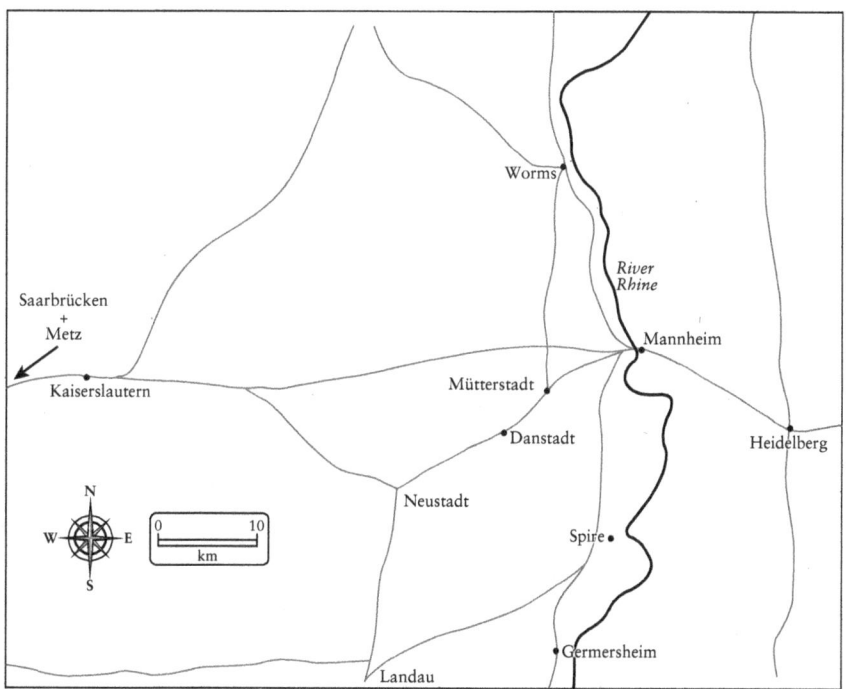

The regiment stayed at Germersheim and surrounding area from the 3rd to the 7th November; it then occupied various other cantonments amongst others Danstadt from the 4th to the 26th December and Spire from the 27th to the 30th. During all this time, I found myself under the orders of General Curto. I had patrols on the Rhine from Germersheim as far as opposite Mannheim, to observe the enemy's movements on the right bank. I had sent from the depot, which was at Metz, all the available men and horses, and had sent back all that which was unserviceable, clothing, equipment, harness, etc.

My regiment was not spared from the epidemic which then reigned in the French army and there were times when I had up to a hundred sick at any one time. I established an infirmary like the one that I had in Catalonia. The three *médecins-chirurgiens* [doctors] of the regiment treated the sick there, but independently of the orders of the chief doctor, I prescribed on my own account that each sick man was to have a bottle of wine per day, white bread with fresh butter, prunes, etc., and above all, good soup and good broth. All this was executed to the letter because I supervised it myself. Almost all my hussars got sick, but I did not lose a single one; most had recovered before the 1st January 1814.

The *duc de Raguse* [Marshal Marmont] commanded the troops stationed between Landau and Worms, and consequently, I found myself under his orders. After having passed my regiment in review, that he found superb, he did me the honour of inviting me to dinner and without doubt, he noticed during the meal that I had the simple cross of *légionnaire*[43], for one of his aides de camp told me that he was surprised that I did not have the cross of officer and that if I wanted to draw up a proposal, he would add to it so that I would obtain this cross. This manner of attaining it displeased me and I replied to the

---

[43] The lowest level of the *Légion d'Honneur*.

aide de camp that I was much attached to my cross of legionnaire, won by me when I was a non-commissioned officer, and that when I did something to merit his protection in such a way when I was under his orders, I would ask him for the cross of officer myself, on which the aide de camp retired very confused. I now agree that I was wrong not to accept this proposition that the *duc de Raguse* made through his aide de camp, but then I was sure that I would obtain the cross of officer at the first occasion and without any other protection than of my sabre.

On the news that the enemy was conducting large movements on the right bank of the Rhine and was preparing to cross the river, my regiment was concentrated at Duttenhoffen near Spire on the 31st December 1813. Towards 2am the next day, the 1st January 1814, cannon could be heard from the direction of Mannheim. It was the enemy crossing the Rhine, who captured our guns and the few men who were charged with the defence of this position. During the day, the troops received the order to move forwards and to concentrate at Mutterstadt. The enemy's scouts occupied the village where we arrived a short time before dark and from where we chased him for half a league. But the entire army had crossed the Rhine and the French troops received the order to retreat; we marched all night and then took up the rear-guard, not giving this up until Nogent-sur-Seine. On the 2nd, we arrived close to Neustadt where we took position and where the enemy came to observe us; we took several horses from him. We remained there throughout the 3rd and retired as far as Kaiserslautern on the 4th.

The army of the *duc de Raguse* was 12,000 strong; the enemy was put at 100,000 effectives, but this was much exaggerated. Rumours coming from headquarters gave as certain the arrival of the Austrians at Paris on the 25th, without any obstacles; it was said that the Midi had declared in favour of Louis XVIII and, on the other hand, that the Vendée had taken up arms in the same cause. The emperor, it was added, was demented and had abdicated in favour of his son. This is what was being said in the *duc de Raguse*'s small army, but here is what I saw and heard: I had an officer of my regiment and twenty five hussars in permanent service with the duke; on the evening of the 4th, this officer came to see me and gave me a copy of the manifesto of the Emperor of Austria. I returned this piece to him after having read it and forbade him to show it to anyone; but the whole army knew of this manifesto with the exception of my regiment. The next day, the 5th, in our march from Kaiserslautern to Deux-Ponts [Zweibrüken], General Curto came to chat with me at the head of my regiment and after having repeated to me what was being said, as I have already recounted, he added that the colonels of regiment, if they conducted themselves well, would be kept and that their positions would be preferable to that of the generals, of which a great number would not be employed. I immediately proposed that he should change rank with me. Then he took a more joking tone and the general continuing in the same tone asked me if I would be enough of an enemy to myself to follow the poor fortune of a man who was going to be abandoned by the few troops that remained to him. He told me that this man had lost his head and that it was impossible to resist all the forces of Europe united against him. I replied to him, "I will follow Napoleon in his reverses as in his successes." The general did not reply to me and left me laughing.

During the 5th, the regiment crossed at Deux-Ponts to collect some contributions for the government, and it slept, in the night of the 5th/6th, between Bliescastel and Sarreguemines. I had the entry of the village barricaded on the side of Bliescastel; the enemy attacked us at 2am and was repulsed. I was watching when the enemy attacked. We continued our retreat and on the 7th the regiment slept at Neunkirch, near Sarreguemines; we crossed the Sarre on the 8th and the regiment was lodged in Sarreguemines where we cut the bridge. The enemy having appeared on the right bank, we fired some artillery at them, and he crossed the Sarre above the village. On the 9th we skirmished until towards three o'clock in the afternoon, and the retreat was made on Grossbliedersdorf, where we slept.

The army set off on its march at 1am on the 10th. I was warned that we would be cut off by the enemy. I deployed my regiment for combat and warned my hussars that they had to pass over the bodies of the enemy when they appeared, but we arrived at Saint-Avold in the evening without encountering them.

On the 11th, the enemy finally showed himself towards 2pm; it appeared as if he wanted to outflank Saint-Avold, I realised this and sent word to Marshal Marmont, who ordered the retreat to start immediately. However, the enemy infantry entered the town in column, and we beat him whilst retiring. I had two hussars wounded and for myself, I received a ball through my greatcoat. We slept two and a half leagues from Saint-Avold, on the road to Metz. The army continued its retreat on the 12th as far as this town. Beurmann's brigade, composed of two regiments of infantry, my regiment, and a battery of horse artillery, slept at Lauvallières, between the road from Saint-Avold and that from Boulay, having a small river at our back. The general handed over command of the brigade to me and went off to Metz. The position was a poor one because of the river that I had behind me and which was crossed by a bridge commanded by the heights on the right bank. I watched out all night and at dawn I put the brigade under arms when I received the order to go to take position at Colombey. An hour after my arrival in this village, the enemy crossed the bridge at Lauvallières, thus outflanking my left. I immediately formed up the brigade, the infantry in column by *peloton*, the artillery to the left and my regiment flanking the infantry to the right, and thus retired to Borny where I took position to the left of the main road. We skirmished with the enemy, who was repulsed. The *duc de Raguse*, who I had had warned, arrived and was unhappy that I had left Colombey. I explained that my position close to this village would have easily been turned and that it effectively had been, and that the best position was that of Borny, where I had retired. He left the brigade there on the 13th, 14th and 15th.

On the 13th, arriving at Borny, I learnt that the depot of my regiment was still at Metz. I seized this occasion of seeing the *duc de Raguse*, to ask for permission to go to Metz myself to accelerate the movement of this depot and to take before its departure all the men, horses and effects which would be useful to the regiment. I found the depot in a terrible state; dead and dying men had been abandoned in the rooms of the fort's quarters and horses running in the stables without having eaten for two days. Finally, I took everything of use to the regiment and sent off the depot to retire into Normandy.

General Curto, after having come close to me as I have recorded above, to find out my thoughts on the events that were happening, had rendered to the *duc de Raguse* a faithful account of his conversation with me. Also, I left the duke's army in leaving Metz to become part of the division of *gardes d'honneur*, commanded by General Defrance. I was put under the immediate orders of General Picquet, whose brigade consisted of a regiment of *gardes d'honneur* and my regiment; I left at Metz seventy mounted men for the service of the fortress.

Picquet's brigade slept at Mars-la-Tour on the 17th; it set off on its march at half past midnight on the 18th and, after having halted at Manheulles due to terrible weather resulting from the thaw, it went to sleep at Haudainville, near Verdun. General Picquet having received the order to fall back during the night on Haudiomont with the 10th Hussars, his regiment of *gardes d'honneur*, two battalions of infantry and a company of artillery, we left Haudainville on the 19th at 2am. I took position at Manheulles with my regiment and a battalion of infantry, whilst the general remained in the position of Haudiomont with the other troops. At 2pm, I learnt that Fresnes was occupied by three hundred Prussian cavalry. I left immediately with my regiment with the intention of beating them and chasing them off; but I had hardly got halfway than I saw a strong enemy column composed of cavalry and artillery arrive at Fresnes and take position in front of this village. I then covered my march with twenty five men under the command of a good officer, whom I ordered to stop on the main road and to only retire when he received the order from me or after having been forced to retreat by the enemy; then, retiring myself to Manhuelles with my regiment, I placed two squadrons in the rear of the village and the two others in column by peloton[44] on the road in the village itself, the entry of which I had barricaded on the side of Metz and Fresnes[45] with vehicles, leaving only enough space for two mounted men to pass through. I also deployed the battalion under my orders outside the first house of the village behind a large ditch which secured them from being reached by enemy cavalry, and I ordered the commander not to fire until this cavalry was on the road in front of his battalion; the range was twenty five to thirty paces. My deployment was hardly completed than I saw the twenty-five men left back on the road from Fresnes pushed back at a fast gallop by more than 800 Prussian cavalry. I indicated to them the passage that I had organised for them, and they entered the village. The enemy charged up to the barricade and engaged with sabre blows, but they had not noticed my battalion that sent them a volley at the same time as I had my élite company charge them impetuously and they were repulsed. They returned to the charge, received a second volley from the infantry and I had them charged a second time by the 5th Company which, with the élite company, chased them off vigorously. The enemy having retired out of musket range, I returned my hussars into the village to await a third attack, but the enemy had been so well

---

[44] In the French army, a peloton was a tactical unit based on a company. A company, which enjoys more common usage, was an administrative unit.
[45] The road from Fresnes to Manhuelles joins the road from Metz at the entry to the same village.

received that they did not risk it again, and not able to make me leave the village with his cavalry, he advanced his artillery which, instead of firing at my troops, aimed their fire at the houses. Then, to avoid the burning down of a village in my home area,[46] in which I even had my parents, decided to evacuate Manheulles and retire to the position of Haudiomont. First, I filed off my infantry and then my regiment, the élite company forming the rear-guard; the enemy did not dare to attack me during my retreat. In this small affair I lost a mounted hussar, one of the twenty-five, whose horse fell in the precipitate movement to draw the enemy who remained a prisoner; the infantry lost no one and no one on our side was wounded. The Prussians had ten or twelve killed, fifty to sixty wounded, including a superior officer, three prisoners and seven or eight horses were captured. Hardly had I arrived at the position of Haudiomont than the enemy appeared in front of Manheulles. Our artillery sent him some balls which wounded men and horses. However, night had come, and the enemy appeared to lodge in the village of Maneulles. I proposed to the general to surprise them at midnight with just two battalions. The general refused, alleging that not only did he not have the order to attack, but also that he had been told to avoid all combat. I slept with my regiment at Ronvaux.

The next day, we continued our retreat and for a second time made a stopover at Haudainville. After having passed through Verdun, we had successive stopovers at Chattencourt, Charny, Souilly and Clermont, where we stayed on the 24th and 25th. On the 26th, at Sainte-Menehould, we joined the infantry of General Ricard and, after having marched all night, at dawn we found ourselves hardly two leagues from the town. On the 27th the regiment slept two leagues from Vitry, which it passed through in the morning of the 28th. I was

---

[46] Curély was born at Avillers, a village in the canton of Fresnes, just four kilometres to the southeast.

given a regiment of infantry to march with my own men. I slept that day at Arzillières, a large village where the enemy had already appeared, on the 29th at Outines and Dienville on the 30th.

The battle of la Rothière and Dienville took place on the 31st; the affair only started towards 2pm. I was deployed in the plain, having my right on Dienville and my left on la Rothière. The enemy marched all his infantry against the centre on this [latter] village, only my regiment and one of those on the *gardes d'honneur* remained to guard more than thirty guns which did not cease to fire on the enemy. As we could hardly count on the *gardes d'honneur*, a general from the emperor's suite came to tell me that His Majesty confided the guarding of all the guns in the centre to the 10th Hussars and that the colonel of these would answer for it with his head. This was a prickly mission; we had in front of us masses of infantry and cavalry, and if we had been charged, my head would have been in great danger, but the artillery re-doubled its fire with such accuracy that all the masses supporting their right went towards la Rothière. Night arrived, and my head remained on my shoulders. During this battle, my regiment lost several men and horses to the enemy's artillery; it had been engaged in a disadvantageous position to await the *duc de Raguse*, who was coming from Montiérender and lost in his retreat a brigade with almost all his cannons.[47] How much would the emperor have gained to leave him to be taken, him and all his army corps![48]

---

[47] The memory of Curély has let him down here; Marmont joined the army on the 1st February with a very numerous artillery which contributed much to save the army after the losses of the battle of La Rothière. His rear-guard, which had no artillery, did, it is true, fall into the hands of the enemy and he received well warranted reproaches from Napoleon. Curély, whose character was essentially right and honest, judges Marmont harshly in light of his defection later in the campaign.

[48] This is a reference to when Marmont defected with his arm corps forcing Napoleon to accept defeat and eventually abdicate.

In the evening, we slept at Brienne-la-Vieille and the retreat was made on Troyes via Lesmont. On the 2nd February, in passing on the bridge at Lesmont, the emperor said to me, "Colonel, you are to go and scout my march on Troyes and you are to sweep up all you encounter." I found only a few Cossacks who had robbed several *vivandiers* and who rushed off at our approach. The emperor slept at Piney and my regiment in the surrounding area. The next day, having passed through Troyes, I was sent with my regiment and two guns to relieve the troops who were guarding the bridge of la Guillotière; I arrived there at midnight, having covered more than fifteen leagues in this day. Immediately after I had received the order to go there, I had taken care to send two officers, each with twenty-five men, to the right and left of the road to collect up for me some rations and forage at the bridge, near which there was not a single house. These officers carried out their task so well that they arrived at almost the same time as us with all the necessary rations and a barrel of wine that I immediately had distributed to my hussars and gunners. Despite the bad weather, the fatigues and the privations, my hussars were content and said, "No one would be able to do more for us than our colonel."

The Austrians, who were near to us, having heard our movement, thought the post had been evacuated. They approached several times, but they always found the place occupied. Judging by the bivouac fires, on the right bank of the Barse the enemy had a numerous camp, and we also saw fires in the village of Laubressel. From the information I had collected, these fires had only burned for a few hours. I concluded that the enemy had crossed the Barse and wanted to move on our left. I immediately reported all I had seen to General Picquet who had remained near Troyes with the *gardes d'honneur*, but as the officer who carried my letter was not sure of finding the general, I ordered him, if he did not meet him, to take this letter to the *major-général* [the army chief-of-staff, Marshal Berthier] at Troyes, which is what he did. Very early the next morning, the enemy deployed to cross, and indeed he crossed at the bridge of la Guillotière; but the emperor and the *major-général*, who had received my letter, arrived with some troops. Some Austrians were allowed to cross, then I immediately charged them with two squadrons of my regiment. I forced them to re-cross the bridge and took some cavalrymen and infantry. Our artillery then came up and engaged in a cannonade which on one side and the other, lasted until evening.

My letter, arriving directly with the emperor, resulted in a reprimand for five or six generals. A brigade of infantry was supposed to guard the bridge with my regiment, but these *messieurs* had preferred to have supper and sleep at Troyes. When the emperor arrived at the bridge of la Guillotière, a senior officer that I knew galloped up and said to me, "What have you done? People say you are the cause of a terrible anger of the emperor against several generals that he has overwhelmed with reproaches and these generals know that you wrote directly to the emperor, etc., etc." I replied to him, "My dear friend, you come to tell me the pure truth. I have done my duty and possibly avoided a check to the army. If everyone had been at his post as I was, no one would be responsible for the faults of others. Anyway, I fear no one. As long as I am able, I will do my duty, and then we can all march with our heads held high." Not a single one of these generals spoke to me of this affair, nor gave me a sense that they bore a grudge on this subject.[49]

On the evening of the 4th, I slept at Thennelières and remained there on the 5th. The bridge of la Guillotière was guarded by infantry and I occupied Laubressel with a squadron.

We continued our retreat. On the 6th, after passing through Troyes, I slept at Barbery, on the 7th at Vallant, near Méry on the 8th.

---

[49] Who knows if some of them, however, did not do something that was reflected in the treatment of Curély by the government after the restoration?

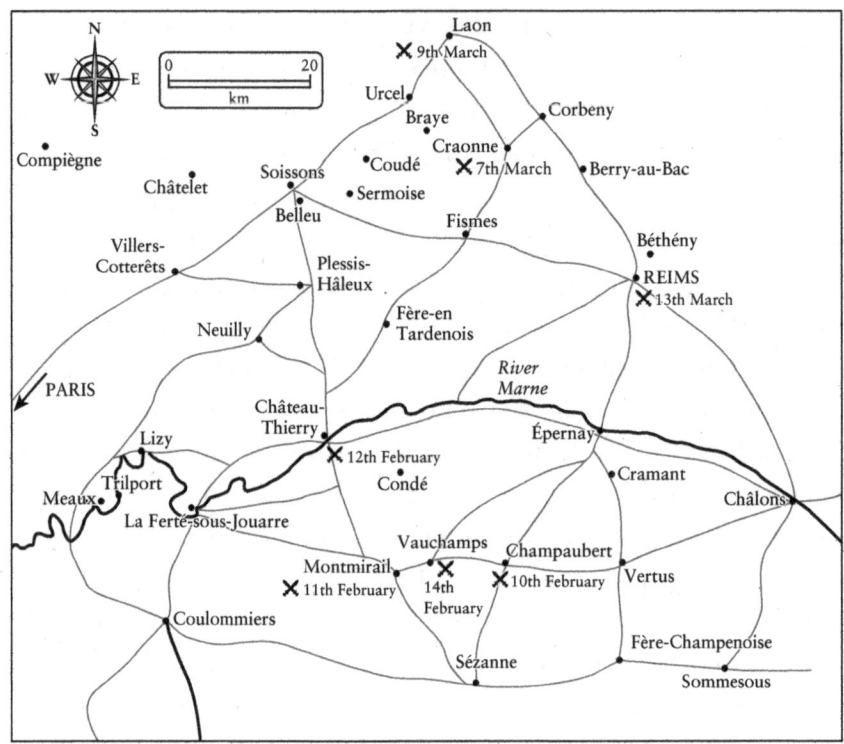

I finally left the rear-guard and, after crossing [the Seine] at Nogent, slept a league from this town.

The emperor, leaving a force to guard Nogent, marched with the élite of his troops to Sezanne where we arrived during the day of the 9th after marching throughout the night and day. The regiment remained there during the 10th, observing the road to Fère-Champenoise and arrived at Montmirail on the 11th to take part in the battle[50] and then to form the rear-guard. We passed the night in front of Montmirail, on the Château-Thierry road, and early in the morning of the 12th, we set off in pursuit of the enemy. The division of *Gardes d'Honneur* of which I was a part, and which

---

[50] Although present, it seems the 10th Hussars took no part in the fighting.

was still commanded by General Defrance, received the order to move around to the right, to get between Château-Thierry and the Russian rear-guard. Arriving a cannon's shot from the enemy, I was ordered to attack his line with my regiment, the *Gardes d'Honneur* remaining in observation. As I was going to be busy with a force of thirty squadrons and my regiment only containing five, I thought it necessary to attack by the left of the line and hold back the centre. By this movement, I attracted all the Russian cavalry against myself, and the emperor was able to profit by this by attacking the right with his guard, which broke it and carried all before it. I then retook the charge and pushed the enemy as far as the vineyards. At this movement, Marshal Ney ordered me to pursue à l'outrance and to attack a battalion square which was in the plain, close to the Marne. I was unable to strike this battalion as it hurriedly re-crossed the river, but, at that moment, two guns were revealed on the opposite bank and sent me several salvoes, which only wounded a small number of hussars of my regiment. I captured a number of men and horses. The emperor's report included this mention, "Colonel Curély of the 10th Hussars should be mentioned." That's all that was said. In the evening, Marshal Ney informed me that the emperor was to nominate me *général de brigade* and the next day I received a letter advising me of this. However, I continued to command the regiment until the arrival of my successor. We remained in bivouac the whole day.

Marshal Mortier's corps, under whose command the division of *Gardes d'Honneur* was temporarily placed, crossed the Marne in order to follow the enemy. After having stopped the same day at Plessis-Hâleux, this army corps established itself at Villers-Cotterêts on the 15th, where it remained until the 22nd. On the 17th, I was designated by the marshal to march on Soissons with seventy hussars of my regiment and a hundred and fifty *gardes d'honneur*. I arrived before this town at midnight, just as the enemy were leaving. I entered and seized the gates. At 8am on the 18th, several Russian wagons appeared at the Laon gate; I had the gate opened and immediately closed behind this detachment, whose men only realised that we were French when I had the wagons taken. At Soissons I received a Danish officer who came to announce to the emperor that his sovereign was abandoning him to join the coalition against him. The same day, I received the order to leave the town and re-join Marshal Mortier, whose army corps moved to Neuilly on the 23rd and crossed the Marne on the 24th at Château-Thierry to go to sleep at Condé and surrounding area, where it stayed on the 25th. Having learnt that the Prussian general Blücher marched with his army on Meaux, the marshal re-crossed the Marne at Château-Thierry and slept at la Ferté-sous-Jouarre with his army corps on the 26th. He continued his retreat on the 27th and crossed the bridge at Trilport, over which Marshal Marmont's corps also crossed, pushed by Blücher. It was a bridge of boats which had been built a little above the stone bridge which had previously been destroyed by Marshal Macdonald, and which was retrieved to our side after our passage. The two French corps guarded the position of Meaux. Blücher's army had tried to cross the Marne close to Meaux, however, because the emperor marched on his rear, it set off in the afternoon of the 27th and precipitously crossed this river at la Ferté-sous-Jouarre; he then retreated on Soissons. The corps of Marmont and Mortier pursued him by the road from Meaux to Soissons. In the evening of the 18th there was an engagement close to Lizy in which the enemy was repulsed and he continued his retreat.

On the 1st March, Colonel Bos having come to replace me at the head of the 10th Hussars, I left this regiment and joined the emperor on the 5th close to Berry-au-Bac, after having slept successively at Meaux, Montreuil and la Fère-en-Tardenois. I then followed the general headquarters which slept at Corbeny on the 6th. The battle of Craonne took place on the 7th and lasted all day. The enemy was forced to retreat.⁵¹ The imperial general headquarters slept the same day at Braye. In the very early hours on the 8th, I received the order to replace General Sparre in command of the 11th Brigade of heavy cavalry, which was part of Roussel d'Hurbal's division and was composed of two regiments of dragoons that had come from Spain. The army marched on Laon and my new brigade slept the same evening at Urcel. On the 9th, the emperor ordered the cavalry to enter the town of Laon at the gallop, but we encountered forces that were too superior; we fought the whole day. The fighting started again in the morning of the 10th and lasted throughout the day. The emperor, unable to dislodge the enemy from their position of Laon, retired on Soissons where we arrived on the 11th. In the morning of the 12th, I received the following order:

> *Monsieur le général* Curély, on the emperor's orders you are to provisionally leave your brigade of the 6th [Cavalry] Corps to go to Châtelet, between Soissons and Compiègne, take command of the *brigade des escadrons réunis*, composed of detachments belonging to the 2nd and 5th Cavalry Corps and organised in the manner of the attached order of His Majesty the Emperor.
>
> You are to go immediately to your destination and occupy yourself in carrying out the emperor's intentions for the organisation of this brigade and to observe the river Aisne, between Soissons and Compiègne. Major Douldener, who is currently in Châtelet, will pass on to you the orders and instructions that he has received to guard the ferries on the

---

[51] The battle of Craonne was something of a pyrrhic victory for Napoleon whose army suffered very heavy casualties.

river and to collect up all the boats which are to be sent some to Soissons and the others to Compiègne.

At Châtelet there are already detachments of the 5th Hussars, 11th and 23rd Chasseurs and of the 2nd Carabiniers and 5th Cuirassiers of the 2nd Corps, as well as detachments of the 2nd, 19th, 20th and 25th Dragoons of the 5th Corps.

General Roussel has ordered detachments of the 1st Carabiniers and 5th Cuirassiers of the 2nd Corps to be sent to Châtelet; tomorrow detachments of the 13th Cuirassiers and 24th Chasseurs, which are part of the 2nd Corps will also be sent there, as well as of the 15th Dragoons, which are part of the 5th Corps; these three detachments are coming from the *duc de Reguse*.

You will have under your orders Colonel Planzeau, Major Demonand, Major Dordonnel, and another colonel or major who will be nominated tomorrow; then you will have four superior officers that you can place as you judge best. Be sure to let me know where you place them.

When all the detachments are concentrated, this will be at least 1,200 men. The emperor's intention is that a battery of horse artillery will be attached to the *brigade des escadrons réunis*; it has been ordered to leave tonight to go to Châtelet.

Immediately that you have completed the organisation, you are to send me a state of the new formation of the *brigade des escadrons réunis*, with an exact break down of all the men and horses present.

You will see from the orders and instructions given to Major Douldener, the measures that need to be taken to observe and guard the river Aisne, from Soissons to Compiègne; you are to take every care, General, to ensure that His Majesty's intentions are carried out.

Signed, Alexandre *Le Prince vice-connétable, major général*

P.S. The lieutenant colonel or major that you were to have under your orders will be Major Bro[52], who is in the suite of imperial general headquarters, I have ordered him to join you at Châtelet immediately.

ORDER

ART. 1. A brigade will be formed that will be entitled *des escadrons réunis*.

ART. 2. The organisation of this brigade will be as follows:

1st Regiment, light cavalry; 1st Squadron; 23rd and 24th Chasseurs; 2nd Squadron; 11th Chasseurs; 3rd Squadron: 5th Hussars; 4th Squadron; 5th Chasseurs.

2nd Regiment, heavy cavalry; 1st Squadron: 13th Cuirassiers; 2nd: 5th Cuirassiers; 3rd: 2nd Carabiniers; 4th: 19th, 22nd, 25th and 2nd Dragoons.

---

[52] Bro was an old friend of Curély's and his successor as aide de camp to General Edouard Colbert' He commanded the 4th Lancers at Waterloo and died as a major-general.

In addition, it is necessary to join to them the cuirassiers and carabineers which are with General Roussel and which belong to the 2nd and 5th Corps, which will augment the regiment with another squadron.

ART. 3. Each of these regiments will be commanded by a colonel or a major.

ART. 4. As and when march regiments arrive at Soissons, all those that belong to the 5th Corps are to be placed in the *brigade des escadrons réunis*, all those that belong to the 1st Corps are to be sent to this corps, and all those that belong to the 6th are to be sent to General Roussel. Immediately that he has sufficient men, four regiments will be formed, one of light cavalry which are part of 2nd Corps, one of light cavalry which are part of 5th Corps, one of heavy cavalry belonging to the 2nd Corps and one of heavy cavalry that are part of 5th Corps.

ART. 5. The *major-général* is to make all the necessary arrangements for the execution of this present order.

Signed; Napoleon

I also received the following orders:

Soissons, 12th March 1814.

Monsieur le général Curély, the Emperor's intent is that as well as the *brigade des escadrons réunis* that you command, you are to have under your orders the town and garrison of Compiègne; which includes the battalion of the 9th Regiment of Tirailleurs [a regiment of the Young Guard] commanded by *chef de bataillon* Theillon and all the other troops which are in Compiègne are under your orders.

The Emperor's intention is that you are to take measures to raise the national guards of all the country from Soissons to Compiègne. You will require at Soissons the necessary men, as national guards of the *levée en masse*, to complete all the cadres of the 2nd Battalion of the 14th *de ligne* and the 136th *de ligne* which are at Compiègne, to a hundred and forty men per company...

Take care to organise the urban national guard everywhere it is necessary and send me, if it is possible, a state showing the situation of the troops that are in Compiègne. It appears that an artillery convoy for the provisioning of Soissons has arrived in Compiègne. Order Major Ottenin, who is fulfilling the functions of the commandant of arms at Compiègne, to have it leave immediately for Soissons. It appears that fourteen guns have also arrived at Compiègne. It is not necessary to have them leave, but let me know about these fourteen guns, if they have crews, the necessary teams, where they have come from and by whose orders they have gone to Compiègne. When I have this information, the Emperor will give orders for this artillery, of which it would be good to keep four pieces for the defence of Compiègne. Let me know this information as promptly as possible.

Also order a *tambour* [a circular fortified emplacement] constructed on the right bank of the Compiègne bridge.

Signed Alexandre

Soissons, 12th March, 5pm.

Monsieur le général Curély, the Emperor orders that with the *brigade des escadrons réunis* that you command, and which is at Châtelet, you are to leave at dawn tomorrow, the 13th, to go to Soissons; take care to take along your artillery and only leave a few patrols to observe the ferries as far as Compiègne.

I have ordered the battalion of the 9th Tirailleurs, which is at Compiègne, to leave early tomorrow morning to go Soissons; give them the same order.

Signed Alexandre

Général, after having provided five hundred cavalry for Sermoise, what remains of the *escadrons réunis* are to go to establish themselves in the village of Belleu, near Soissons; you will take bread for four days to all the *escadrons réunis*.

Le Colonel général, aide-major général

Signed Auguste Belliard

Soissons, 14th March 1814, 4 o'clock.

Monsieur le général Curély, I send you the table of organisation of the *division des brigades des escadrons réunis*; occupy yourself with the formation of the brigades, regiments and squadrons conforming to the table attached.

This division will be under the orders of General Berckheim; you will command the brigade of light cavalry and General

Mouriez that of heavy cavalry. This general, as the most senior, will tomorrow take command of the division until the arrival of General Berckheim.

Let me know this evening the names of the colonels and majors who command the regiments as well as the *chef d'escadrons*.

It is necessary that as soon as the work is done, that you give me an exact situation report of the number of officers and the true strength in men and horses.

Bonsoir.

Signed: Belliard

Soissons, 15th March 1814

Monsieur le général Curély, the *division des escadrons réunis* is, after the orders of His Majesty, to have two batteries of horse artillery. The one that already exists is destined for your brigade and you are already in possession of it. A second battery of Polish horse artillery will leave this morning on my orders to go to Fismes and this is for General Mouriez to keep with his brigade of heavy cavalry. Consequently, I request of you *général*, pull back to Sermoise in order to be at the disposition of General Mouriez.

Inform me of the orders you give in this regard.

Signed: Auguste Belliard

Charged by the Emperor to form into squadrons, regiments and brigades all the detachments coming from the depots and to guard with these troops the river Aisne from Compiègne as far as Soissons, and above Soissons as far as Berry-au-Bac, on the 12th to the 15th March, I received 2,400 carabiniers, cuirassiers, dragoons, chasseurs and hussars that I formed into five regiments, of which two were of heavy cavalry and three of light troops. These last three formed a brigade with a strength of 1,600 men, of which I held the command and with which I was given a battery of horse artillery.

On the 13th March, I sent Major Bro with five hundred cavalry and the artillery to observe the course of the Aisne. I remained at Soissons to receive the detachments which arrived and to form them into regiments.

On the 14th, I continued to receive several detachments.

On the 15th, I received the order to follow the emperor's movement on Reims; I slept with my brigade at Fismes on the 15th and on the 16th at Béthény, near Reims. On the 17th, the emperor headed for Épernay, the army crossed the Marne near this town and my brigade slept at Cramant.

I received the order to leave Cramant at 1am and to fall back on Épernay, to take the route across the plain and to march on Vertus; we continued to march as far as Fère-Champenoise where we slept on the 18th.

Early on the 19th, the emperor went with the guard, the cavalry and the foot grenadiers to Méry, passing by Plancy. I flanked the right with my brigade, heading for a village situated about two leagues above Plancy. The bridge had been cut. I received the emperor's order to swim across the Aube and to march on Méry; we pursued the enemy and made him re-cross the Seine. Arriving close to Méry, the emperor ordered me to swim across the Seine below this town to then to march on Méry by the left bank to chase the enemy out. In this engagement I captured fifty Austrian cavalrymen. The enemy

1814, the Campaign of France   199

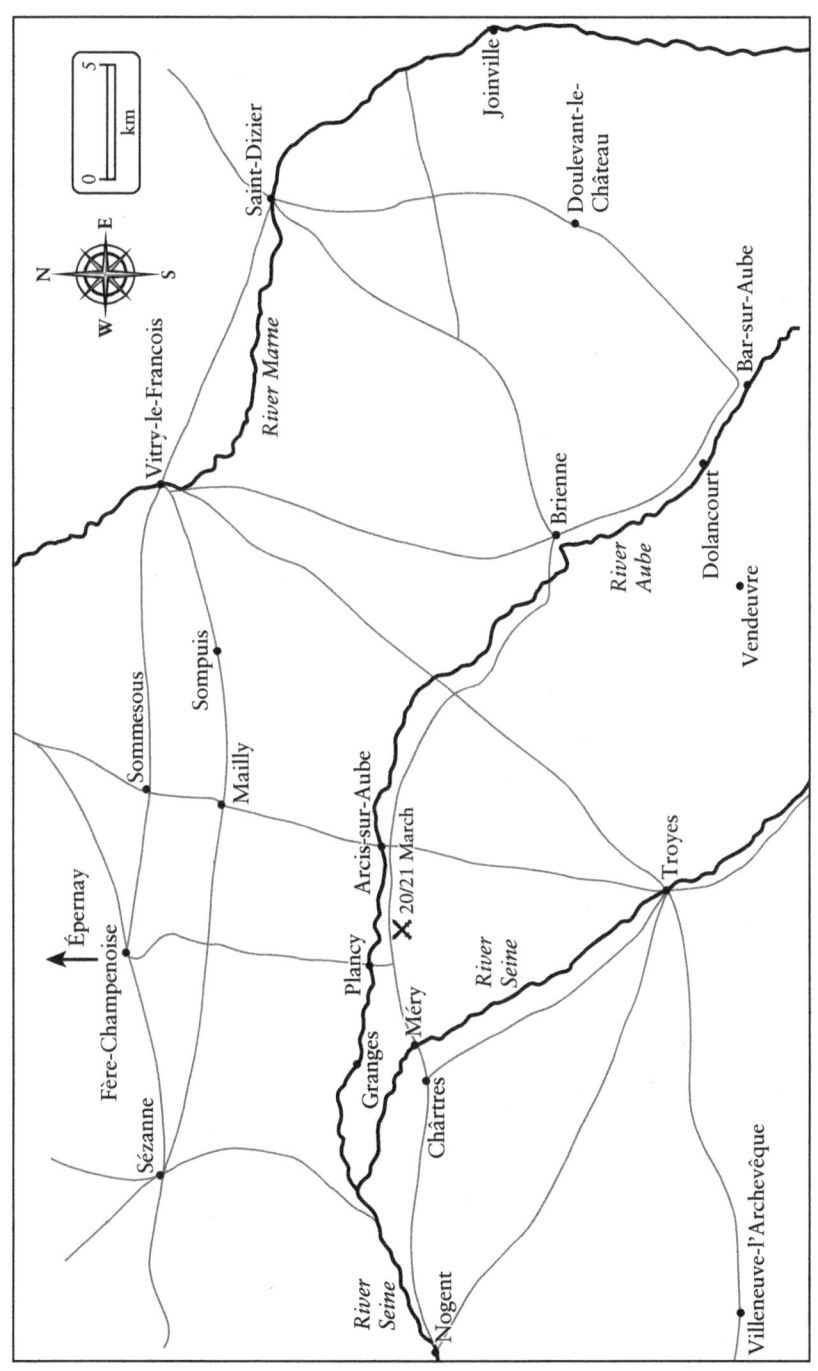

retired on Troyes and the same evening the emperor slept at Méry with part of his guard. For me, I was with my brigade at Châtres.

Early on the 20th, the emperor left for Plancy. Here is the order I received;

Plancy, 20th March 1814, midday.

Monsieur le général Berckheim, give the order to *général de brigade* Curély to guard Méry with his brigade, to send patrols on Troyes by both banks of the Seine and to correspond with general headquarters at Arcis-sur-Aube; order him to send officers in post to communicate with Nogent because there are no enemy in this direction.

Signed: Alexandre [Berthier]

In consequence of this order, I took position with my three regiments and my company of horse artillery at Méry. Towards 4pm, the grenadiers and chasseurs à cheval of the guard set off to join the Emperor at Arcis-sur-Aube. Hardly were they a league from Méry when they were attacked by a numerous cavalry supported by artillery. I immediately deployed to support them, and I sent, to this end, my aide de camp to take the orders of the general who commanded the cavalry of the guard. He returned to tell me that the commander had replied, "I do not need any help and I know how to pass with my cavalry despite the enemy." However, the guard cavalry fell back and soon they were broken and thrown into disorder. I immediately advanced with two of my regiments and my artillery, which I ordered to fire canister shot when it was in range. The enemy stopped and replied to my fire with his own guns. Seeing his forces superior to mine, including cavalry of the guard, and having learnt that this cavalry was commanded by a *chef d'escadron*, I immediately ordered this officer to cross to the left bank of the Seine with all his troop, whilst with my brigade I would delay the enemy. The guard having crossed the bridge, I made my retreat on Méry in the best order, the enemy not daring to attack me. Night approached, and I crossed the Seine with my brigade except for fifty men, who I made dismount to defend the bridge on foot using a ditch which was impracticable for cavalry. I then barricaded the main road. I then started to breathe, I had saved the guard from complete destruction, and I had retired to a secure place with my brigade without suffering loss. The enemy, having scouted my position, I showed him dismounted men on the edge of the ditch and he thought that I had some infantry and he contented himself by forming a line of posts all around my position on the right bank of the Seine.

One will be surprised to always see me say, "I did," when I had a *général de division* to command me. To this I will observe that this general, as good as he had been otherwise,[53] was very tired as a result of the Russian campaign. We only addressed orders to him for form; I was informed to do whatever I thought was appropriate. He never wanted to give me orders.

Night having arrived in the critical position in which I found myself, I thought however I should correspond with the emperor. I sent off two officers and two local people at different hours by different routes with my letters. One of these officers was obliged to turn back; I had no news of the two locals, but the other officer, after having passed through the enemy posts, reached Arcis-sur-Aube and gave my letter to the emperor. This same officer, after having passed through the enemy posts for a second time, brought me the following order at 4am:

---

[53] General Berckheim had particularly distinguished himself at the first battle of Polosk and in the famous charge of cuirassiers of Doumerc's division at the Bérésina.

Arcis-sur-Aube, 21st March 1814, 1.45am.

The Emperor orders *M. le général* Berckheim that Curély's brigade and the division of guard cavalry which are coming from Méry, are to continue their journey this evening to go to Sommepuis [Sompuis], if that is possible; the detachments of Curély's brigade are then to re-join their regiments and this brigade will be dissolved.

Signed, Alexandre, *Le Prince vice-connétable, major général*

At 6.30am, the enemy was still surrounding my position on the right bank, at seven o'clock I saw with pleasure that they retired with most of their troops. Immediately, I warned General Berckheim who had been sleeping with the guard cavalry at the village of Granges, to go straight away to Méry with this cavalry because, the enemy leaving the position, we left straight away to re-join the emperor. At nine o'clock, the guard and my brigade were together, and I set off to cross the Aube at the village where I had crossed on the 19th above Plancy. The guard marched in column by *peloton* and formed the left, my brigade marched to the right in the same order, having scouts on the right to observe the enemy; the artillery marched in the centre, between the two columns. We were about an hour away from the Aube when the enemy noticed our movement. He sent several troops in our pursuit, but they arrived too late; we had crossed onto the right bank of the Aube. We continued our march to Arcis, where the emperor was with the army and where he was fighting. There were the corps of cavalry of which the detachments of my brigade were a part. Conforming to the emperor's orders, each detachment went to its own regiment... to my great satisfaction. These detachments were composed of young men who had still not seen the enemy, which did not know how to either ride their horse or to care for it, men from whom we could expect nothing good. I was happy however, not to have had a bad experience whilst I commanded them.

I had been ordered to follow imperial headquarters.

The emperor's army had already started its movement to Saint-Dizier to cut the allied retreat. On the 21st I slept near Sommepuis. On the 22nd, the whole French army (less a single battalion that remained to defend the bridge of Arcis-sur-Aube) headed for Saint-Dizier, crossing the Marne a league above Vitry-le-Francois. This town was occupied by the Russians; the emperor had the commandant summoned to surrender the town, but he did nothing, and we arrived at Saint-Dizier in the evening. On the 23rd, we were at Doulevant where we stayed on the 24th to await news of the direction taken by the enemy; we had sent patrols from one side on Vitry, on the other to Joinville and Bar-sur-Aube. The patrol sent to Vitry returned to say that the Russian army was marching on Saint-Dizier. The emperor went to this town in the morning of the 25th and reached it just as the Russian General Wintzingerode's corps was entering, which was taken as the allied advance-guard. This corps was beaten and dispersed in less than a quarter of an hour. Anxious and annoyed not to have encountered the allied Grand Army, on the 26th the Emperor made a big reconnaissance on Vitry, thinking that the enemy army was coming behind Wintzingerode's corps; we found nothing and on the 27th we marched again, on Doulevant and there we learnt definitively that the allied army was marching on Paris, only having in front of it the corps of Marmont and Mortier who had been ordered to cover the capital. The emperor had been deceived in his forecasts, thinking that, if he moved on the rear of the allied army, this army would retreat as quickly as possible so as not to be cut off. The allied sovereigns had decided, contrary to all expectations, that instead of retiring, they had covered their advance with Wintzingerode. In this critical situation, the emperor left Doulevant on the 27th, marched on Troyes. Arriving at the bridge over the Aube near Dolancourt, he received a despatch from the empress, informing him that she had left the capital. He immediately left with the cavalry that he found, and the same day reached as far as Troyes. The army was ordered to make forced marches to Fontainebleau. I slept near Vendeuvre on the 28th, on the 29th near Villeneuve-l'Archevêque, on the 30th near Montereau and at Fontainebleau on the 31st.

The army concentrated at Fontainebleau and in the surrounding area in the best positions. There it learnt with indignation of the capitulation of Paris; each burnt with the desire to avenge this cowardice.[54]

I remained at Fontainebleau on the 1st and 2nd April and in the morning of the 2nd I received the following order:

Fontainebleau, 3rd April 1814

Monsieur le général Curély, I inform you that you have been nominated to command a brigade in the cavalry division under the command of General Roussel d'Hurbal; go immediately to this destination.

Signed: Alexandre

I went straight away and arrived the same day at Mennecy, near Essonnes, where I remained on the 4th. Early in the morning of the 5th, Marshal Mortier, under whose orders was Roussel's division, called together all the generals close to him and announced to them the desertion to the enemy of the *duc de Raguse* and his army corps, which had occupied Essonnes and the surrounding area. The marshal proposed to six or seven generals who were around him for one of

---

[54] Here Curély reflects the sentiments of the army, which did not know how such a thing could have happened. He was, however, unaware that the capitulation had been preceded by an unequal and heroic battle in front of Paris.

them to leave immediately to stop, at the barrier of Essonnes, if there was a way, anything that remained there of this army corps outside the barrier. Not one of the generals opened their mouth. "I will go with pleasure," I said to the marshal. "Well, take my guard and leave at the gallop; I will send you some troops which will be under your orders, and guard this point in our line.

I left at the gallop with twenty or twenty-five dragoons. Arriving at the Barrier d'Essonnes, I found many enemy general officers with troops placed beyond the barrier and several French stragglers of the corps of Raguse[55], heading for the enemy side. I turned these back, telling them that they had been deceived, that they were being led to the enemy and that they were betraying their country. They immediately turned about, indignant at having been deceived in this way. The enemy generals who were at the barrier to watch the corps of the *duc de Raguse* file through, screamed, calling to me and demanding who I was, by whose order I was turning back the troops. I still had on my uniform of colonel of the 10th Hussars but I replied to these '*messieurs*' that I was a general and that on my private authority I would stop Frenchmen who gave themselves up to the enemy on the march order of a traitor, that they could do what they wanted, that I was ready to defend myself if they wanted to attack. In speaking thus, I had my hand on the hilt of my sabre. They hastened to inform me about the abdication of Napoleon and that Louis XVIII was going to rule France[56]... I invited these generals that they should remain inside the gate, and I would stay outside.

Meanwhile, the troops that Marshal Mortier promised me arrived. I left the barrier to give them my orders, then I retired out of the way and close to the first houses of Essonnes. I dismounted and reflected on the events of the moment when, despite the order that I had given to the dragoons that I had left on guard at the barrier not

---

[55] Note how he no longer refers to him as marshal or *duc de…*
[56] It seems a bit premature to be speaking of Napoleon's abdication.

to give passage to anyone under any circumstances, I saw arrive at the gallop, a Prussian officer with his sabre in his hand. Half in German, half in French, he told me to follow him immediately. I replied to him that I would go, but he must give me time to mount. Immediately in the saddle, I drew my sabre and charged the Prussian officer, who only just had the time to reach the barrier. I thought there was going to be an engagement; I deployed my troops to receive the enemy, but the allied generals only wanted me for stopping the movement of desertion. They waited to see a large part of our troops pass to their side, for someone had painted the French army as discontent.

All the men that came under my orders at Essonnes (there were 4,000 of all arms), loudly expressed their indignation in learning of the desertion of the *duc de Reguse*'s corps. I remained in this position for forty-eight hours and received from the *major-général* the invitation to let pass the general officers or superiors who were carrying an order signed by him to treat with the enemy. Several appeared, going to Paris, or returning; I let them pass. The French army was soon to know of the events; emissaries arrived in crowds from Essonne and other points in the line of advance posts with proclamations attempting to provoke desertion and discouragement. No one deserted, but everyone was discouraged. After two days, I was ordered to leave some troops at Essonnes and to send back the others into their cantonments and myself to return to Mennecy, where I remained until the 9th April. During the painful days of the 5th to 9th, here is the notification that was addressed to us:

Paris, 7th April 1814, 9.30pm.

To the Messieurs, Marshals and Generals of the French Army

Monsieur le général, your chief of staff arrived here to announce to us that you had received no orders and that you feared that in consequence, you would be attacked. This fear is unfounded. The armistice has just been prolonged to settle the articles for a general peace. Thus, remain calmly at your post keeping guard. French honour requires it and needs also that you only take orders from your own chiefs. The *major-général* will send you orders for the cantonments that you are to occupy after the armistice.

Please make known the direction contained in this letter to the generals of the other corps, tell them above all to maintain order in their troops and warn them that the painful state of our situation will cease and that it is the honour of the chiefs not to give themselves up to the discretion of the enemy, who nevertheless treat with us with all the regards that the reputation of the army merits.

Signed: The *duc de Vicence*, Marshals Macdonald and the *Prince de la Moskowa*.

Fontainebleau, 9th April 1814

Monsieur le général Roussel, the 6th Cavalry Corps is to canton in the Department of the Eure with the 7th Army Corps under the orders of the *duc de Reggio*; tomorrow you are to march to your new location.

Immediately send an officer to General Gressot, chief-of-staff of the 7th Army Corps at Vivesoux near Villers-en-Bière to be informed of the route that you are to follow.

Tomorrow you are to sleep at Malesherbes, on the 11th at Angerville, the 12th at Chartres, the 13th at Dreux and the

14th at Évreux; unless General Gressot only tells you we are authorised to pass by la Ferté-Alais and Dourdan, although this is part of the Department of Seine-et-Oise, which by the convention of the armistice it not available to us. If we are authorised to go that way, you are to sleep tomorrow at la Ferté-Alais with the 7th Corps, the 11th at Dourdan etc.

Ensure you take your artillery along with you and everything else that is part of your division; march your troops in good order, maintain discipline, prevent desertion, send your commissary of war ahead to procure rations along the route.

Signed: Alexandre

General Roussel left for Paris on the 9th [almost certainly to pledge his allegiance to Louis] and gave me command of the division. The army was informed of Napoleon's abdication by the following piece:

MINISTER OF WAR

Abdication of Napoleon Bonaparte

His Majesty the Emperor Napoleon renounces for himself, his successors and descendants, as well as for each of the members of his family, all rights of sovereignty and of domination of the French Empire and Kingdom of Italy and all other countries.

The island of Elba was given to the Emperor Napoleon with an annual revenue of *** Francs[57] that France was to pay him; he took

---

[57] This total was left blank in the original manuscript, but was two million by the treaty of the 11th April 1814.

with him some generals and close to twelve hundred French and Polish troops from his guard.

On the 10th, I left with Roussel's division composed of four regiments of dragoons under my orders, and slept the same day at Nanteau and surroundings; near Malesherbes, on the 11th at Arbouville, near Angerville, on the 12th close to Chartres, on the 13th at Saint-Remy, near Dreux and on the 14th at Grosseuvre near Évreux [to the east of Paris], where the division went into cantonments. I remained in this village until the 18th and then established myself at Prey on the 19th, a village closer to Évreux. During this time, some evil men, who were not satisfied with the misfortune of the army, again tried to excite the troops to desert. I did everything in my power to calm the dragoons of the division and made them remain at their posts; I received the following letter from General Roussel on this subject,

Paris, 17th April 1814.

My dear General, I have received a letter from my aide de camp which informs me that you have been obliged to take precautions to prevent desertion. He tells me that the *sapeurs* of the 7th Dragoons, a *maréchal des logis* at their head, had deserted through one of the villages in my divisional area and that they had spread the rumours which had been on the point of causing desertion of some of my own men. I am relying entirely on your zeal, my dear General, to contradict all the bad rumours which are only spread by bad spirits; there is no question of carrying away the troops. That my troops have confidence in me, I have not lost sight of, even though I am in Paris. I will do all that is required of me to ensure that those who remain are treated as men of honour as is necessary. It takes time to organise everything, and I think we are assured that we will be treated as the army which has given so many proofs of courage.

Général de Division Roussel d'Hurbal

The division was asked for a detachment of three hundred mounted men to go to Paris on the arrival of the king in his capital. Colonel de Saint-Amand was nominated to command this detachment. I remained at Prey and the division conserved its cantonments until the 10th May; it was then dissolved and each regiment left for its garrison. After having stayed successively at Chartres, Paris and at Nantes where I mostly stayed from the 23rd June to the 24th September, on the 1st October I came to Saint-Benoît [on the Loire], where I established myself and where I passed the months of October, November and December 1814, and January and February 1815. I bought the château of Jaulny [in northeast France, southwest of Metz] on the 1st March 1815 and moved there immediately.

Chapter 12

1815, Waterloo and the Loire

*I*t would have been interesting for Curély to tell us of his feelings towards Napoleon's return from exile in 1815, but unlike many of his contemporaries who wrote at length about this topic, he reveals none of his emotions. Given the loyalties he expressed towards his emperor in the dark days of 1814, one would have expected him to have enthusiastically embraced Napoleon's return. However, despite his evident love for Napoleon, perhaps he, like many other senior officers, felt that Napoleon's cause was hopeless in face of opposition from the whole of Europe and that he was content to have put a life of danger behind him. His account of the Waterloo campaign is thin and pedestrian, lacking in much detail and in which he does not display the calm but professional and perceptive narrative of events as he does in many of the previous chapters. It is hard to know whether this is because of a lack of enthusiasm for the whole enterprise or because he was writing in the depression of total and final defeat.

It may even be that he was disappointed that he had no opportunity to take a significant role in the fighting and perhaps to even have helped turn the campaign around. He would surely have had this opportunity, as well as the satisfaction of serving in the Imperial Guard, if Marshal Ney's recommendation, and Napoleon's agreement, to place him in the guard had been implemented before the fighting started. Instead, Curély was to lose his initial command, that of a brigade of dragoons, to a reorganisation, and then remained unemployed through the battles of Ligny and Quatre Bras, only taking command of a brigade after it had largely fallen apart during the catastrophic defeat of Waterloo. Having finally gathered together almost two hundred men of his brigade in the chaotic retreat, he was then reassigned to command what must have been a very weak brigade of cuirassiers (consisting of the 2nd and 3rd Cuirassier Regiments) which had formerly been commanded by General Donop (who in the official returns was listed as 'missing' having been seriously wounded and thrown from his horse at Waterloo), part of the 12th Cavalry Division of General Roussel, in Kellerman's 3rd Cavalry Corps.

As the French army retreated to Paris, the Prussian army attempted to cut it off by outflanking their defensive line on the river Aisne and advancing down the river Oise before cutting east across their line of retreat. In an effort to stop the Prussian movement, Curély was sent to seize Senlis only to find it already occupied by the Prussians. The following skirmish, which almost resulted in his capture along with both Generals Roussel and Kellerman, was Curély's only engagement of the campaign, and a rather ignominious one with which to effectively finish his career.

The rest of the chapter follows the withdrawal of the army south of the river Loire after the second abdication of Napoleon and the eventual surrender of the provisional government. Here Curély leaves the story to be told by the official correspondence that he received, the whole campaign being a decidedly underwhelming end to an otherwise glorious career.

Hardly had I established myself at Jaulny than I learnt of the departure of the emperor from the island of Elba and his re-entry into France; it was easy to anticipate new combats.

On the 29th April, I was nominated to the command of a brigade of dragoons in Jacquinot's division. After having gone to Metz to take the orders of this general, I returned to Jaulny to arrange my affairs and the next day I left to take command of my two regiments of dragoons, cantoned in Saint-Avold and the surrounding area. The division was passed in review at Metz on the 23rd and on the 25th the brigade was sent into cantonments at Kédange and environs, near Thionville.

1815, Waterloo and the Loire   213

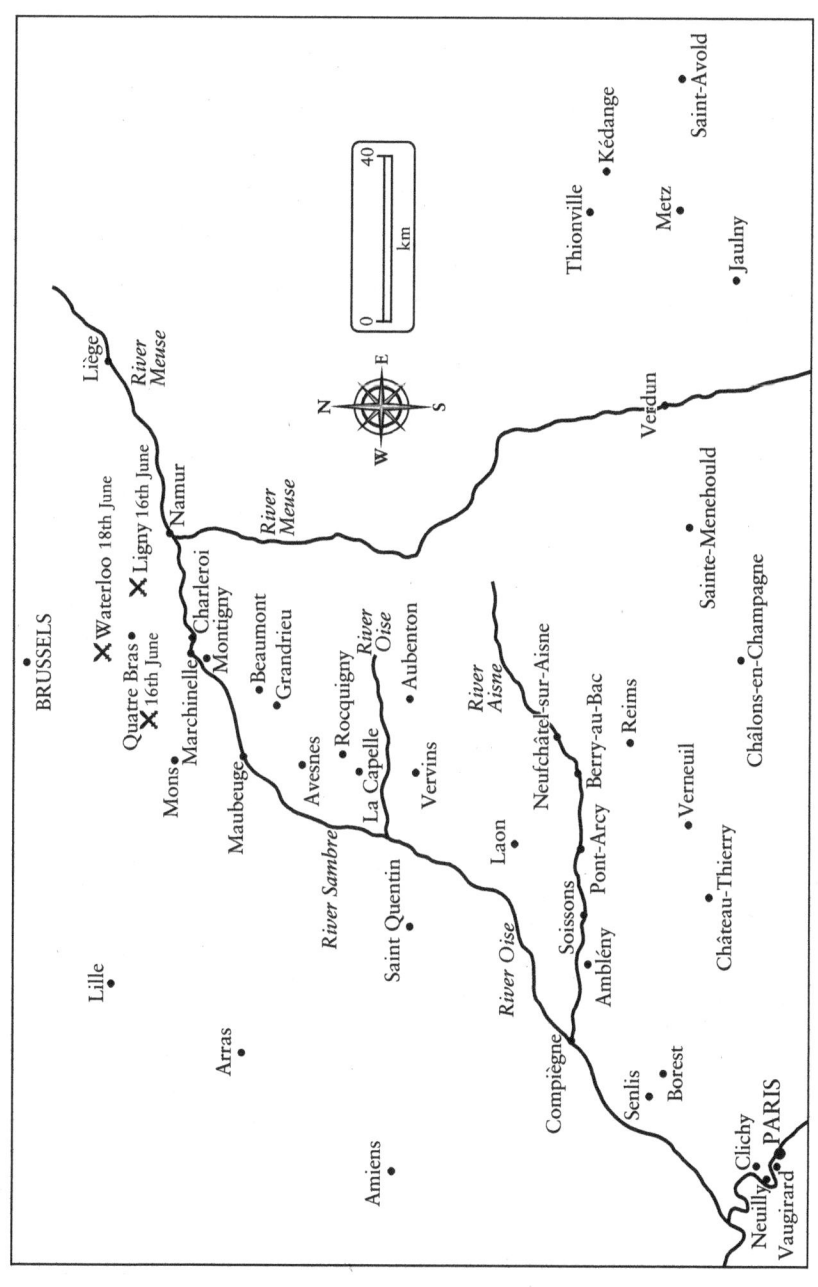

On the 6th June, I received the order to go myself to the emperor's headquarters at Laon; the division was dissolved and its regiments moved into different army corps. I sent off my horses to march in stages from Metz to Laon and I returned to Jaulny to start again by post on the 11th and to sleep the same day at Sainte-Menehould, on the 12th at Berry-au-Bac, the 13th at Laon, where I found my horses but from where the emperor had already departed. On the 14th I was at Vervins, on the 15th at Avesnes, the 16th at Montigny, near Charleroy [Charleroi]' I heard the cannon and I burnt with the desire to get there.[58] Finally, on the 17th, I joined the army. In the morning of the 18th, Marshal Ney presented me to the emperor, who asked me what regiment I had been in, from here did I come and if I had been employed by the king. The marshal said to the emperor, "Sire, this is a man like those who you will need in your guard." The emperor replied, "You put him there." After this interview, Marshal Ney said to me, "Remain with me today, tomorrow I will place you in the guard." During the battle[59], I carried the marshal's orders to several corps. Towards evening, I was sent by the emperor to take command of a brigade of chasseurs who had lost their general.[60] On my arrival, the brigade had melted away; I only found eight or ten chasseurs of the 4th Regiment. I was then carried along by the crowd during the first moments of the retreat. Throughout the night we marched all mixed up and I arrived at Charleroi at 8am. The town was blocked by guns and caissons.

I retired close to Marcilly with my aide de camp to watch our last fugitives pass and the arrival of the enemy. It was only at 1pm

---

[58] The battles of Quatre Bras and Ligny were fought on this day.

[59] Of Waterloo, fought on the 18th June.

[60] This must have been Dommanget's brigade (4th and 9th Chasseurs) of Domon's division. Interestingly, Dommanget was not killed or wounded and no reason can be found for why Curély had to take over command from him.

that two to three hundred Prussian cavalry entered Charleroi; I then took the group and retreated. I arrived close to Beaumont without meeting a single French soldier their flight was so rapid. I slept at Grandieu between Beaumont and Avesnes.

On the 20th, in retiring on this latter town I found nearly fifty chasseurs of the 4th Regiment who I ordered to follow me and when I arrived at Avesnes, I had brought together nearly two hundred men of the brigade of which I had become commander. From Avesnes, Prince Jérôme sent me with my troop to reconnoitre the routes to Beaumont and Mauberge. On my return, I had the honour to dine with him; there were fifteen generals at this dinner. I refused the command of Avesne which was offered to me, and I left the same day with my troop to go to sleep at Rocquigny close to La Capelle, the 21st at Aubenton, the 22nd at Signy-le-Grand, the 23rd at Neufchâtel-sur-Aisne, the 24th at Verneuil close to Pont-Arcy and finally, on the 25th, at Soissons. There I left the few chasseurs that I had with me and I was given two regiments of cuirassiers with which I slept on the 26th at Amblény close to Soissons.

On the 27th, the part of the army that was concentrated at Soissons, marched on Compiègne to hold this post and guard the line of the Aisne. But the enemy had preceded us and occupied Compiègne. It was necessary for us to move to the left to retire through the woods to Senlis. After a very difficult march, we arrived before Senlis at 10pm. A brigade of cuirassiers of the corps of the son of General Kellerman, of which I was a part, passed through this town to retire on the road to Paris. My brigade, at the head of which was found with me General Kellerman and General Roussel, commander of the division of which I was a part, set off to follow the first and we entered Senlis. We had arrived close to the middle of the town which was lit up as if it was daylight, when five or six shots suddenly rang out from a small road that ran into the one we followed, and a ball struck the knee of a *chef d'escadron* of cuirassiers. We continued our march to reach the exit of the town, but arriving close to the Paris gate, I noticed a group of men under this gate. I advanced alone at the gallop to reconnoitre them and when I was ten paces away from them I and the head of the column was welcomed by the fire of a company. As they continued to fire, it was impossible to leave on the Paris side. We withdrew in disorder to the Compiègne gate, but it had also been occupied by enemy infantry so that three generals and two regiments of cuirassiers found themselves stuck in the town of Senlis. There was no option; either to become prisoners or to fall suddenly on the enemy. We did not hesitate; we re-took the road by which we had entered and retired that night to Borest; our loss was a general's hat and a few men wounded.

Early in the morning on the 28th, all the rest of the column that had passed by Senlis headed for Paris. My brigade was posted at Clichy and remained there on the 29th. The enemy appeared at the same time before the capital. On the 30th, I was sent with my brigade to Neuilly. The enemy, having crossed the Seine below Paris, passed all his cavalry and part of his army onto the left bank by the Jena bridge. Our cavalry was posted at Vaugirard. Conforming with the convention agreed with the enemy, the French army retired beyond the Loire. We crossed this river at Orléans on the 11th. After successive stages from Mareau, Pierrefitte-sur-Sault, Saint-Benin, where I rested from the 19th to the 22nd, I arrived on the 23rd at Ainay-le-Château. The army was then put into cantonments, and I remained in this small town until the 1st August, on which date the troops were dispersed across wider cantonments. I followed the 3rd Cuirassier Regiment which was under my orders, and which went to Poitiers. In this town I learnt that Marshal Macdonald, who had replaced Marshal Davout in the command of the army, had sent an individual order to each general officer. Not having received mine, I decided to go to Bourges, where general headquarters was located. I arrived at Châteauroux on the 9th, the 10th at Issoudun and the 11th at Bourges and presented myself at

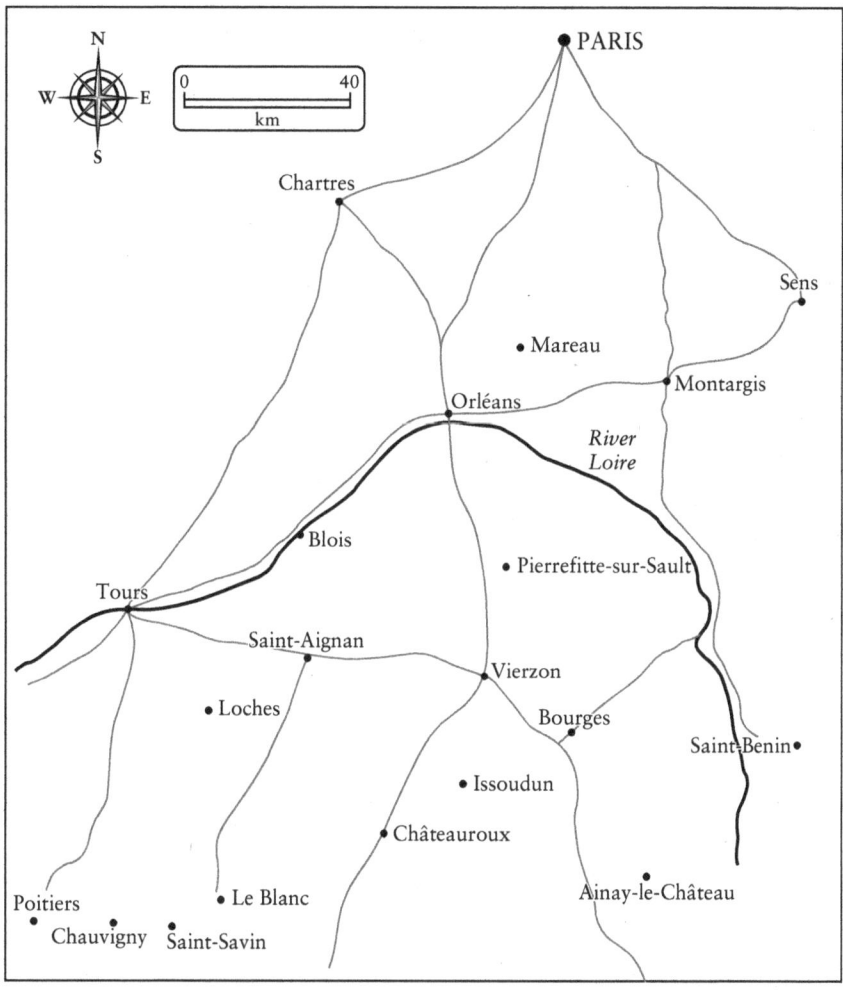

the marshal's house. He gave me the order to take command of the 3rd and 9th Cuirassiers, cantoned at Poitiers. I returned to this town where I arrived on the 18th, after having travelled by stages (Issoudun, Châteauroux, Saint-Gauthier, Le Blanc, Saint-Savin, Chavigny and Poitiers). There I commanded the two regiments of cuirassiers as the provisional inspector of cavalry. The army had been re-named the Army of the Loire.

Here is the content of the order that I received,

Army of the Loire

Bourges, 3rd August 1815.

Monsieur le Général, His Excellency the Minister Secretary of State of War having ordered that the regiments of cavalry of the army were to go into garrisons where they were to be united with their depots, the 3rd and 9th Cuirassiers have received the order, as well as their depots, to go to Poitiers.

His Excellency the Marshal *duc de Tarente*, commander-in-chief of the Army of the Loire, has nominated you to provisionally command these two regiments.

You will be under the command of a lieutenant general, who will soon be nominated and who you will come to know of on his arrival at Poitiers, where he will establish his headquarters. You are then to correspond with him on all that is relative to the service.

His Excellency the Minister Secretary of State for War particularly recommends the maintenance of discipline, to prevent any disorder and above all to prevent desertion. You are to give instructions to the commanders of the regiments to fulfil his intentions in this regard.

On your arrival at Poitiers and when the regiments are established there, you are to prepare their inspection and you are to send an account of your actions to the lieutenant general under whose orders you find yourself.

Le Maréchal de camp chef de l'état major général,

Signed Comte Hulot.

Later, and by an order dated 21ˢᵗ October, the 4ᵗʰ squadron of grenadiers of the old guard, also cantoned at Poitiers, was added to my garrison and I was ordered to provisionally replace for the transmission of orders, *Lieutenant-Général comte* Milhaud, who had been called to Paris.

The same day that I received this letter, I received the following one,

To *Monsieur le Maréchal de camp* Curély, provisionally employed in the inspection of cavalry, retiring to his home at Jaulny, Arondissement of Toul, Department of the Meurthe.

Monsieur le Général,

I regret to inform you that in execution of the orders of the Minister of War of the 18ᵗʰ of this month, your functions as the provisional inspector are to cease as well as the service relations that I have had with you, and you are authorised from this moment to return to your home.

You are to inform His Excellency where you choose to establish your home and inform him of the day that you will arrive there so that he can send you the orders that the government judges it appropriate to give you and to lay down your conditions.

I invite you to handover the papers of your office of inspector to the house of the general officer or superior, commanding the department where you reside so they can be handed on to the new inspector who will replace you.

Agreez, etc.

Maréchal duc de Tarente, commander-in-chief of the French troops on this side of the line of demarcation.

Signed: Macdonald

The generals before being classed into categories, according to the greater or lesser part that they had taken on the return of Napoleon, I had to send, before my departure from Poitiers, to His Excellence the *duc de Bellune*, chief of the commission of purification, the following piece,

JEAN-Nicolas Curély, *maréchal de camp*, member of the *Légion d'honneur*, being on half-pay at Jaulny, close to Pont-à-Mausson, department of Meurthe; left his home on the 30th April 1815, by an order of the 23rd April, received on the 27th, to go to Metz in order to take there the command of a brigade of Jacquinot's division, commanded in this army the 15th and 16th Dragoons from the 1st May until the 8th June.

On the 8th June, received the order to leave the Army of the Moselle to go to Laon by normal stages and independently then to retire to Soissons with the army where he received the order to take command of a brigade of the 12th Division of cavalry under the orders of Lieutenant General Roussel d'Hurbal.

To command the 2nd and 3rd Cuirassiers, to follow the army beyond the Loire and remain there.

On the 3rd August he received the order from His Excellence Marshal *duc de Tarente* to take command, in the quality of provisional inspector, of the 3rd and 9th Cuirassiers in garrison at Poitiers.

On the 26th October 1815, received the order from His Excellence Marshal *duc de Tarente* to return to his home.

Left to go to Jaulny, close to Pont-à-Mousson (in Meuthe) on the 1st November 1815.

Appendix

Editor's introduction. It appears that Curély, who had educated himself, never ceased in saying that he worked on this until his final days. In his retirement, as during his campaigns, at night, and even in the middle of the mud of Poland, he was copying in his own hand work that he read and often added long annotations. Several of these copies have been conserved and the annotations show how he developed his intellect and drew on his own experience to make comment. As an example of this work, below are some extracts drawn from his comments on the book *Mémorial de Sainte-Hélène*, written by Las Cases, who recorded Napoleon's conversations and activities during his time in exile on Saint-Helena. This book was read and copied in full by Curély at the time of its publication, and he added his own annotations in the margin. I have added my own comments to give further context but also to challenge Curély where his own statements may not be entirely accurate.

EXTRACTS FROM MÉMORIAL DE SAINTE-HÉLÈNE

A. The Battle of Eylau

Napoleon: I encountered the enemy at Eylau, the affair was murderous and indecisive; if the Russians had attacked us the next day we would have been beaten.

Curély's observation: It is impossible that the emperor has spoken these words. Before evening on the 8th, the battle had been won by the French. At this moment, I would like to say that at three or four o'clock in the afternoon Marshal Ney's corps arrived by the road from Kreutzbourg after having cut into two equal parts the corps of Lestocq; the last part of which had been thrown back and forced to retire on Koenigsberg by the Kreutzbourg road and the other part had joined the Russian army on the ground of Eylau. Marshal Ney's corps marched principally on Eylau, except for nearly a brigade which remained to follow and observe the part of the Prussian corps which had retired on Koenigsberg on the Kreutzbourg road. By this movement, Marshal Ney took the enemy in his right flank and rear. The enemy realised this and made a night attack on Marshal Ney but did not succeed. After 10pm the enemy started his retreat in the greatest disorder. I was with the guard as officer of the advance-posts, all that I have said I saw for myself; the battle was won at the appearance of Marshal Ney and the enemy could not attack the next day without exposing his whole army.

This Editor's Note: In this instance, Napoleon was rather closer to the truth than Curély. Marshal Ney had been given the mission of stopping Lestocq's force reaching the battlefield; this he failed to do, and the Prussian commander made a telling contribution in the repulse of Davout's attack on the Russian left flank. Although Ney did attack the Russian right and took the village of Schloditten, he later drew back and came into line with Soult's corps on the left of the French line. His intervention had achieved little, though it did convince Bennigsen, the Russian commander-in-chief, to withdraw during the night against the urging of many of his generals who felt they were winning and wanted to continue the struggle the next day.

B. Napoleon's Coronation

Napoleon: The throne was hereditary in my family; it thus started a new dynasty that time had to consecrate as it had legitimised all the others, for since Charlemagne no crown had been given with as much solemnity. I received it with the wish of the people and the sanction of the church.

Curély's observation: Weakness! The church sanctions nothing in such a case, the people must be everything.

C. Marshal Marmont

Napoleon: I accused Marshal Marmont of having betrayed me. I render justice to him today, no soldier betrayed the faith he owed his country.

Curély's observation: That he does not displease Napoleon, Marshal Marmont deserted with his army corps; this corps did not know, apart from some generals, that it was passing to the enemy. I stopped a very small part of this corps at Essonnes, which had not then passed the barrier. I think that this is called treason.

This Editor's Note: Curély rightly states that Marmont passed his corps into the allied lines without the majority of his troops realising what he was doing. After a creditable defence of Paris in conjuncture with Marshal Mortier, the latter left Marmont to negotiate the surrender of the capital. Tallyrand used this opportunity to suborn the marshal. Marmont was one of Napoleon's oldest companions-in-arms, having met at the siege of Toulon in 1795 and fought together throughout the ensuing wars. Although Marmont re-joined Napoleon after leaving Paris to be occupied by the allies, he remained in contact with Tallyrand and in the night of the 4th/5th April 1814, Marmont marched his corps into the allied lines. Outraged when they realised they had been duped, they were only calmed when they learnt of Napoleon's abdication. After the restoration, Marmont was made part of the king's bodyguard; he did *not rally to Napoleon on his return in 1815 and took no part in the Waterloo campaign. It was Marshal Marmont's actions in 1814, along with the actions of some of the other marshals, notably Ney, Oudinot and Macdonald, in forcing Napoleon to abdicate, that led to the lack of trust of the army in its leaders in 1815.*

D. Waterloo

Napoleon: He spoke of Waterloo... The armies advanced. In mine there was devotion and enthusiasm in the soldier, but there was no longer any in the chiefs, they were tired, they were no longer young, they had made war a lot and they had land and palaces. The king had let them keep their fortunes and properties...Perhaps it was too much to ask of human nature.

Curély's observation: *There was no longer any enthusiasm in the chiefs!* Then why did they take up arms for you, just for you, since they were rich in palaces and land. They could have done like many others, remained at home, if they had not wanted to fight.

They were tired! They proved the contrary at the battle of the 16th against the Prussians [Ligny] and on the 18th against the English [Waterloo].

Perhaps it was too much to ask of human nature! Here, I agree. The battle of Waterloo was the convincing proof. This battle was lost due to the fault of the commander-in-chief. The enemy army had forces four times the size of ours and two French army corps were left promenading behind a few fugitives! In such circumstances, one should concentrate all your troops and pass, at the favourable moment, over the belly of the enemy. We should have done this at 1pm and we would only have had the English to fight instead of trying it at 5pm, at the moment when the French army had been turned on its right by the arrival of the Prussians corps. Napoleon complained, with reason, that wherever he was not, things went badly. Why, in the most decisive moment of his life, did he confide two independent army corps to a Marshal of the Empire of two days, who had only ever commanded his division of cavalry? At least he should have kept him close.

This Editor's note: Here Curély follows one of the standard French excuses for the loss of Waterloo; the failure of Marshal Grouchy to prevent the Prussians from arriving on the battlefield, whilst arriving himself with the two corps that he commanded. For good measure, Curély exaggerates the superiority of the two allied armies over the French and also belittles Grouchy's previous command experience. For a thorough analysis of Grouchy's actions during the Waterloo campaign, see the editor's book, Grouchy's Waterloo *by* **Pen & Sword.**